Hawaii
Islands Under the Influence

D0104646

HAWAII
Islands Under the Influence

Noel J. Kent

Foreword by Dan Boylan

University of Hawaii Press
Honolulu

Printed in the United States of America

98 97 96 95 94 93   5 4 3 2 1

Library of Congress Cataloging-in-Publication Data

Kent, Noel J.
   Hawaii, islands under the influence / Noel J. Kent ;
   foreword by Dan Boylan.
       p.   cm.
   Originally published: New York : Monthly Review
   Press, c1983.
   Includes bibliographical references and index.
   ISBN 0-8248-1552-1
   1.   Hawaii—Economic conditions.   2.   Hawaii—
Dependency on the United States—History.
3.   Hawaii—Social conditions.   4.   Hawaii—History.
I.   Title.
HC107.H3K46   1993
996.9—dc20   93–25169
                                                       CIP

University of Hawaii Press books are printed on acid-free
paper and meet the guidelines for permanence and dura-
bility of the Council on Library Resources

*For the people of Hawaii, in solidarity,
and for my mother and father, in gratitude*

Contents

Foreword

When Noel Kent's *Hawaii: Islands Under the Influence* first appeared a decade ago, I was asked to review it for the *Journal of Pacific History*.

I wrote a negative review. After five years of teaching classes on the history of Hawaii, I found Kent guilty of rehashing the obvious—that is, that Hawaii, from the moment of Captain James Cook's landfall on January 18, 1778, had been a pawn of world economic forces directed from the European, American, and Asian continents.

The journal's book review editor wrote back, asking if perhaps, just perhaps, I was being too harsh on Kent. Didn't he provide an analytical construct for Hawaii's history that heretofore had been lacking? Incensed that someone would ask me to soften my criticism, I responded by withdrawing my review.

Of course, the book review editor was correct, and I stubborn and myopic.

A decade later I welcome the University of Hawaii Press' decision to reissue *Hawaii: Islands Under the Influence,* and I am honored to write a foreword to it.

Why my change of heart? First, because I have team-taught another decade of Hawaii history classes at the University of Hawaii at West Oahu. In most of those classes, we have given our students the opportunity to read Kent's book, and they have reacted positively to it. As well they should. Noel Kent writes with insight and vigor. He is, in the best sense of the word, a provocative writer. No reader of *Hawaii: Islands Under the Influence* can dismiss it.

Second, what appears obvious to academicians is not necessarily obvious to everyone else. Whole generations of American, Hawaii-based, and foreign businessmen, generals, admirals, kings, queens, governors, senators, mayors, and labor leaders have seen themselves as the decisive actors in the drama of Hawaii's history. And throughout most of Island history professional historians and economists have written accounts that supported their sense of efficacy.

Yet every epoch of Hawaii's history demonstrates anew the comparative powerlessness of Island leaders in the face of economic forces from afar. The inexhaustible greed of New England China traders denuded Hawaii's sandalwood forests and drove *alii* into debts of such size that the kingdom's independence was threatened. Beginning in 1820, New England missionaries intent on proselytizing the world undermined a native Hawaiian culture, leaving Hawaiians with a malaise that would contribute mightily to their downfall. And whaling turned too many Hawaiian subsistence farmers into wharf rats.

But sugar undoubtedly had the most profound effect. The American planters' need for an abundant labor supply transformed the demographics of the kingdom, turning the Hawaiians into a minority in their own land. The planters' demand for a secure market for their crop resulted in the overthrow of the Hawaiian monarchy in 1893 and the annexation of Hawaii to the United States in 1898; in the mid-1930s, that same fear of a market loss contributed significantly to the Hawaii statehood movement.

The Islands became the plaything of imperialists and military strategists, most notably the naval theorists of the age of steam-driven ships. They lusted after Hawaii's strategic location in the northwest Pacific quadrant and its fine harbor at the mouth of the Pearl River.

These imperialists and strategists were both American and Japanese. The desires of the first contributed to the United States' decision to annex Hawaii; the desires of the second resulted in Hawaii being the only U.S. property attacked during World War II and the first territory since Reconstruction to suffer four years of martial law. The long Cold War—and its Pacific fires in Korea and Vietnam—insured that much of Hawaii's modern economy would be determined in the state and war departments of Washington, Moscow, Beijing, and any number of smaller capitals.

Kent's dependency model fits Hawaii perfectly, even more so today. Indeed, *Hawaii: Islands Under the Influence* seems to grow more relevant with each passing year. In Kent's concluding, and arguably most persuasive, chapter, "Epilogue: The Harsh Nineties,'' he argues that Hawaii's postwar reliance on a tourist economy owned in the mainland, Japan, Canada, and Europe is increasingly producing a two-class society: one rich and the other poor.

A drive through Honolulu neighborhoods from Waianae to Hawaii Kai supports Kent's contention. Almost everywhere, single-family homes sprout second stories. The combination of tourism's low-paid service jobs and the speculative nature of Hawaii real estate has made it nearly impossible for young families to purchase homes of any type.

Despite my new-found appreciation of Noel Kent's work, however, I still have some reservations.

The first is not with Kent specifically, but with analytical models in general. Their strength is the view of the forest they provide; their weakness is in their failure to show the health of the individual trees. In short, social science models—and certainly one as deterministic as Kent's—too often leave out people, thus missing the complexity and the humanity of history.

Hawaii may well have been, as Kent argues, a colonial economy with a history of labor exploitation. But many of the exploited, or their children, did well. Indeed, they did far, far better than the inhabitants of the third-world countries on which the dependency model was built.

For example, Hawaii's material success stories include former U.S. Senator Hiram Fong, Capital Investment's Chin Ho, Servco Pacific's George Fukunaga, and Garden Island Realty's Masao Yokouchi—names representative of Hawaii's many ethnic groups.

More common than the accumulation of great wealth among children of Hawaii's plantations are the endless tales of the families who rose to secure middle-class status. All of us know several such stories.

Consider one of mine. Pedro and Placida Ramelb, an illiterate Filipino couple from Ilocos Norte, arrived in Hawaii in the early 1920s. They worked their entire lives in the sugar fields of Pahoa on the Big Island and Kahuku on Oahu.

In their lifetimes the Ramelbs knew few luxuries. But they saw four of their six children earn university degrees. One became a lawyer, another an elementary school principal, a third a nurse, and the youngest an engineer. All six of their children owned their own homes, earned good livings, and now enjoy comfortable retirements.

It is also important to note that amidst the exploitation, the economic hierarchy, and the manipulations from afar, somehow Hawaii has realized a degree of racial harmony unknown in most parts of the world. That is no small achievement in a time when phrases like "ethnic cleansing" are common and where many American cities are often just a police arrest away from a riot.

Finally, I would take exception to Kent's almost relentless Marxism. Kent writes of the imminent "crisis of capitalism," the "land-developer bourgeoisie," and "the ruling class." He dismisses governors William Quinn and John A. Burns for becoming the servants of corporate America. He even faults labor leader Jack Hall for abandoning his socialist roots and allowing himself to be coopted by capitalist Hawaii.

I don't think that's fair. Many intelligent, moral men and women have studied Marxism and ultimately embraced it; just as many or more have followed the same process and rejected it. It's my firm belief that Burns and Hall were both thoroughgoing pragmatists. In the 1930s Hall used a class analysis of society in order to win a better life for Hawaii's workers, but he never sought a full-blown Marxist society. And neither did Burns; he was always, as he willingly admitted, a "Jeffersonian with a little bit of the Jacksonian mixed in." Kent's treatment unjustifiably diminishes them.

Nevertheless, Noel Kent's *Hawaii: Islands Under the Influence* is an audacious, ultimately successful attempt to see the Islands whole. For the past decade it has served as a welcome antidote to the more conventional historical treatments of explorers and whalers, native kings and territorial governors, triumphant democracy and benevolent capitalism.

Thanks to the University of Hawaii Press, it will be around at least another decade to provoke, enlighten, and forewarn.

April 1993   Dan Boylan

Acknowledgments

This book, of course, remains solely my responsibility. Nevertheless, no one makes a journey (much less an intellectual journey) alone and acknowledgments are in order. A number of fine teachers have assisted in my various passages over the years: during the mid-1960s, John Smail and Hans Peter Krosby of the University of Wisconsin history department and Robert Van Niel of the University of Hawaii history department; a decade later, there were Robert Stauffer, Ben Kerkvliet, Deane Neubauer, and Michael Shapiro of the University of Hawaii political science department. In Hawaii, a small circle of people have been simply invaluable. Mimi Sharma has provided excellent and incisive criticism. Another fine scholar, John Reinecke, offered marvelous suggestions for revisions in the text; George Cooper and Sam Pooley have been concerned and helpful. John and Marion Kelly have shared their vast knowledge of Hawaii and theory with me. Franklin Odo of the Ethnic Studies Program has been tremendously supportive. Nem Lau was a fount of caring. My deepest thanks to the staffs of both the University of Hawaii Library (especially the Hawaiian Pacific division) and the Hawaii State Library for providing generous access to all materials. Rob Britton and Herb Hiller, two of the most adept critics of international tourism, have given me numerous insights. And *mahalo* to the people at Monthly Review Press for whom I've come to have real affection: Jules Geller, Judy Ruben, and especially Susan Lowes, my editor, who has performed wonders in transforming a manuscript into a book.

Honolulu, October 1982

Introduction

Much has been written about the Hawaiian Islands. Since James Cook and one of his shipmates, John Ledyard, set down their thoughts in diaries two centuries ago while their ships lay at anchor in Kealekekua Bay, a cascade of literature has materialized around a host of Hawaiian themes. This represents a powerful testimony to the enduring ability of what Mark Twain once called the "loveliest fleet of islands that lies anchored in any ocean" to evoke a response from so many.

Certainly, there is an abundance of chatty travelogues of eighteenth- and nineteenth-century Hawaiian "adventures," in at least four languages, along with a plethora of missionary memorials recounting the conversion of the "benighted" to the faith and a goodly number of (sometimes extremely revealing) portraits and self-portraits of the plantation elite that ruled Hawaii as its own for nearly a century. And yet, despite all this, the serious student of Hawaiian society looks in vain for scholarship that can provide a comprehensive, incisive analysis of the dynamics of past and contemporary social, political, and economic development. In our own time, a key juncture in Island history when a series of sharply etched crises have brought the much touted "celebration of Hawaii" so popular in the 1950s and 1960s to a rather abrupt end, the absence of a literature specifically addressed to the most critical questions of Hawaiian development is both distressing and unacceptable.

The dominant historical studies reflect these limitations. Ralph S. Kuykendall, whose importance stems from his influence on later studies, in his massive three-volume *The Hawaiian Kingdom, 1778–1893*, remained content to provide the reader with a prodigious number of facts, while refusing to examine issues in depth or to explore the possibility that a variety of interpretations might exist. By treating watershed issues as "factual" history needing little if any creative analysis, his work merely served to reinforce existing

1

stereotypes of Island development as both inevitable and beneficial to Hawaii's people and as a triumph of progress—in other
words, the viewpoint of the plantation elite which controlled the
society in which he lived and the university at which he taught.

Unlike Kuykendall, the two most widely read and influential
histories of Hawaii—*Hawaii Pono* by Lawrence Fuchs and *Shoal of
Time* by Gavan Daws—brought the reader into contact with modern Hawaii and took positions strongly critical of the despotism of
the pre-Pearl Harbor plantation structure. But for Fuchs and
Daws, and others like them, the period of conception was crucial—
the hallucinatory years around the passage of statehood, the "celebration of Hawaii" era, a brief but euphoric time that saw hotels
sprouting over Waikiki rooftops, a rampage of tourism and land
development that gave promise of endless boom, land prices doubling fortnightly, and the sons and daughters of immigrant plantation workers entering mass consumption society as fully
enfranchised citizens and consumers. Fuchs and Daws were describing a society at its zenith of performance and social legitimacy;
neither was able to foresee the growth of unresolvable contradictions, the coming fall from grace.

Fuchs was particularly enthusiastic about the Hawaiian model of
development. He argued that the full integration of the Islands
with the mainland, their "Americanization," had finally broken the
stranglehold of the plantation oligarchy on socioeconomic life; that
the rise to power of a liberal corporate establishment (whom he
identified as progressive local politicians, labor union leaders, and
entrepreneurs, a new generation of "enlightened" corporation
managers, and liberal mainland capital investors) meant a fundamental break with the old society. He thus provided the intellectual
rationale for the liberal-corporate developmental model (basically
the New Deal–post-New Deal national strategies of organized
labor–Big Business collaboration with a massive governmental role
in rationalizing the economy—as transferred to the Islands) that
was being consolidated even as the book appeared in 1961. And
Fuchs was confident that since Hawaii had proven the viability of
developing a multi-ethnic, underdeveloped society along liberal
capitalist lines, it would now furnish a shining example for others
throughout Asia and the Pacific: "Hawaii illustrates the nation's
revolutionary message of equality of opportunity for all regardless

of background, color or religion. This is the promise of Hawaii, a promise for the entire nation and indeed, the world."[1]

The more perceptive Gavan Daws, writing in 1968 with the advantage of hindsight, expressed his dismay at the consequences of the two-century-long assault on Hawaiian culture and some ambivalence about contemporary trends, but he still concluded that the "future seemed open and the present was enjoyable enough."[2] This was echoed by a number of other writers: local historian Theon Wright, for instance, hailed the "peaceful revolution" in Hawaii. "It is an aggressive, highly industrialized and economically flourishing society, quite peaceful and wholly American," he wrote. Others were scornful of the days when Hawaii was "paradise" for the few and fulsome in their praise of the "New Hawaii."

This, then, is the dominant paradigm of Hawaiian historiography. Its tendency toward a simple reductionism and its reluctance to discuss some of the nasty dilemmas generated by the very "success" of the model are critical weaknesses. These are bound up with the paradigm's world view and the inner logic of its assumptions. Indeed, the lack of self-awareness of the kinds of values (always middle class, mid-twentieth century, United States-oriented) that inform the paradigm, the lack of theoretical grounding in the scholarship—all of these make this body of work deeply flawed as a point of departure for the study of Hawaii's development.

The dominant paradigm carries the basic assumption that the "New Hawaii" is a central component of the U.S. metropolis and has a modern, sophisticated economy. Thus the "New Hawaii" is justified precisely to the degree that it is perceived as a radical break with the most restrictive and obnoxious aspects of the old plantation society. If the old Hawaii was essentially a mid-Pacific backwater, a quasi-colonial maze of sugar and pineapple fields directed by an inbred power structure, then the dominant scholarship hails its long-awaited liquidation and the introduction of a modernized and "enlightened" capitalist order. Harmony and consensus are viewed as the most significant elements of historical continuity in the Hawaiian pattern, the "peaceful revolution" is the final realization of democracy and pluralism. These claims are the cornerstone of contemporary Hawaiian historiography's *celebration* (rather than analysis) of the Island experience.

Yet these historians tell us nothing about the crucial dynamic of a society in transition. Critical to any understanding of the Hawaiian development process is an examination of the ongoing dialectic between global capitalist development and local development, and of the special role of the state in relationship to capital—not a narrow focus on internal development in Hawaii to the exclusion of the dynamic interplay between the Islands and the developing world capitalist economy, not an ignoring of the ties and linkages uniting the interests of local and overseas elites. In short, a political economy—who benefits and who sacrifices in the process of development, and the essential question of whether or not what is occurring really *is* "development" (informed by the concepts of "power," "class," "mode of production," etc.)—is needed.

Hawaii: Islands Under the Influence will make, I hope, a humble beginning toward such a political economy. The study uses the dependency framework first formulated in the 1960s to explain the widespread failure of development strategies in the Third World. By then, of course, the evidence was overwhelming that not only were underdeveloped countries in Asia, Africa, and Latin America not achieving genuine development, but in point of fact they had emerged as peripheral societies attuned to the economic needs of the advanced capitalist center and dependent upon it for technology, capital, skills, and organization. The pattern was clear: these countries suffered from a distorted emphasis upon primary export production, the lack of a soundly balanced, integrated economic structure, foreign domination of strategic economic sectors and of the local bourgeoisie, and a sharply stratified and increasingly dichotomized class structure, in which ever increasing numbers of people lived in misery. In what today comprises a substantial body of literature, dependency thinkers such as Andre Gunder Frank, Samir Amin, Norman Girvan, Paul Baran, Suzanne Bodenheimer, and Johann Galtung have made a powerful case for the historical basis of dependency and underdevelopment: that the loss of control by the peripheries has been a consequence of a historically determined series of interlocking global structures and strategies.

What is valuable about the dependency model is its attempt to work out a coherent analysis of the global economic structure, and then to use this to analyze development in individual societies, to eliminate the boundaries between national and international processes and between the political, economic, military, and ideological dimensions of social interaction. The real strength of the dependency model as an analytical tool derives precisely from its orientation toward dynamism, its concern with assembling patterns of intersystemic and international linkages, and its use of history as an instrument to reveal the dynamics of social change and transformation.

To subject Hawaii's development to a dependency analysis is to open a door that has been closed too long and to provide a new dimension to Island (and Pacific) studies. The dominant scholarship denies that Hawaii as a state retains important structural characteristics of the oppressive plantation society that was the Territory of Hawaii. It insists upon Hawaii's secure place as a mature, developed state of the most powerful nation on earth. This study will examine and challenge these assumptions by analyzing the structures and linkages imposed upon Hawaii by two centuries of steadily increasing interaction with the global capitalist system.

For the past two centuries, virtually from the time that Western ships began to call regularly at Hawaii, the Islands have been "under the influence." Under the influence of sea captains, fur traders, sandalwood merchants, whaling ship owners, sugar planters, presidents, congressmen, admirals, banks, life insurance companies, land developers, and airlines. Under the influence of powerful metropolitan forces, which have profoundly shaped the course of the Islands' economic, political, and social development, and have molded it in their image. Change in Hawaiian development has corresponded historically to the development of the forces of production in the advanced capitalist world, from a center radiating influence and change out to this mid-Pacific periphery. In short, Hawaii's development for the last two hundred years has been *peripheral* in nature, a reflex of expansionist needs in some metropolitan center.

During the period of mercantile capitalism in the United States and Western Europe, Hawaii was used as a provisioning center for the trans-Pacific trade, as a supplier of sandalwood for the China market, and, finally, as a whaling port. Later in the nineteenth century, as capitalist development spread rapidly across the U.S. continent and a West Coast market for agricultural commodities evolved, Hawaii's role shifted to that of sugar supplier. The plantation society was born. By the mid-twentieth century, however, because of changes emanating (again) from the metropole, the plantation economy stagnated. Tourism, an industry built upon the unprecedented post-World War II expansion of global capitalism and a number of striking technological advances, now emerged as Hawaii's economic base.

The pattern is thus clear: each transformation of the Islands' economy received its impetus and direction from economic and political change occuring at the center. Hawaii's role and possibilities for development were *not* (as most observers have argued) completely circumscribed by its relatively small geographic size and population or limited resources. These limitations, while certainly real, could have been overcome but for the ironclad grip of metropolitan elites (and their local allies) over the development process. Moreover, we should appreciate the importance of Hawaii's "potential surplus" being squandered, at every historical stage, through conspicuous consumption by Island elites or repatriated back to the metropole. The misappropriation or loss of this potential surplus made a real developmental strategy impossible in Hawaii—even if a force had existed capable of implementing it. In fact, at each stage, as we shall see, Hawaii became bound more tightly to the world capitalist system.

A second major theme in Hawaiian history is the critical role played by the alliances between elites in the metropole and in Hawaii. These were strategic alliances which delivered Hawaii over to a plantation and then to a tourism economy. And in every case, the aims and desires of the metropolitan elite were dominant. In the last analysis, the elite has wielded (as it still does) far greater power than the "boys on Merchant Street"; it has always been in a position to make or break the Hawaiian economy. Not only have the Islands' internal elites proved incapable of launching a real development strategy, but they have (at least in the tourism–land development period) readily accepted the role of aiding and abetting the overseas penetration of Hawaii.

The task of the first part of this book is to establish a general model of the development of a plantation society as it emerged during the first century of contact between the Islands and outsiders. The formative events of Hawaiian history will be examined within the context of core-periphery relationships, particularly the growth of United States power and economic interests in the Pacific, and it will be seen how Hawaii gradually assumed the role of an integrated periphery within the sphere of U.S. control. Finally, the plantation society of the 1900–50 era will be analyzed in terms of class and social dynamics, economic relations between Hawaii and the United States, and the interplay between the dominant classes in Hawaii and the metropole.

Part 2 will examine the transformation of a plantation society into a tourism-oriented society. It is an attempt to answer the fundamental question: in terms of power relationships, economic and political control, and mass participation, how genuinely *new* is the "New Hawaii"? More directly, has change in Hawaiian society resulted from the continuation of the core-periphery axis described in Part 1, or does the advent of the "New Hawaii" mark a break with past developmental mechanisms? The focus in Part 2 is Hawaii's role in the Pacific Rim strategy formulated by overseas multinational corporations, the incorporation of the post-World War II Island political elite and old-line plantation companies into an enlarged "establishment" under the direction of overseas interests, and the nature of Hawaii's tourism society.

A pair of *caveats* should be stated at this point. For one, although I certainly believe that dependency formulations are of great value in the study of Hawaii's political economy, I also recognize the somewhat unrefined nature of the paradigm. Critics have rightly pointed out that dependency models need more finesse in terms of such questions as how "degrees of dependency" are to be established and what the distinctive forms that constitute a dependency relationship are. On various levels, there is a need for critical reevaluation and a greater degree of attention to nuance and subtlety. Yet, if used with sensitivity and discernment, the dependency paradigm provides an eminently viable way of investigating the dynamics of past and contemporary Hawaiian development.

A second *caveat* about the context in which the book has been written: I make no claim that this work is in any way "definitive," or that it constitutes a new "history" of the Hawaiian Islands. I believe that the historical analysis at the core of the study is both accurate and clearly argued. However, given the fact that the broad sweep of the study has been gained at the expense of in-depth description of many important issues, this cannot be considered a genuine academic history of Hawaii. It is rather an attempt to show how dependency has applied to the Hawaiian case over the last two centuries, and thus can be used to critique existing scholarship, and as one foundation for a new political economy.

The book is based on a project begun in the early 1970s as a personal inquiry into Hawaii's political economy. During a period when I was unemployed and also deeply depressed about the war in Indochina, I began researching such subjects as the power structure in the Islands, local history and politics, and the role of tourism in the economy. This research eventually resulted in a number of articles and academic papers and drew me into the political science department of the University of Hawaii, where I did the bulk of the research and writing.

What my background and experience have made of me is someone committed to the idea that quite "ordinary" men and women are capable of building a social order that I would define as "rational," democratically accountable, socially just, and as ecologically sound as possible: in short, a society that answers *real and universal* human needs for dignity, self-respect, and genuine solidarity with other people. If my academic work has any validity, I feel that it is as a catalyst to help ignite people to play a creative role in the great social dramas of our time, as a means to *empower* them in their struggles. The touchstone of my frame of reference is always what I conceive to be the real interests and welfare of the great majority of my fellow human beings.

Part 1

THE TIES THAT BIND

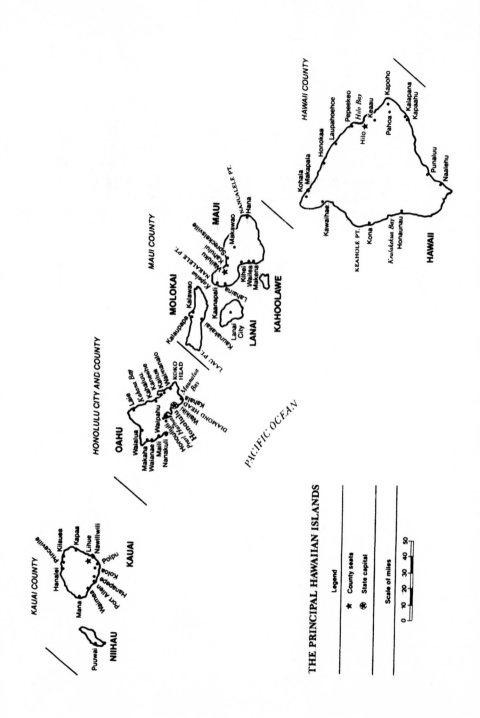

THE PRINCIPAL HAWAIIAN ISLANDS

Legend

★ County seats

✪ State capital

Scale of miles

0 10 20 30 40 50

1
To Kealekekua Bay and Beyond

We are in the eighteenth century. It was a busy century, in science
and speculation and writing, in economic experimentation and war,
in building and art; a revolutionary century, far beyond the confines
of politics and social relations.

—J. C. Beaglehole,
The Life of Captain Cook (1979)

"In the morning of the 18th, an island made its appearance bearing
north by east and soon after, we saw land bearing north and entirely detached from the former. Both had the appearance of high
land."[1] So noted one James Cook, captain of His Brittanic Majesty's
Navy, in January 1778, his hard-traveling ships a source of awe and
mystery to those Hawaiians gazing across from the shore at what
they called the "forest that has slid down into the sea."[2]

On the threshold of that contact which would so indelibly mark
the future of Hawaii, we can appreciate this voyage as but one
more culmination of almost a millenium of European development. The sudden appearance of British vessels on Hawaii's
shores in 1778 was neither an accident nor, as some would have it,
an "act of fate." Indeed, this voyage may be viewed in retrospect as
simply another logical step among so many, another outward
thrust of Western European power in a process of expansion that
had commenced in the eleventh century.

James Cook and his hardy tars were thus the inheritors of a
dynamic tradition stretching back over a score of generations: this
era was marked by the emergence of Western Europe from the
economic and social breakdown of the early feudal age and the rise
of an urban civilization with a market economy geared to generating demands for scarce commodities, valuable minerals, and the
far-off lands where these could be found. That Cook and his companions were British is significant: England had become over the
previous two centuries a prominent European and world power.
This relatively small island kingdom, once an economically primi-

11

tive raw-wool exporter for the more sophisticated Flemish textile industry (in the fourteenth and fifteenth centuries), had become a nation about to take the unprecedented leap into the Industrial Revolution.

Mercantile activities overseas (a natural consequence of *internal* development within England) became the foundation for the massive accumulation of capital upon which English commercial and industrial preeminence was to be based. By the sixteenth century, English commercial interests had established themselves in a dominant relationship to the more economically underdeveloped lands of Eastern Europe (Poland, Russia), from which they secured needed lumber (for shipbuilding) as well as foodstuffs and other vital primary products. They had also established a similar relationship along the coastal regions of Africa, where they obtained slaves for their own West Indian plantations or carried them elsewhere, often making profits that were nothing short of stupendous. North America and India furnished monopoly markets for English manufactures, being themselves restricted from competing with English goods by tariffs and other prohibitions from London, while sending enormous amounts of raw materials and specie to lubricate the commercial apparatus of the "mother country." England, more than any other country in the late eighteenth century, had the motivation and the ability to mobilize resources for expansion overseas.

Hence the James Cook who disembarked in Hawaii in 1778 carried a most significant inheritance. He was heir to the initial thrust of the Industrial Revolution, an age of unprecedented, undreamed of change and innovation in which technical miracles were the order of the day. Coking coal was revolutionizing the process of iron smelting. Nine years before Cook's two ships, the *Discovery* and the *Resolution*, reached the Hawaiian Islands, Richard Arkwright had patented the spinning frame and James Watt had done likewise for his new invention, the steam engine. A year after Cook's voyage, the first iron bridge would arch across an English stream.

Cook, a fifty-year-old Yorkshireman, was the quintessential new Western man. Son of a laborer, his rise from able-bodied sailor to officer represented the miniscule, yet nevertheless significant, new social mobility that allowed a small minority of men of ability to occupy positions that in Asia or Africa would have been unthinkable. He was also the progenitor of a kind of professional who has only come into his own in our era: the technician, intellectual, and scientist at the service of the wide-ranging schemes and stratagems of businessmen and diplomats. Cook was one of the first of this species and he knew that his presence in Hawaiian waters was the consequence of a mission entrusted to him by the British Admiralty: to discover what was then believed to be a Northwest Passage across northern Canada that would provide England, increasingly dependent upon international commerce for economic prosperity, with a shorter, more direct route to Asia and assure its strategic control over the vital trans-Pacific trade with the China coast. Cook thus represented the leading wedge of an official England increasingly influenced by manufacturing-merchant-financial-shipping interests determined to spread commerce (and reap profits) by virtue of a host of overseas strategies, including exploration.

The Hawaii to which the English came in 1778 was a world removed from the Great Britain of George III. The economy was based on subsistence agriculture and fishing, and life moved in harmonious patterns around the cycles of field and sea. Taro and other crops were cultivated on elaborate terraces, fed by a network of complex irrigation facilities carrying water from high above, and were exchanged for food from the sea. A *kapu* system of strict prohibitions, strongly Polynesian in form, guided the daily lives of the people; political authority was a monopoly of the chiefs (*alii*), the most powerful of whom controlled large areas, or even whole islands, within the eight-island chain. Nowadays, amid so much cynicism and despair, it has become all too easy to romanticize precontact Hawaii and ignore evidence of the sometimes harsh rule of the *alii*, the rigidity of the social structure, and the brutal punishment meted out to those considered wrongdoers. Yet one does sense the presence of strong elements of sharing and mutual concern, of communal work and play, and of human solidarity that makes it very attractive to us today.

By 1778, when the dynamic forces of Western expansionism appeared upon the scene, the two cultures were already irreconcilably different and the violence that flared from the moment of first contact was only a reflection of deeply rooted differences between their aims and their cultures. To James Cook, arriving from an

aggressive, commercially minded England on the way to industrialization, preoccupied with property rights and material wealth,
the Hawaiians seemed remarkably nonchalant about their possessions. Cook seemed somewhat puzzled that "not only their plantations, which are spread all over the country, but also their houses,
their clothing were left unguarded without the smallest apprehension."[3] A Hawaiian named Samuel Kamakau later expressed this
different world view rather poetically, when he said, "You foreigners regard the winds, the rain, the land, and sea as things to make
money with; but we look upon them as loving friends with whom
we share the universe."[4]

Cook's voyage broke Hawaii's millenium of isolation from the
world beyond Polynesia: within a few years, a varied assortment of
Westerners were touching at the Islands on their way across an
increasingly traveled Pacific. Hawaii's role in the late eighteenth-
century trans-Pacific trade became that of a provisioning station for
the handful of U.S. and English fur traders bound yearly for
China. As one merchant wrote with gratitude, "What a happy discovery these islands. What would the American fur trade be without them to winter at and get every refreshment?"[5] The impact of
this early European intrusion was unevenly felt. The foreigners
introduced the previously unknown concept of trade for profit in
their dealings with the fishermen and agriculturalists: island foodstuffs and primary products—pigs, fowls, fruits, vegetables, yams,
firewood—were bartered for simple manufactured iron objects
and tools. (In 1795, for example, the going price was 1 English
musket for 9 large hogs, while a chisel fetched 6 pigs.)[6] The women
quickly learned that their favors would be readily rewarded with
the bright calico cloth and trinkets that every sailor had crammed
into his sea chest. Some basic cultural beliefs were shaken. And yet
the subsistence economy remained viable, with most Hawaiians living much as had their pre-contact ancestors.

As early as a decade after Cook's landing, then, we can discern
the pattern that was to last for the next two centuries: Hawaii as a
resource base for the dominant economic-political interests in the
Pacific, repeatedly shifting its economic role in reaction to much
greater economic transformations originating in the world's economic centers. Thus in the eighteenth century, Hawaiians began to
become integrated (in a marginal yet significant manner) in the

economic grid that led from the fur-trapping camps of the Pacific Northwest to the entrepots of South China. Provisioning was the first mode of integration into this global economy, and yet when expansion from the center decreed change—in this case, when food production on the Pacific Coast reached the point where it could adequately supply merchant vessels—the trade quickly expired. This pattern was to be repeated with other goods and services throughout the ensuing centuries.

Political cooptation of the Hawaiian elite was the essential prerequisite for integration of the Hawaiian economy into the emerging global economy. From the first, many of the chiefs were enamored of the new commodities and weapons brought by the foreigners and sought to use them—and their carriers—as a new source of status and power against their political rivals. As one contemporary wrote:

> Many inducements are held out to sailors to remain here. If they conduct themselves with propriety, they rank as chiefs . . . at all events they are certain of being maintained by some of the chiefs, who are always anxious to have white men about them. The king has a considerable number in his service, chiefly carpenters, joiners, masons, blacksmiths and bricklayers.[7]

Perhaps the most influential of these *haoles*, as these (and subsequent) white outsiders were called, was Captain George Vancouver, one of Cook's junior officers at Kealekekau Bay, a wildly moody man who made five trips to Hawaiian waters and enjoyed cruising around the 300-mile-long archipeligo exhorting the chiefs to live "righteous" lives. Always a man ahead of his time, he envisioned the Hawaiian Islands as a mid-Pacific link between British possessions along the west coast of Canada and the new colony of Australia. He even landed a bull and cow in Hawaii in anticipation of future needs. His most ardent protegée, a ruthlessly ambitious Big Island chief named Kamehameha, was deeply engaged in a bitter conflict with the powerful kings of Maui and Kauai. In return for military assistance, Kamehameha agreed to cede the Big Island to Great Britain, and the Union Jack was hoisted to the intonations of Hawaiian chants. Much to Vancouver's disappointment, however, the era of worldwide imperialism had not yet arrived and the Foreign Office in London, more concerned with events closer to home than with an obscure island in a remote part of the world, ignored this act of annexation. The flag came down.[8]

Kamehameha used his contacts with Westerners to secure arms and technology that gave him a decisive superiority over his opponents and eventually enabled him to unite almost all of Hawaii under his rule. Thus two European sailors managed the king's guns at the crucial battle of Iao, while late in 1795 the army of Oahu's King Kalanikipule was largely broken by artillery fire directed by Europeans. One of Kamehameha's critics, Kekuaolani, was strongly anti-foreign and charged after Kamehameha's death (in the words of the English sailor John Young) that the monarch was a creature of the Europeans: "These were the ones, according to him, who had contributed most to enslave them and to concentrate the sovereignty in the hands of a single individual."[9]

Western guns may have placed Kamehameha on the throne, but his successors were to pay an extravagant price for that victory. The king's proud declaration that "I have made my Islands an asylum for all nations" would return to haunt later monarchs,[10] for political consolidation would prove beneficial primarily to the outsiders, who could now deal with a single centralized authority, one heavily indebted to, and easily coopted by, them. In unifying the Hawaiian Islands under the auspices of Western patronage, the new monarch became their client, gaining foreign support for his political aspirations (and need for personal aggrandizement) in return for Hawaiian resources and labor power. Indeed, the immense supplies of sandalwood, so highly valued by Western merchants for the China trade, being hoisted into the hulls of U.S. and English schooners to pay for the king's firearms and luxuries were already having a crushing impact upon the Hawaiian commoners. In the process, the king forfeited his maneuverability. How ironic that in retrospect the unification of the Hawaiian Islands was an important step toward dependency, external control, and loss of sovereignty.

2

A Tale of Sandalwood and Whaling

If a big wave comes in, large fishes will come from the dark ocean which you never saw before, and when they see the small fishes they will eat them up. The ships of the white man have come, and smart people have arrived from the great countries which you have never seen before. They know our people are few in number and living in a small country. They will eat us up.

—David Malo (1837)

Precisely how vulnerable the Hawaiian subsistence economy was to Western capitalist penetration was revealed by the sandalwood trade, which began in earnest around 1810. Dorothy Shineberg notes that the "sandalwood trade of the Pacific Islands owed its existence to a domestic revolution in England," the replacement of coffee by tea as a mass popular drink. This necessitated finding commodities that could be traded profitably to the Chinese suppliers of tea in Canton and stem the one-way flow of gold and silver out of English coffers—a cause of grave concern in this mercantile age when balance of payments deficits were regarded with horror.[1] Sandalwood—a fragrant wood found in the forests of some Pacific islands and used by Chinese craftsmen for making fans, wood ornaments, and incense—was in great demand for this purpose. Fijian and Marquesan sandalwood supplies were exhausted even before the Hawaiian trade began to peak, and Hawaii soon became known in the entrepots of South China as the "sandalwood mountains."

The sandalwood trade reversed the post-Cook primacy of British interests in Hawaii. Almost from its inception, the trade was U.S. dominated, with New Englanders playing the major role: three of the four commercial houses represented in Hawaii were based there. Each maintained a ship in Hawaii to collect the wood and had vessels scattered throughout the Pacific engaged in other trading activities.[2] New England was economically diversified and ad-

17

vanced, with whaling and textile manufacture replacing agriculture as its economic mainstay. Boston was one of the three centers of international shipping on the Atlantic seaboard, and both Massachusetts and Rhode Island, highly urbanized and food deficient, had adopted the road of industrial specialization. Textiles, iron tools, agricultural implements, refined sugar, and rum flowed out of these New England ports to the other states and overseas. Samir Amin sums up this process well:

> The function fulfilled by New England was a special one from the outset. A model, such as history has rarely provided, of a society based on petty-commodity production, it took England's place as the new center in relation to the periphery constituted by the slave-owning colonies of the South and the West Indies. Having thrown off control by the monopolies of metropolitan merchant capital, New England became a fully developed center.[3]

New Englanders were not strangers to the Pacific. By the time of the sandalwood trade, they could already claim a generation-old acquaintance with the Hawaiian Islands and points further west. Indeed, the first American millionaire, Elias Derby of Salem, Massachusetts, had reaped his fortune in the China trade, and by 1800 scores of New England-based ships were cruising the Pacific-Asian shipping lanes in pursuit of pepper, nutmeg, cinnamon, silk, and oriental curios. Profits on these cargoes were enormous, reaching as high as 700 percent in some cases. The fact that Hawaii now possessed something of value on the international market, a commodity that could be lucratively exchanged at Canton (sandalwood cost 1¢ per pound in Hawaii and brought 34¢ per pound in China),[4] provided an adequate incentive to lure a host of merchants into the Islands, ready to foist unseaworthy ships, beads, silk hats, handkerchiefs, scissors, and even billiard tables upon a gullible monarch and his chiefs, all of whom were only too eager to sign promissory notes. From Boston, the owners of the brig *Ann* advised her captain, "If you can, sell the king any articles of your cargo on advantageous terms, to receive your payment in sandalwood when you return from the coast."[5]

The transition from British to U.S. dominance was to be consolidated by subsequent U.S. control of whaling and plantation agriculture. But the pro-British Hawaiian royal family regarded U.S. designs with suspicion. As late as 1822 the king of Hawaii, in a letter to George IV, offered to place the Islands under the British crown; and James Jackson Jarves, a contemporary historian, also commented upon the fairly widespread Hawaiian "sentiment that England was their protector and exercised a species of guardianship of their country."[6] Nevertheless, U.S. influence became steadily more noticeable. While very much a second-rate power in comparison with Great Britain, the new country increasingly saw itself as the future colossus of the Western hemisphere. In 1823 President John Q. Adams dispatched an agent to Colombia, and advised him: "As navigators and manufacturers, we are already so far advanced in a career which they are yet to enter."[7] The Monroe Doctrine, proclaiming Latin America to be essentially a U.S. sphere of influence, was issued the same year.

If Hawaiian society was vulnerable to Western intrusion because of its lack of military power and its relatively primitive technology, then the unwillingness of the elite to confront the multifaceted threats posed by external forces to Hawaiian integrity spelled another kind of ruin: the destruction of existing social relationships and of the subsistence economy. The rigidity of the politico-social hierarchy of old Hawaii (like that of sixteenth-century Mexico and Peru), the fact that the elite occupied a position of absolute authority, confounding all attempts at innovation, compounded this failure of leadership. Kamehameha, who held a royal monopoly on the sandalwood trade until his death, became a fervent consumer of high-priced Western goods, including telescopes, cannons, and even ships. He is described in one contemporary account as something of a dandy, clad in "a colored shirt, velveteen britches, red waistcoat, large military shoes and worsted socks, a black silk handkerchief around his neck."[8] Nevertheless, he was still something of a restraining influence on the unbridled exploitation of the Hawaiian commoner and the sandalwood forests, and with his passing the trade came into the hands of more rapacious *alii,* who soon assumed the role of agents and accomplices in the destruction of their own culture. Their background of privilege and prerogative, their attachment to conspicuous consumption as a leading component of status, and their refusal to broaden the base of community decision-making to include new groups from lower classes all made them unfit for the role of leadership that inheritance had thrust upon them.

It was not long before any respect for the rights of commoners gave way to a harsh exploitation—new taxes, new claims on the produce of the soil, and so on—as the chiefs ordered the commoners deeper into the mountains in search of fresh sources of the wood. Visitors saw long lines of people returning down the twisting mountain paths, logs strapped to their shoulders. A contemporary observer reported: "On one occasion, I saw two thousand persons laden with fagots of sandalwood coming down from the mountains to deposit their burdens in the royal storehouse, wearied with their unpaid labors."[9] The pressure to deliver ever increasing quantities became so intense that the subsistence economy began to disintegrate as agriculturalists lacked the time necessary for food production. Famine stalked the Islands, and it became a common sight to see "men driven by hunger to eat wild and bitter herbs, moss, etc."[10] In frustration, embittered commoners tore the *iliahi* trees out of the ground—roots and all—to destroy the trade.

As both the quality and availability of sandalwood diminished, it left the impecunious *alii* with staggering debts to the handful of merchants resident in Honolulu, a group insignificant in numbers but conscious of their economic interests and prepared to resort to power plays against a weak Hawaiian monarchy equally easily influenced by both strong outsiders and powerful *alii.* "Respecting our own debts, I am at a loss what to say, our prospects darken and brighten alternately," was the report of Dixie Wildes to his New England commercial house. He added ominously, "I hope you and Bryant and Sturgis will make a strong representation to the government. A ship of war here or I fear we shall not get our debts."[11]

The merchants' pleas for aid brought about the first incidence of gunboat diplomacy. In 1826 Captain Thomas of the U.S. Navy moored his vessel in Honolulu harbor and pressed the Hawaiian government for the repayment of various outstanding debts. Sometime later the *Vincennes* arrived to apply further pressure on the chiefs, who eventually acknowledged $50,000 in debts and agreed to continue to shepherd the commoners into the mountains to cut still more wood.[12]

Sandalwood, once among Hawaii's most plentiful upland tress, is today probably unrecognizable to at least 90 percent of the people in the Islands. Yet, ironically, Hawaii may have been spared the greater calamities reserved for those in lands containing riches far more coveted than sandalwood. Consider the fate of Latin America, where large numbers of people were enslaved for generations so that fabulously rich gold and silver mines could be pillaged for the ultimate benefit of merchants, bankers, and aristocrats in London, Paris, Amsterdam, and Madrid. Only ghosts haunt Potosí, Bolivia, from whose mines legend tells us poured enough silver to form a bridge across the Atlantic to Seville. And Guanajuato and Zacatecas, the fabled Mexican gold mines, are now just a desert of slag and gaping craters, seen only by impoverished peasants walking by on dusty roads.

The end of the sandalwood trade provided only a momentary pause on the road leading to Hawaii's further integration into the evolving global capitalist economy. By the third decade of the nineteenth century, Hawaii was emerging as the principal field base for New England's newly booming Pacific whaling industry, and a new group of resident merchants soon became a fixture in the Islands. The exhaustion of North Atlantic whaling grounds, at a time of high prices for whale oil (widely used in lubricants, oil lamps, soaps, paints, varnish, etc.), diverted hundreds of whalers into the plentiful hunting grounds of the Central and North Pacific. Hawaii was only a forty-day sail to the Japanese coast, fifteen days to the Gulf of California, and thirty days to the Kodiak coast of Alaska. It was thus a natural stopping point for captains anxious to refit and reprovision and allow their crews some sorely needed relaxation while they transshipped their accumulated catch of whale bone and oil to swift, graceful clipper ships standing by for the run to the United States. Once again, a combination of factors *exogenous* to the Hawaiian Islands—high whale oil prices, the decision by New England whaling interests to transfer their activities to the Pacific, and consequently the huge expansion of the U.S. whaling fleet (aggregate tonnage of whaling vessels increased from 1230 tons in 1815 to 136,927 in 1840)[13] involved Hawaii in the whaling industry. And, like the sandalwood trade before it, whaling was overwhelmingly American: between 1845 and 1854, 4,402 ships from the United States docked in Hawaii, as compared to 405 from all other nations combined.

Whaling had a much greater impact on Island economic and social structure than did sandalwood. For the first time, the Hawaiian masses were drawn into the cash economy as workers and producers on a regular basis. Attracted by the promise of town life, many young people journeyed to the leading whaling towns, Lahaina and Honolulu, to seek work, engage in casual prostitution, or even to set their mark to a ship's book for a two- or three-year voyage. In the years 1845–47 alone, two thousand Hawaiian men signed on as sailors; hundreds of others crossed the ocean to labor for the Hudson's Bay Company in the Oregon Territory. A local proletariat appeared amidst the steadily growing port facilities of the two whaling towns, earning from $50 to $200 a year or more through skilled and unskilled labor.[14]

Hawaiian agriculturalists in inland areas started growing food crops expressly for sale, sending vegetables and potatoes to town markets and ships' purchasing agents, thereby taking a step toward the extinction of the fading subsistence economy. This commerce was orchestrated by the local chiefs, who claimed two-thirds of the receipts as their own.[15] Yet they remained unable and unwilling to employ these capital resources in constructive economic ventures; they existed, instead, as a financial sieve to enrich the *haole* merchants, and money in their possession quickly flowed back into the hands of the traders.

Honolulu and Lahaina became the foci for the more than 1,700 whaling ships that docked in Hawaiian waters between 1829 and 1843, disgorging the first tourist onslaught to the Islands; by the 1840s, 600 whalers were appearing every year. Some 5,300 visitors came in 1834, and this figure had reached 19,700 by 1846.[16] Lahaina's Front Street—the scene of New England sailors wearing checked shirts and bell-bottomed trousers, who stormed about, casting off the rigors and harsh discipline of months at sea, of escaped slaves, and of footloose Europeans arranging liaisons with their ladies of the night—witnessed a lucrative wholesale and retail trade whose aggregate value amounted to well over $100,000 per year by the 1840s.

With the advent of whaling, another facet of Hawaii's incorporation into the world capitalist system appeared: uneven economic development—the overdependence upon those sectors of the economy linked to the international market—at the expense of a more evenly balanced, Hawaii-centered, and locally managed development. In the 1830s, for instance, income from whaling at Honolulu ranged from a low of $69,200 to a high of $129,750 annually, while exports from all of Hawaii for the year 1838 were only $65,850; whaling was thus more significant in dollar volume than all other exports taken together.[17] This was recognized by one of the most influential of the many *haole* ministers and advisors in the Hawaiian government, R. C. Wyllie: "The prosperity of these islands depends mainly on the whale ships that annually flock to their ports. Were the whaling fishing to fall off, the islands would relapse into . . . insignificance."[18] Meanwhile, the colonial type of trading pattern, which had started with provisioning, was reinforced by the whaling trade: Hawaii imported finished manufactured goods like cotton cloth, naval stores, iron products, furniture, cordage, etc., and paid for them with services and foodstuffs sold to the whalers.

Honolulu experienced a meteoric rise in importance under the impact of whaling, and began to establish what was to be its complete political, economic, and cultural domination over the rest of the Island chain—its role as *a center within the periphery*. Fifty years earlier it had been an obscure fishing village near the Nuuannu Stream; by 1810 it was still little more than a shabby camp containing some thatched pili-grass cottages and adobe trader shacks lodging the sixty resident foreigners. By the next decade it was a bustling little port, handling the business of a fair number of merchant ships and offering the services of its public houses and taverns (complete with billiard tables and "all kinds of spirits") to entertain the two hundred foreigners now comprising the mercantile establishment.[19] By the 1830s, we hear of a town of ten thousand fast becoming an adjunct of New England: Yankee English spoken, Yankee ships in the harbor. There were four American mercantile houses and two English ones—worth between $15,000 and $100,000—as well as eleven shopkeepers, mostly American, and, as one visitor reported, "Mercantile business is almost entirely in the hands of the foreigners and they are growing rich rapidly."

At least two of the Big Five firms which were later to dominate Island life had their origins in this era, their profits derived almost totally from the wholesale and retail business and services, rather than from the production of goods. Doctors, ministers, businessmen, carpenters, all lived in three-storied frame houses with verandas and window shades. Numerous street-level shops and warehouses were alive with business, while general merchandising firms prospered through their provisioning and repair work. Chinese tea and silks, specie from Mexico and timber from California were consumed locally or warehoused and transshiped elsewhere. As a Pierce and Brewer advertisement in 1840 put it: "Having constantly on hand and for sale on liberal terms merchandise imported from the United States, England, Chile, and China and adopted to the trade of the North Pacific."[20] To be sure, this was not a sophisticated town, even by the standards of the day. However, the six hundred foreigners were increasingly directing their commercial activities toward a grid of what would eventually become "downtown Honolulu"—Mauna Kea, King, Hotel, and Beretania streets, intersected by Queen, Merchant, and Bishop.

After 1860, as whales became scarcer and voyages therefore longer and more costly, the whaling industry fell into a gradual, but ultimately fatal, decline. Its final death throes occurred in a horrible incident in 1871 in which the bulk of the whaling fleet was trapped within the massive glacial icefields of the Arctic, swallowed up in an abyss of ice. But it would have ended soon in any case: petroleum was coming into widespread use, displacing the whale oil market. Moreover, New England shipowners had turned their attention to the more profitable opportunities of acting as commercial carriers for that region's expanding factories and mills. The whaling that did continue in the Pacific homeported out of San Francisco.[21]

If whaling had been an unpredictable, sometimes wildly cyclical industry (in 1847 and 1848, for example, the industry temporarily collapsed), over which the merchants of Hawaii could exercise almost no control, and if they had become far too dependent on it as a source of income, it nonetheless laid the foundation for a bourgeoisie that was to dominate Hawaii for many years. This was a stratum of confident New Englanders, Englishmen, Scots, Germans, and others who possessed the capital, commercial acumen, and skill to seize upon whatever seemed to them the most promising venture of the moment. Hawaii's period of mercantile capitalism, with its service-based commerce, was passing; the day of substantial investment in productive assets and agro-industrial capitalism was about to begin, and they were here to take advantage of it. The outcome of this next phase of Hawaii's development would find the Islands bound immeasurably closer to the world market economy and confirmed in their role as a periphery. But before we turn to this, it is important to consider the fate of the Hawaiians themselves.

3
Dispossession of a People

The land is a mother that never dies.

—Ancient Polynesian epigram

The social order and moral standards of the coming generations of Hawaii *nei*, whatever their blood, are inevitably to become English in type as well as language. By English, of course, we mean not British but "The Greater England": and America being our nearest and overshadowing neighbor, it must be Anglo-American. Our literature, our art, our manners, our moral and political opinions will be mainly American. . . . The coming form of government will be that of America.

—Reverend Sereno (1884)

The dramatic changes that transformed the Hawaiian economy from subsistence to mercantilist-based within the space of three-quarters of a century were accompanied by an increasing sophistication of the governmental apparatus. The impetus for this lay with the commercial revolution that rendered obsolete old Polynesian institutions and demanded a governmental structure and legal system that could respond to the needs of a capitalist class of entrepreneurs and merchants; and much of the day-to-day work in creating this was carried out by a group of New England missionaries who had first arrived in the Islands in 1820, charged with nothing less than "raising up the whole population to an elevated state of Christian civilization."[1] These missionaries conducted the business of proseletyzing with much the same strategy as those other New Englanders, the merchants and ship captains, conducted the business of making profits: they cultivated the Hawaiian nobility assiduously, and used the conversion of some influential individuals at the top of the hierarchy to spread conversion on a mass basis throughout the populace.[2] Thus gaining spiritual influence with royalty, they soon approached the levers of political power, at first as advisors to the government and later as staff for the upper echelons of the bureaucracy—and the *real* power behind the throne.

Missionary intervention soon modified the autocracy of the monarch to bring it more in line with the system of constitutional parliamentary government that was developing in Western Europe. Tenacious, strong-willed clergymen like Gerrit Judd and John Riccord wrote a constitution in 1852 that granted decisive powers to themselves as ministers of the king. One admires their versatility. Later, former Maine Congressman Elisha Allen, a bespectacled sugar planter, would be, in turn, minister of finance, chief justice, and minister of foreign affairs. As minister of education, Richard Armstrong, pastor of Honolulu's Kawaihae Church, played an important role in consigning the Hawaiian language to obscurity and Americanizing the school system. By 1842, one foreign observer was commenting, "Much expectations for the new government. Missionaries now have everything in their own hands."[3] Five years later, *The Sandwich Islands* editorialized: "The king is king in name only, all executive prerogatives and functions of the king have been assumed by individuals constituting themselves a Privy Council. Either Dr. Judd or Mr. Richards presides at the legislative council and explains the law, then raises his hand to vote for final adoption, and they all vote with him."[4]

One cannot (as many in Hawaii do today) attribute base and opportunistic motives to *every* facet of these missionaries' behavior. Some members of the mission operated out of deep personal attachment to Hawaiian welfare (as they perceived it), intending to safeguard the territorial integrity of the small island kingdom by modernizing governmental structures and commercial relations as rapidly as possible. When, with the blessings of the Hawaiian royalty, they created a Westernized system of government, built an infrastructure of harbors and roads to accelerate commerce, and encouraged internal economic expansion, they believed that the preservation of Hawaiian sovereignty was fully compatible with the promotion of a capitalist economy. They agreed with the views of William Miller, an English visitor in 1831, who warned the Islanders of the need to expedite commercial relations with the capitalist powers and streamline the workings of the Hawaiian economy as a means of self-preservation: "It can barely be supposed that foreign nations will permit so important a source of commerce to be impeded or seriously molested by caprices and arbitrary measures of the native rulers."[5]

Heirs to a startlingly bleak perspective of the human condition, deeply pious, often humorless, the missionaries brought with them a harsh Calvinism whose emphasis on the godliness inherent in the accumulation of private property and material blessings ("Seest thou a man diligent in his business. He shall stand before kings.") had provided the guiding principles for a society in the early stages of industrial capitalism. This was the ideological baggage of the neat and prosperous merchants, factory owners, shopkeepers, and bankers who wielded power in New England. Complaints about Hawaiian "shiftlessness" and "lack of thrift" suddenly became legion. The missionaries were horrified at a Hawaiian lifestyle that was at once casual and oriented to human gregariousness. As the Reverend John Emerson wrote to his brother, "I cannot go on preaching to a lot of people sitting on their haunches with no purpose in life."[6] Samuel N. Castle, one of the founders of today's mighty multinational corporation, Castle and Cooke, spoke in the moralistic homilies so many of those associated with the missions used when he advocated the establishment of a new sugar plantation to benefit workless Hawaiians: "As it is true that indolence begets vice, so it is true that industry promotes virtue. All successful efforts taken to produce industry by proper means tend to promote virtue and must be beneficial to that people on whom they are bestowed."[7] The missionaries' automatic response was to expunge those Hawaiian customs that seemed to undermine the grand objective of material accumulation—in effect, most of the indigenous culture: traditional art, language, dance, sexual mores, nudity, etc.

Ultimately, however, the missionaries' most profound contribution to the destruction of the old society was something for which their capitalist values, personal stake in the new sugar economy, and national loyalties had prepared them well. This was an alliance with, and ultimately integration into, the existing mercantile class, so that the two together could guide Hawaii along the next stage of dependent economic development.

This did not happen automatically, however. During the initial years of missionary activity, certain conflicts arose between merchants and clergy as the early missionaries attempted to protect the Hawaiians from undue exploitation and abuse by unscrupulous foreigners. By 1826 there were open confrontations at public meetings. The merchants charged that missionary influence was encouraging people to neglect their fields in favor of reading books. These merchants, whose profits depended upon regular deliveries of locally grown foodstuffs and related products for sale to foreign vessels, opposed clerical practices that limited their access to Hawaiian production. Some comments were most unkind. Trader Stephen Reynolds spoke of missionary leader Hiram Bingham as the "most impudent puppy I have seen in many a day . . . a blood sucking, cash sucking, lazying, lying wretch."[8]

But by mid-century the interests of both groups were on their way to being reconciled. Even those missionaries sincerely interested in maintaining Hawaii as a sovereign nation wanted this to take the form of a modern capitalist economy intimately linked with the United States. And this growing identity of interest was cemented as both came to own land and have an interest in the plantation economy that was emerging as the result of a new land tenure system. The first sugar plantation was established at Koloa, Kauai, in 1836 and was a definite financial success. This acted as a spur to other investors, and sugar production doubled between 1837 and 1847, leading planter William Ladd to predict confidently: "That this will become a sugar country is quite evident, if we may judge from the varieties of sugar cane now existing here, its adaptation to the soil; the price of labor and a ready market."[9] But if this was to happen, Hawaii's laws and customs had to reflect those in England and the United States, and land legislation and agricultural practices had to be brought in line with foreign notions. With more and more at stake—world traveler J. Henshaw Belcher, passing through Hawaii, noted that, "The Americans alone have at least $572,000 worth of property at stake upon Hawaiian grounds. They have two or three sugar mills in successful operation and two extensive silk plantations on Kauai alone."[10]— foreigners in and out of government pressed the king for basic changes in land tenure arrangements, primarily aimed at making tenure more secure.

In 1836, when the U.S.S. *Peacock* dropped anchor off Oahu, gold-braided Commodore Kennedy paid an official visit to the king, advising him to establish firm property guarantees for foreign landholders, and to allow U.S. businessmen to do business without interference from the monarchy. The Hawaiians demurred, insisting on the validity of their thousand-year-old landholding traditions. This was not an adequate response in a world where Western arms were battering down every barrier to the penetration of commerce. The British, on the eve of the Opium War—which was to force China into a role of vassalage for the next century—still regarded Hawaii as something of a sphere of influence and threatened "an end to good understanding between the two governments if British commercial interests were not secured."[11] Next came the French, in the person of the swaggering Captain La Place and his frigate the *Artemise*, demanding (at gunpoint) and receiving economic privileges for French residents. All of this culminated in an 1839 law protecting building lots from confiscation. "The visits of the American, English and French men-of-war during the last sixteen months established the inviolability of property and person and the natives made to fear the law of nations," reflected merchant Charles Pierce with a measure of contentment.[12]

Nevertheless, dissatisfaction remained rife among the new landowners, to whom the existing land arrangements seemed vague and murky, too crippling in their restrictions and too subject to the irrational whim of chief or king. They wanted land to be not merely available but also a transferrable commodity, with laws protecting ownership rights and facilitating large-scale investment. Their concern was intensified by events on the West Coast of North America. The California Gold Rush and U.S. acquisition of the Oregon Territory had stimulated a population influx and opened up vast new opportunities for Hawaiian producers to supply potatoes ($27 a barrel was the going price in California, as compared to $2 in Hawaii), butter, sugar, and coffee, and to reap windfall profits.[13] As early as 1846, the Reverand Richard Armstrong (owner of 1,979 acres in Maui) was informing a correspondent: "A brisk trade is opening with Oregon and California. . . . The sugar and molasses of the islands will be in demand in these territories and they will bring lumber, flour, salmon, etc., in exchange."[14] The resulting economic boom had reached such a level four years later that this same Armstrong was writing that "every bean, onion, potato or squash that we have to spare is at once snatched away to California to feed the hungry multitude there."[15] Exports to U.S. Pacific coast ports doubled from 1848 to 1851, to over $25,000. The Reverand William Alexander informed his relatives: "These islands feel more and more the effects of the mighty state that is springing up so near us at California. . . . Every lot and garden is planted and the islands will be able to freight a great number of vegetables during the coming year."[16]

"By 1845," writes Neil Levy, "the land tenure system could neither maintain itself in the face of a hostile foreign world nor accommodate itself to the wishes of that world."[17] A clamor arose demanding the radical revision of land tenure policies in the interest of establishing capitalist agriculture. Under intense pressure to act, the government finally appointed a land commission under the leadership of the Reverand Judd (also a sugar planter of some substance): the Great Mahele, or Division of Lands, of 1848 was the outcome of its labors.

Under the provisions of the Great Mahele, 60 percent of the land in the Hawaiian archipelago (2,479,000 acres) was allocated to the crown and government, 39 percent (1,619,000 acres) to 208 chiefs, and less than 1 percent to the 11,000 commoners. Additional laws conferred the right of ownership upon foreigners, and through the Kuleana Act (1850) granted fee-simple rights to tenants on the land they already occupied (their *kuleanas*). The bourgeoisie hailed the new arrangement as a watershed in the liberation of the Hawaiian commoner: "I thank God that these things are now at an end, and that the poor *kanaka* may now stand on the border of his *kalo* patch and holding his fee simple patent in his hand, bid defiance to the world."[18] Yet they also were ready to blame the inevitable consequences of the new land policy on the failings of those destined to be its victims. In the words of Judge Lee, who had played a significant role in the new land legislation, "We shall advise the Hawaiians to keep their lands, but if they fail to, on them the responsibility."[19]

And the inevitable did happen: the Hawaiians were severed from the land that had been the basis of their subsistence economy. In theory afforded the opportunity to secure small freeholds, the commoner found the path to becoming the solid yeoman farmer popularly advertised as his future blocked by a series of frustrating and often unintelligible rules and obstacles, derived from an utterly different cultural and economic context from the one he knew. The new system required personal applications for land deeds, proof of occupancy and of having "really cultivated" the land (particularly serious obstacles),[20] and a relatively sizeable cash fee for surveying and registering the land title. Some commoners simply ignored the new legislation and tried to continue the old ways. Western concepts, such as "land title," "land tax," and even the conception of land as a marketable commodity, lay outside the realm of ordinary Hawaiian experience.

Only 28,000 acres were ultimately awarded to the commoners and many of these were subsequently alienated for nonpayment of taxes or noncompliance with some facet of the law. "Once obtained, the *kuleanas* passed rapidly into the hands of the rising sugar plantation operators, or to land speculators," according to Morgan.[21] Indeed, a host of opportunistic "men on the spot" loitered around tax and land offices eagerly snapping up land declared legally vacated. Land baronies were created instantaneously. In addition, the *alii*, incurably addicted to Western luxuries, sold off vast crown holdings for a fraction of their real worth. This was the germination time for a number of the *haole* families that would eventually rise to prominence. In 1856 only 209 of 15,514 land claims were held by foreigners; by 1886 foreigners held two-thirds of all government allotted land.[22]

The ouster of the Hawaiian people from the land was an irreparable blow which doomed them to cultural debasement, economic destitution, and a third-rate status in their own homeland. It continued the policy of appropriating Hawaiian resources to further the ends of capitalist accumulation and had the ultimate effect of undermining, once and for all, the viability of the "Hawaiian way." To quote John Bodley's broad indictment of such Western practices, "The significance of these policies is that they create conditions under which a tribal lifestyle can no longer be a viable alternative for those wishing to pursue it."[23]

For the rising foreign bourgeoisie, however, the dispossession of the Hawaiians was an essential precondition for the flourishing of capitalist export agriculture. Marx speaks of this as a *general* tendency of capitalist development (exhibited in areas far removed from the Hawaiian Islands):

> The transformation of the individualized and scattered means of production into socially concentrated ones, of the pigmy property of the

many into the huge property of the few, the expropriation of the great mass of people from the soil, from the means of subsistence and from the means of labor, this fearful and painful expropriation of the mass of the people forms the prelude to the history of capitalism.[24]

The Great Mahele and the onset of the plantation economy were thus the culmination of a complex, interconnected series of events whose beginnings may be dated from January 1778—or even from centuries before in Europe. The Hawaiians, after an initial, short-lived enchantment with the curious strangers from across the sea, abandoned any illusions about the place they would occupy in a capitalist Hawaii at the service of more economically developed areas. The smoldering discontent against foreign political domination, the destructive nature of the cash- and market-oriented economy on those more accustomed to subsistence modes of production, the land-grabbing and speculation, found expression, in the mid-1840s, in a spate of petitions and memorials addressed to the throne. "If the nation is ours, what good can result from filling the land with foreigners," pleaded one petition from Lahaina, a center of such agitation. "The Hawaiian people will be trodden underfoot by the foreigners. Perhaps not now or perhaps it will not be long before we shall see it. . . . Another thing, the dollar has become the government for the commoner and for the destitute. It will become a dish of relish and the foreign agents will suck it up."[25] And after a meeting in Lahaina, Baldwin reported, "Something seems to have stirred the natives to the bottom. I do not know what was done at the meeting, but I am told the object is to bring about no *haole* rulers."[26]

There were other responses from the grassroots. These included drunkenness—"In rural districts, natives are commonly drunk at all hours of the day, a thing almost unheard of years ago," noted one missionary—suicide, and apathy. Most revealing was the appearance of a number of messianic cults similar to those arising from Zululand to Central Luzon, Wyoming to Burma, as age-old cultures crumbled under Western intrusion. During the 1840s in black, volcanic Puna, a cult of the new "trinity"—Jesus, Jehovah, and Hapu—arose, promising refuge for believers in a world about to be destroyed. And we know of a Kamuela woman, calling herself Lono, who spearheaded a revivalist movement on Oahu's North Shore in 1845. On Kauai and Oahu, hundreds of Hawaiians engaged in never-before-seen rituals under the direction of persons claiming divine sanction. Two decades later, prophets still appeared on the Big Island whispering of ancient mysteries and a world to be reborn.[27] One perceptive observer, the itinerant sailor-novelist Herman Melville, paused to make this notation while wandering around Honolulu: "Are these, alas! the fruits of twenty-five years of enlightenment?"[28]

4
The Rise of King Sugar

> We must cultivate entirely for a foreign market to pay for our importations. We import all our building material and all our clothing and drinks. We can't go back to the times of Kamehameha I and live on *poi* and wear a *malo*.
>
> —Charles Bishop (1874)

What the Great Mahele took from the Hawaiian people was used to lay the foundation of a sugar plantation economy that formed the base of the *haole* elite's economic and political power over the next century. Theodore Morgan, for one, stresses the significance of the Mahele and of the new capitalist land tenure arrangements: "Capital could now be invested with security; the road was clear for the rise of the sugar industry which has chiefly dominated the course of Hawaiian economy since."[1] The forced alienation of thousands of Hawaiians from the soil not only provided the bourgeoisie with vast acres of fertile land for cultivation, but also with a ready-made labor force, which furnished the great bulk of plantation workers until the mid-1870s. R. C. Wyllie, a planter and Hawaii's foreign minister from 1845 to 1865, outlined three ingredients for the commercial success of the sugar industry: "Three fundamental elements essential to our progress are cheap land, cheap money and cheap labor."[2] The Mahele and new land policies delivered at least two of these.

Since the international market defined the economics of sugar production, Island planters adopted many of the same strategies for profitable operations as did their fellow planters (and possible competitors) in other sugar-producing areas. In practice, whether in the Caribbean, the U.S. South, or elsewhere, this meant a substantial concentration of land, labor, and capital in order to produce a cost-efficient crop. These imperatives had a massive socioeconomic impact upon the societies playing host to "King Sugar." To quote Ralph Davis's description of the dynamics of the Caribbean sugar industry:

35

Sugar transformed society in every area it touched, because of the economies of scale that large productive units offered. . . . The sugar plantation changed colonial societies in much the same way that the factory for a time changed English society. The efficient scale of operations required a large concentration of fixed capital and the owner of the capital wanted a completely subordinated and rigidly disciplined labor force.[3]

Sugar societies thus generally came to be characterized by a series of interlinked phenomena: a heavy concentration of political and economic power in the hands of those in control of the production apparatus, a sharply stratified class structure with a strong racial and/or cultural component, and a concentration on one export to the metropolitan areas of North America and Western Europe.

When discussing any facet of Hawaiian development after 1778, we must always be aware of the external influences at work. As noted earlier, it was the steady march of the United States across the Great Plains, over the Rockies, and to the Pacific Coast that had set the stage for a sugar plantation economy in Hawaii. Strategies of continental domination—embodied with notions of "manifest destiny"—along with high world market prices for gold and other Western products, created an enticing market for Island sugar. This was noted in a statement issued by the newly formed Royal Hawaiian Agricultural Society in 1850:

The extension of the territory and government of the United States to the borders of the Pacific, the wonderful discoveries in California and the consequent creation of the mighty state on the western front of the American continent, has as it were, with the wand of a magician, drawn this little group into the very focus of civilization and prosperity.[4]

The composition of the new plantation-centered bourgeoisie was diverse. Some were experienced in Island commerce, old hands in the whaling trade like Charles Pierce, or missionaries released from their obligations by the American Board (in 1850), including Henry Diamond, E. O. Hall, and Walter Rice, all of whom immediately launched business enterprises, as well as S. N. Castle and Amos Starr Cooke, New Englanders who had been acting as purchasing agents for the missions. Their status as ex-missionaries or mission associates aided them immensely, for they were able to benefit from a government policy of selling land to mission members at a fraction of its customary price. Others were newcomers like Charles Bishop, who stepped off an Oregon-bound packet for a brief stay and within three years had become the king's Collector of Customs—and within a dozen years was a prominent merchant, banker, and planter, having married a Hawaiian princess, heir to vast estates. Other such newcomers included Benjamin Dillingham, a Massachusetts sailor who founded a commercial dynasty, and James Campbell, a one-time Maui carpenter who accumulated 15,000 acres in Kahuku and 40,000 more in Ewa, Oahu, in addition to 25,000 on the Big Island.

The setting, typical of the pre-monopolistic stage of capitalist industrial development, was one of numerous small enterprises, lacking adequate capital, frequently going bankrupt, while the industry consolidated itself into larger and larger productive units. By 1847 only five plantations had survived this vigorous "weeding out" process.[5] The origins of the economic domination of Hawaii by the Big Five companies thus lay in this period, as entrepreneurs moved into the vacuum created by the rapid expansion of the plantations, gradually assuming the role of factors for the planters. They performed such essential functions as banking, floating loans, making contacts with shippers and purchasers, and warehousing, and in the process gained control over almost every aspect of the Hawaiian sugar industry. Henry Hackfeld, proprietor of a small fleet of vessels running between Bremen and Honolulu, early realized the possibilities presented by the new industry and became the agent for Koloa and East Maui plantations. Charles Brewer, a relatively venerable merchant house, made the transition from whaling provisioner to sugar factor. A shrewd Englishman, Theophilius Davies, owner of a well-known Honolulu emporium, also began to dabble in the "white gold," while two former members of the mission party, Messrs. Castle and Cooke, operating out of their general merchandise store at King and Fort streets, handled an increasingly lucrative sideline in sugar marketing and loans. Two members of the Maui missionary contingent—Samuel Alexander and Henry Baldwin—became involved in the large-scale cultivation of sugar in Maui. Thus from such a humble start evolved the Big Five: Hackfeld and Company (Amfac), C. Brewer and Company, Theo Davies Company, Castle and Cooke, and Alexander and Baldwin.

Beginning in the late 1840s, a number of approaches were made to officials in Washington by Hawaiian planters with a view toward securing a treaty of reciprocity between the two nations, thus guaranteeing Hawaiian sugar duty-free entry to the continental market. These attempts floundered until the removal of Southern sugar from Northern tables during the Civil War opened the continent to a sizeable influx of Hawaiian sugar. Unprecedented prosperity came in its wake. Sugar prices rose from the rather mediocre level of the 1850s ($.0695 per pound) to a highly profitable $.1719 by 1864, and demand was consistently high.[6] According to a *San Francisco Bulletin* correspondent, sugar in Hawaii had "surmounted all difficulties and is now in the fulltide of success."[7]

High profits stimulated a number of years of rapid expansion, marked by the introduction of newly engineered irrigation systems, modern fertilizers, and ultra-modern machinery. Indeed, those at the apex of the sugar industry, the planters and factors, and their managers and engineers, met the challenge of bringing water to Oahu's central plain and to Wailuku with the same painstaking thoroughness their contemporaries were applying to the design of the Suez Canal and the intercontinental railroads, to the construction of massive new armaments and steel bridges, and to the penetration of remotest equatorial Africa. In this mid-Victorian age of technical miracles, it seemed that no force could stand before determined men armed with powerful new technologies. What was happening in Hawaii, in California, in New England, in the English Midlands, and in so many other places had a common cause: a capitalism impelled toward technological change and innovation to maintain its rate of growth.

Honolulu in the 1860s numbered 13,000 or 14,000 souls and was the focal point of the new plantation economy. Called by one observer, rather extravagantly, the "metropolis of the North Pacific,"[8] its dusty roads and three-story wood-frame houses, where merchants sat in comfortable armchairs and entertained friends around handsomely finished walnut tables, seemed to echo the Western boom town of the same vintage. Elsewhere, the visitor might wander across a scattering of Hawaiians, not yet overtaken by the age, living their time out in pili-grass houses in isolated valleys or remote fishing villages, clinging to the ancient ways in a land long since passed from their hands.

Soon after the onset of large-scale sugar production, it was apparent that the Hawaiian was neither an adequate (disease had reduced the population to *one-sixth* that of the pre-contact era) nor dependable source of labor. Hot-tempered William Hooper, manager of the Koloa Plantation, was driven to the heights of frustration by the casual attitudes of the three hundred or more plantation workers under his employ and was convinced that the Islanders were completely "worthless" as plantation wage labor. "It requires the concentrated patience of a hundred Jobs to get along with these natives," he once muttered in disgust.[9] And so, lacking what they regarded as an adequate, disciplined, domestic workforce, the planters turned to the systematic importation of foreign labor: here is the origin of what would later (erroneously) be labelled the "melting pot of the Pacific."

In retrospect, it seems only natural that in their quest for workers the plantation interests would reach across the ocean to East Asia. Caught up in the extended death throes of the Manchu dynasty, beset by stronger Western intruders and its own internal corruption, burdened with a failing economy and massive regional and national rebellions, mid-century China proved to be a lucrative source. It was not long before pigtailed Chinese coolies, some purchased from mandarins by labor recruiters (in turn financed by the Hawaiian government), some bought at street auctions, were being shipped to Hawaiian plantations to work as contract laborers. Foreign Minister Wyllie, who played a major role in arranging for Chinese labor recruitment, wrote approvingly to a friend about the recently arrived workers: "I agree with you fully in regard to the character of the Chinese laborers. Both in industry and morals, they are vastly superior to our Hawaiian Christians."[10]

The recruiters took their search beyond China. By 1868 they were scouring the provinces of Hiroshima and Yamaguchi in southern Japan in search of hardy, landless peasants interested in working for what they were told would be high wages and good housing: over two hundred thousand Japanese arrived at Honolulu Harbor during the next half-century in pursuit of this dream of a good life.

Numerous studies have documented the sparse wages and

benefits, the atmosphere of brutality imposed by callous overseers
(lunas), and the authoritarian regime under which the indentured
laborers worked (i.e., fines of a month's pay for missing a day's
work and imprisonment for absences, all legally enforceable under
legislation written by the planters). Above all, the immigrants were
regarded by the plantation elite as less than fully human, as inter-
changeable cogs in the productive apparatus—as *commodities* to produce commodities. In the fields, conditions were harsh enough to
exhaust the energies of the most resilient. Housed in camps that
were abominable, even by the standards of the time, carefully seg-
regated by ethnic group to reinforce interethnic animosities, vic-
timized by bosses and foremen who cheated them of part of their
wages, forced to carry passbooks and endure a regimentation bor-
dering on prison conditions, their general situation was neatly
summed up by the San Francisco *Chronicle* (hardly a friend of
working people): "It has been for a good while reported that the
labor system of the Islands is little if any more humane toward the
laborers than Cuban slavery and certainly much worse than slavery
on the Southern cotton and sugar plantations used to be."[11] Yet
these conditions provided the basis for the substantial accumulation of capital by the Island plantation complex during the next
hundred years. Sharply exploitative labor practices resulted in the
accumulation of fortunes from the labor of thousands of plantation
workers who lived at the margin of economic survival.

If the importation of foreign workers solved the planters' labor
problems, the lack of a secure and dependable market for their
agricultural goods still constituted a deep source of concern. The
United States, birthplace and cultural home of a large majority of
the foreign businessmen and nearest point of population concentration, had always seemed the prime market for Island sugar exports, and had proven to be so during the expansion westward and
the Civil War. The war's end, however, brought a sharp drop in
demand—and economic depression to Island growers. By the
1870s the planters found themselves in even more desperate need
of a trade agreement that would make their product competitive in
the American market.

There had for some time been a growing move toward outright
annexation. As early as 1837 the *Pacific Commercial Advertiser,* a
faithful mouthpiece of business views, editorialized that immediate
annexation would mean "national prosperity instead of adversity.

It means the glorious life of the people instead of gradual decay and death."[12] The 1850s brought annexationist sentiment to a fever pitch. Rumors circulated wildly that armed-to-the-teeth toughs—"fillibusterers," as they were called—recruited from California goldmining camps were gathering to embark on an expedition to Hawaii, capture it in gangster fashion, despoil it, and sack, loot, and enslave the population. This never happened, but a number of the king's "loyal" ministers (including Wyllie) acted in collusion with the U.S. consul in Honolulu to try to entice the monarch to accept a treaty of annexation. There was also an offer by New York commercial interests to buy the Islands for $5 million—which led one skeptic to observe that "these ambitious gentlemen can then sell their conquest to the United States on their own terms and pocket something by the operation." A statement signed by nineteen prominent merchants and planters in 1853 solemnly advocated an annexation that "would restore prosperity and security." In his description of this group, U.S. Commissioner Gregg (himself an ardent annexationist) called them "chiefly a party of foreigners—to a large extent American foreigners . . . impelled to favor a new political order by the numerous advantages they may reasonably hope to derive from it."[13]

In the United States, various politicians and newspapers also began calling for annexation. California Congressman J. W. McCorkle declared: "It is essential to our Pacific interests that we should have possession of the Hawaiian Islands." That this was voiced by a California politician is significant, for by 1850 San Francisco was already emerging as a port city of importance with a definite Pacific-Asian commercial orientation.[14]

We also begin to hear military voices drumming up support for the taking of Hawaii as a military necessity. In 1851 Admiral DuPont of the U.S. Navy stated that, "It is impossible to estimate too highly the value and importance of the Hawaiian Islands, whether in a commercial or a military sense." He continued, "Should circumstances ever place them in our hands they would prove the most important acquisition connected with our commercial and naval supremacy in those seas."[15] This was, of course, the very time when Captain Perry—ordered by Washington to open Japan to a trade for which "no limits can be assigned to its further expansion"—was sailing into Tokyo Bay.

U.S. Secretary of State Seward (who had once issued the biblical-like injunction to U.S. merchant capital, "Multiply your ships and send them forth to the East"),[16] having already outflanked Great Britain in the North Pacific by purchasing Alaska, was now determined "to build such an empire as the world has never before seen." Seward's vision of global economic strategies anticipated those of the multinational corporations of a century later: "The nation that draws most from the earth and fabricates most, and sells most to foreign nations must be and will be the greatest power on earth. You want the commerce of the world. This is to be looked for on the Pacific."[17] Hawaii was an important pawn in Seward's plan for Pacific domination, and shortly after the end of the Civil War he sent a blunt message to the United States minister to Hawaii: "It is proper that you should know for your own information that a lawful and peaceful annexation of the Sandwich Islands is deemed desirable."[18]

Yet all this amounted to naught, for annexation was politically impossible at this time: the government in Washington was still far too preoccupied with pulverizing Indian tribes west of the Mississippi and grabbing the Southwest and California from Mexico under the cloak of "Manifest Destiny." Nevertheless, there was undeniable interest in Hawaii, and it would intensify as the century wore on and the United States consolidated itself as an economic and political unit of continental dimensions, developed agriculturally and industrially, and burgeoned as a commercial and military power. This interest was officially recognized by U.S. Secretary of State Daniel Webster in 1842, when, during the course of establishing diplomatic relations with the Hawaiian government, he enunciated the doctrine of special U.S. interest in the Hawaiian Islands:

> The United States . . . are more interested in the fate of the Islands and of their government than any other nation can be; and this consideration induces the president to be quite willing to declare that the Government of the Sandwich Islands ought to be respected . . . that no power ought to seek for any undue control over the existing government . . . or for preferences in matters of commerce.[19]

Then, in 1842, President Tyler issued what was essentially a Monroe Doctrine for Hawaii, asserting that the "United States possesses so very large a share of the intercourse with those islands" and threatening a "decided remonstrance" against those who would menace Hawaiian sovereignty. The Tyler doctrine was issued at a time of growing U.S. awareness of the country's potential role in Pacific commerce, and served to warn rivals away from the Islands. As one writer put it, "Far-sighted Americans were increasingly absorbed by the problem of expanding our interests in the Far East. The industrial economy had reached the take-off point; by the mid-fifties the domestic market was saturated by its products and the price index was falling at an alarming rate."[20]

In Hawaii, however, such global concerns were of less immediate interest than protecting the price of sugar, and the oligarchy turned its attention to winning the passage of a reciprocity treaty, which would guarantee tariff-free access to the U.S. markets—and huge profits as well. Samuel N. Castle, for instance, wrote to his son, "I am almost coming to feel that the only door to temporal prosperity is reciprocity with or without annexation to the United States, by either of which sugar would be made to net some 30 to 50 percent more than it now does. . . . [Otherwise] I fear a more or less general failure of our sugar interests."[21]

By the 1870s the dependence of Hawaiian sugar upon the U.S. market was generating an economic crisis as that market proved fickle indeed. Prohibitive tariffs limited the access of Island sugar to markets garnered during the Civil War period. Sugar production was not expanding and the lack of confidence in the industry on the part of investors meant stagnancy. A continental observer wrote: "Not more than one-quarter of the area of cultivation is at present under cultivation. Large tracts suited to cane are neglected, or devoted only to grazing from want of capital and labor."[22] Nevertheless, a number of key figures within the U.S. Congress, avid annexationists convinced that a reciprocity treaty with Hawaii would only serve to hinder and delay the ultimate absorption of the Islands, collaborated with other anti-reciprocity elements in sabotaging passage of a commercial agreement between the two countries.

In Hawaii, the plantation-controlling class came into direct conflict with Hawaiian determination to preserve at least some degree of sovereignty. For almost half a century, despite the presence of a monarch whose powers were in theory quite extensive, the politics of Hawaii had been the politics of the rising bourgeoisie of Honolulu, anxious to use government expenditures to further its own capital accumulation. It had done this in a myriad of ways. Government monies were used to subsidize labor recruiters seeking workers for Hawaiian plantations in far-off lands, government coercion was used to enforce a harsh law-and-order regime on the plantations, and government funds were used to create the essential infrastructure upon which the merchant-planters' export economy depended.[23] In 1854, for example (fiscally a relatively poor year for the government), $40,000 was expended on harbor improvements and $15,000 more on wharves; the following year, $30,000 more was spent on harbors. These allocations were made at a time of great misery and destitution for many landless Hawaiians, legitimately in need of a public support not available to them.

In late 1872, with the death of the popular King Lunalilo, a vigorous contest was waged for succession to the throne. There were enthusiastic mass meetings and renewed political interest among the people. Two prime contenders came to the fore. One, David Kalakaua, was a descendant of Big Island alii. A dapper man-about-town, well known for his addiction to all-night poker games and horse racing, he also was prone to occasional anti-elite nationalist rhetoric. The second candidate, Queen Emma, was the granddaughter of an English sailor, a strong-willed woman closely attuned to the bitter frustrations of the Hawaiian masses. In speaking out against the land thievery and annexationist intrigues that had characterized a good part of the century, the Queen was sharply eloquent: "There is a feeling of bitterness against those rude people who dwell on our land and have high ideas of giving away someone else's property as if it were theirs."[24] According to novelist Charles Nordhoff, then traveling in the Islands, Hawaiian nationalism was emerging as a force to be reckoned with. He found people everywhere "very strongly opposed to annexation. They have a strong feeling of nationalism and considerable jealousy of foreign influence."[25]

Kalakaua, initially the object of some mistrust among the planter-merchant elite, was able to solicit their support at a secret meeting with businessman Alfred Castle and became their candidate. Charles Bishop rendered the final stamp of approval when he pronounced Kalakaua to be "reasonable, impartial, and careful"— the highest virtues of the bourgeoisie. A brief but spirited campaign followed, in which Emma demonstrated great popular support. But when the thirty-nine electors gathered at the courthouse at Queen and Fort streets in February 1873, the verdict was a foregone conclusion: through bribery, threats, and cajoling, Samuel Wilder and a few others (it was said) had "fashioned thirty-nine votes for Kalakaua's crown."[26]

What happened next revealed that the Hawaiians had swallowed one humiliation too many. A large crowd of pro-Emma partisans, enraged by the decision, set upon the three delegates appointed to deliver the victory message to the new king. They then stormed the courthouse itself, scattering the electors and injuring half a dozen of them. More ominously for the future of law and order—and thus the protection of the prevailing economic and social order—the Royal Hawaiian Police, swept up in the maelstrom of excitement, tore off their badges and joined the demonstrators. "The army has disbanded, the police proved ineffectual; the volunteer troops were divided in their sympathies," wrote a frightened Laura Judd.[27] With any real leadership and organization, the Hawaiians in one bold stroke might have regained at least temporary control over the Islands. Neither, however, was available.

Threatened as never before, the business oligarchy acted in concert to defend its interests. Vastly outnumbered (90 percent of the population was ethnically Hawaiian), it instinctively turned to outside allies. Banker and plantation owner Charles Bishop, acting in his capacity as minister of foreign affairs, immediately requested the commanders of U.S. and British warships docked in Honolulu Harbor to land troops to crush what he called "a riotous mob."[28] One hundred and fifty U.S. marines and British sailors were duly landed and marched up Fort Street, dispersing the demonstrators and arresting key leaders. Government buildings were occupied by marine detachments.

The facade of Hawaiian political sovereignty was irrevocably shattered. External military intervention in Hawaiian affairs disarmed resistance, as it did in Hawaii's Pacific neighbors—Fiji, Tahiti, and New Caledonia. Yet the Hawaiian people still smouldered with a sullen hatred. In 1874, a year after the courthouse incident, the British commissioner to Hawaii privately admitted, "The king is not popular on this island and were Honolulu left without the protection of a ship of war, there would be a revolution in which he would lose his throne and possibly his life. . . . it is fear of foreign intervention which keeps the Hawaiians quiet."[29]

Now that a dependable servant of their interests occupied the throne and the populace was properly intimidated, the oligarchy began again to negotiate reciprocity. Taking the cue from his patrons, the new monarch embarked on an extensive trip across the United States, where the appearance of foreign "royalty" was a public relations triumph of the highest order. Speaking before a joint session of Congress, the king proved worthy of those who had sent him: "Today, our country needs the aid of a treaty of Commercial Reciprocity with America in order to insure our material prosperity."[30] By bringing notice of Hawaii's importance and its "yearning" for closer ties with the United States to public attention, the king's mission was a factor in hastening passage of the reciprocity treaty—albeit a fairly unimportant factor when compared with the persuasive arguments by such representatives of the Hawaiian government as Foreign Minister Charles Harris, who now turned the previous argument on its head and argued reciprocity was a logical step toward annexation:

> The annexation of the Hawaiian Islands by the United States sooner or later must become a national necessity, to guard the approaches against hostile attempts on the Pacific States. If reciprocity of commerce is established between the two countries, there cannot be a doubt that the effect will be *to hold these islands with hooks of steel in the interests of the United States, and to result finally in their annexation to the United States.*[31]

The Treaty of Reciprocity, removing trade barriers between the United States and the Kingdom of Hawaii, was passed in 1876. It allowed—indeed, encouraged—the further transformation of Hawaii into what one writer has called the "sugar-raising slope of the Pacific,"[32] and in doing so guaranteed the subordination of *all* alternative strategies for economic development and the allocation of virtually every available resource (land, water, human labor power, capital, and technology) to sugar production. In such an encompassing monoculture economy, "economic diversification" meant at most the production of a few agricultural export crops, like coffee and rice, for the same markets to which sugar was sent. Thus by reinforcing the high profitability of sugarcane cultivation, and at the same time making Hawaii a captive market for U.S. industrial products, the treaty effectively precluded Hawaii's ability to develop into an autonomous, self-directed, somewhat self-sustaining economic entity.

Morgan has succinctly summed up the economic scene at this point: "By 1876, the *haole* merchants and planters and missionaries had reformed the Island economic structure essentially after their own image. Their plantations, stores, steamships, churches and weekly brass band were drowning out the traditions of the past. Hawaii was bound tightly in the existing commercial network of the world; and Hawaii's future was the future of its plantation economy."[33]

For the sugar planters and agents, the advantages of reciprocity were well worth the long struggle to obtain it. Most significantly, the treaty provisions added $50 to $60 a ton to the received price of sugar (which had been only $120–$135 a ton). This "bonus" was responsible for an enormous increase in profits, and in turn stimulated a dramatic rise in production. During the first four years of Reciprocity, sugar production doubled, and by 1890 ten times as much sugar was being harvested and exported to the United States as in 1876. The 20 plantations of 1875 expanded to 63 by 1880, as land in sugar increased by 20,000 acres. Methods of production were also transformed to take advantage of new technology and economies of scale: new boiling techniques, centrifugal separation of sugar from molasses, deep plowing, and the intensive use of fertilizers all began to be employed. Efficient large-scale plantation-mill combines replaced smaller, more primitively engineered sugar estates. These new combines, requiring large inputs of capital to finance the import of costly machinery—physical capital on plantations rose 227 percent in the 1870s and 228 percent in the 1880s[34]—and to irrigate lands being brought under cultivation, intensified the already pronounced plantation dependence upon the sugar agencies' myriad of services, including financing, marketing, purchasing, shipping, and warehousing.

An entire financial apparatus grew up around the plantation economy. Banks were established specifically to serve the needs of the sugar interest. Bishop and Company, for instance, was founded in 1870 with a very "generous" loan from the Hawaiian government, $125,000 at 7 percent interest (money which the bank president, Charles Bishop, reloaned to planters at 10 or 12 percent interest) and became an important source of capital for new investment in sugar. Bishop was later joined by the Hawaii National Bank, established by landowners Samuel Parker and James Campbell. Insurance companies, sugar agencies, ranches, shipping companies, and banks all worked together—indeed, their directors were often the same men—exchanged favors and friendly deals, and became steadily more interlinked.[35]

In the United States this was the heyday of such singleminded industrial empire-builders as Rockefeller, Carnegie, Vanderbilt, Gould, and Fisk, ruthless entrepreneurs in the grand style who used armed gangs, price cutting, and political muscle provided by bought politicians and judges to drive their competition to extinction. Since the Island economic and political situation was rather different, however, the use of other strategems was necessary to accumulate capital and acquire monopoly control. Isolated by twenty-five hundred miles of ocean from their compatriots, located in the midst of a large, ever more hostile non-Caucasian majority, in what was after all still a foreign country, unable to rely upon U.S. working-class elements in the population, or even at times on the non-U.S. bourgeoisie, it was logical that the small clique of *haole* businessmen saw mutual aid as indispensable to their survival. The compactness of the Islands, the limited resources, and the precariousness of a sugar industry all directed those who might, in the United States, have been fierce competitors toward cooperation.

Thus the kinds of no-holds-barred struggle that characterized the freewheeling capitalism of the emergent oil, steel, and railroad trusts on the continent never appeared in the Islands. The dominant pattern was instead one of closely interlocked family and company alliances concentrating economic decision-making within a very small elite circle at the apex of society, and there was a remarkable degree of cross-fertilization between landed estates, financial institutions, and agricultural interests. In a series of deals, Benjamin Dillingham leased Honouliuli and Kahuku (Oahu) lands from James Campbell, then subsequently subleased Honouliuli to W. R. Castle and promoted the establishment of the Ewa Plantation in conjunction with Castle and Cooke. Later, when the leeward side of Oahu began to thrive, James R. Castle, in cooperation with Robert

Lewers and John Paty, helped Dillingham obtain financing for his Oahu Railway and Land Company's project to run a commercial and passenger railroad through their canefields. Similarly, when Alexander and Baldwin desperately needed credit to expand its sugar production, Bishop and Company were on hand to supply timely infusions of capital. Charles Bishop then became a director of the Hawaiian Sugar Company—sitting side by side with such powerful planters as Henry P. Baldwin and George MacFarlane.[36] In this manner, the interlocking group of men controlling the Big Five companies came to dominate every important segment of the Islands' economy.

Despite their need for capital, at no time did this agro-mercantile oligarchy permit "outsiders" to gain control over its economic base. Although by 1885 Hawaiian plantations had about $3.5 million in loans outstanding from San Francisco banks, stockholder investment came almost entirely from Island sources. And given the high rate of profit earned by Hawaiian sugar plantations during this period, this was not difficult: as one historian of the Hawaiian sugar industry put it, "So great were the profits that all problems of capital scarcity disappeared. The development of the Hawaiian sugar industry after 1875 was largely through capital of its own creation."[37]

Local ownership of the dominant industry defined the unique relationship of the Hawaii plantation elite to the elites in the United States, with whom it was to negotiate Hawaii's future. Although Hawaiian economic dependency was conditioned by an ongoing reliance upon access to the U.S. market and U.S. sugar technology, it was also affected by the fact that the local business elite managed—at least in this period—to retain financial control over the basic economic sectors. This gave the bourgeoisie in Hawaii a certain flexibility in dealing with metropolitan elites, as well as a high level of political leverage within the Islands. The elite in Hawaii was thus not a typical collaborationist class, as was (and is) found in many areas of Africa or Latin America, functioning primarily as a commercial intermediary for the penetration of foreign capital. In Hawaii, it was a class that was able to establish a real grip on the productive and financial apparatus, and to maintain it until well after World War II.

This did not mean, however, that U.S. capital was content to be excluded from the bonanza promised by Reciprocity. In fact, the most acute nineteenth-century threat to the power of the new elite in Hawaii was *personally* carried to Honolulu on the same vessel that brought news of the passage of the treaty. This was Claus Spreckels, the "Sugar King," whose venture into Hawaii represented the first substantial challenge from overseas to the local elite's monopolization of the economy. Spreckels' was one of the great Horatio Alger stories of his day, and he almost instantly became the most controversial man in the Islands. Born in 1828 in a German village, son of a poor family, Spreckels migrated to the United States in his youth and achieved great financial success, first in the New York grocery business and later in sugar refining in the San Francisco Bay area. When Reciprocity was finalized, Spreckels, whose control over the California Sugar Refining Company (which had both a West Coast monopoly and the most modern refining facilities in the world) placed him in a prime position to profit from the new windfall in Hawaiian sugar, was determined to establish a vertical monopoly. He would establish his own sugar production facilities in the Islands, transport the sugar to California aboard his own Oceanic Lines, and there process it in his own refinery. Such complete backward and forward integration would provide him with an economically rationalized operation, capable of great cost-efficiency, and thus give him a definite competitive advantage over his rivals.

Spreckels had the financial resources to carry out his plans. His interests extended far beyond sugar, and included banking, railroads, utilities, and rubber. Like many of his contemporaries, he was utterly ruthless in pursuit of his objectives, prepared to use any tactic to achieve his ends. The *Gazette,* organ of the planters, expressed its opinion of the San Francisco financier thus: "He has found most people with whom he comes into contact either weak or corrupt and always selfish. He uses them to suit his purposes, which is all that they are good for. Those who approach him with hypercritical, high-toned professions get their measure taken every time. They have their price and are either purchased or used, or kicked to one side."[38]

For Spreckels, backward integration necessitated access to huge supplies of raw sugar. To accomplish this, he acquired—by bribery, threats, and purchase—extensive tracts in Maui, lands which were subsequently welded together to form the largest plantation in Hawaii, complete with the most sophisticated new machinery. He spent the then immense sum of $500,000 on a giant irrigation works to carry water from the flanks of Haleakela down to his fields below. When finished, the Sprecklesville complex brought its owner a very substantial annual profit.

The achievements of the man whom the Hawaiians called "ona miliona" (the multimillionaire) were as much a consequence of Spreckels' extraordinary ability to manipulate the Island political process to his advantage as of anything else. He paid only one or two visits a year and entrusted his local affairs to overseers, yet by the 1880s "His Majesty Spreckels" had secured an ironclad financial hold on the king, for Kalakaua, the misnamed "Merry Monarch," was an unstable, impetuous, and spendthrift character, manipulable because of his desperate need for the considerable sums that Spreckels periodically placed at his disposal, and because of his own growing nationalistic, anti-elite sentiments. In 1878, for instance, Spreckels got the king to dismiss a cabinet that refused to grant him extensive water rights in Maui, and two of his leading associates came to occupy cabinet positions. He secured an equally strong hold on the legislature, for which he became financial agent and creditor. Once, when asked about the newly acquired right of foreign corporations to hold land in Hawaii, he replied with customary aplomb, "I had the law passed myself."[39]

Much of Spreckels' success in the political arena was due to his close association with Walter Murray Gibson, certainly one of the most fascinating and enigmatic characters ever to play a prominent role in Hawaii's history. Born on a ship at sea, Gibson was an adventurer, linguist, world traveler, a gentle man of great personal magnetism—and also something of a con artist. His sojourns had taken him to South America and then Asia, where a Javanese girl had helped him escape the Dutch prison to which he had been sentenced after being charged with (in vintage Gibson style) attempting to establish himself as an East Indian sultan. "There was an Oriental fragrance breathing through his talk, an odor of the Spice Islands still lingering in his garments," commented someone who knew him well.[40]

He came to Hawaii as a representative of the Mormon church and proceeded rapidly to transfer a parcel of church-owned land into his own name. He quickly grasped the essential trauma of the Hawaiian people, and in his newspaper and fiery oratory emerged as their protagonist. "It is folly to suppose that the native population of these Islands will sit down contentedly under an exclusive foreign domination," he editorialized in 1880.[41] He was soon top vote-getter in the Islands, and simultaneously occupied the offices of premier, minister of foreign affairs, secretary of war, and secretary of the interior.[42] Yet at the same time—and this is the source of the mystery—he formed an alliance with Spreckels (whose level of cynicism may be judged by his privately expressed thoughts on the annexation of Hawaii: "By and by, sometime, they will be annexed, but not now. I'll guarantee to deliver them at any time.")[43] This, and Gibson's lack of any concrete accomplishments in restructuring Hawaiian society in the years he held some degree of political authority, made him highly suspect as a genuine advocate of Hawaiian interests.

Given their different power bases and interests, the staying power of the unlikely triumverate of king, Spreckels, and Gibson was always in doubt. Ultimately, the militancy of ordinary Hawaiians would either have pushed Gibson and Kalakaua beyond rhetorical promises or destroyed their credibility. And Spreckels, of course, was an enemy of self-determination for the Hawaiian people. Furthermore, the old missionary and plantation elite saw Spreckels as a crudely opportunistic and dangerous interloper, an outsider whose political intrigues and immense economic power threatened the finely tuned structures they had erected in Hawaii. Gibson was regarded as a radical demagogue far too popular with the ethnic Hawaiian voters, who still constituted a firm majority of the electorate, and Kalakaua was seen as their easily manipulated marionette, lavish in his wastefulness and increasingly given to "extreme" nationalist positions.

To such a plantation oligarchy, fearful of the emergence of a grassroots challenge to their interests, remembering still the courthouse incident of 1873, the imperative was for direct and violent action. By 1885 they were organizing a counterattack under the leadership of firebrand Maui lawyer Lorrin Thurston, who demanded of the legislature: "Are we to act for ourselves and make our own laws or are we to be led around like swine with rings in our noses at the will of a man who cares for nothing but for his own interests?"[44]

A series of flagrant scandals involving the king set the stage for the fiercely contested 1886 elections, the oligarchy's last fling at legal constitutional change. The defeat of their Independent Party (headed by what read like a *Who's Who of Finance and Industry in Hawaii*) led them to charge fraud—and begin to plan for a coup d'état.[45] They established a military arm, the Hawaiian League, as their vehicle.

Throughout 1887 the League, whose membership numbered four hundred under the command of planters Sanford Dole, W. R. Castle, and C. Brewer executive J. O. Castle, organized for the confrontation to come. To arm the League's military adjunct, the Honolulu Rifles, guns and ammunition were imported from San Francisco and Sydney; Castle and Cooke took deliveries as if they were ordinary business orders. One thing was certain: they had to strike swiftly. Trouble was coming from the United States in the form the planters most dreaded—the renewal of the Reciprocity Treaty was threatened.[46] Given this unstable situation, control over the internal political situation in Hawaii appeared vitally important to the elite.

Complaints had been voiced in the United States for years that Hawaiian reciprocity was worthless from the U.S. standpoint. Charges were made that the treaty was merely a subsidy to rich planters like Spreckels (who had numerous enemies in Congress and elsewhere). In the face of rising Senate opposition, anxious planters began promoting the cession of the Pearl River estuary, near Honolulu, to the United States for use as a naval base. They reasoned that this would have the effect of stifling the Congressional opposition to Reciprocity by demonstrating the value of a continued association with Hawaii—not forgetting, of course, that a U.S. naval presence on Oahu would also mean increased security for the elite and would buttress the chances of eventual annexation.

Actually, this was not a new idea. As early as the 1840s, U.S. military men had been scouting the Islands for likely sites, and in 1866 the U.S. minister to Hawaii had written to the secretary of state that control of Hawaii, in event of war with France and Britain, was absolutely necessary to the United States. In 1873, scarcely two months before the U.S. Navy suppressed the uprising surrounding Kalakaua's election, two generals, John M. Schofield and B. S. Alexander, ostensibly vacationing in the Islands but in fact on a confidential mission "to assess the capabilities of different ports in Hawaii," recommended to the secretary of war the securing of the area originally known to the Hawaiians as Wai Momi (Water of Pearl). The generals' host in Hawaii was none other than Foreign Minister Charles Bishop, on record as favoring annexation and the cession of Pearl.[47]

Hence it is not surprising that Congress, at the request of the military, had added an amendment to the Reciprocity Treaty of 1886 requiring that the Hawaiian government grant the United States exclusive rights to entry and naval repair in the Pearl River estuary as a condition for renewal. At the grassroots, Hawaiians responded with a rash of angry meetings, denouncing such outrageous demands on Hawaiian sovereignty. This rising national consciousness had the support of at least some forces within the existing government and Reciprocity seemed about to be terminated. To the Reverend Charles Hyde, sitting in his Honolulu home, there was little doubt that the king and his associates were out to "break the missionary influence entirely."[48] As Walter Murray Gibson confided to his diary, "The tempest seems to be rushing to a climax."[49]

Meanwhile, boatloads of arms were arriving at the docks, and at the armory at Beretania Street and Punchbowl Avenue, on June 30, 1887, a public meeting organized by leading planters and businessmen was held and demands were raised for the dismissal of the Cabinet, the rewriting of the constitution, and strict limitations on royal prerogatives. Alexander Young of Honolulu Ironworks expressed the prevailing mood when he cried, "Strike when the iron is hot," while Sanford Dole told the assembly, "This meeting is called to give the king one chance, just one more chance to fall into line for political reform"[50]—"reform" being a favorite phrase among the elite that clothed the rather crude attacks on Hawaiian self-determination.

When Kalakaua balked at accepting these demands, the Hawaiian Rifles seized strategic points in the city and mounted armed patrols. Gibson and his son-in-law were arrested, hustled down to the docks, and bundled aboard a California-bound packet. Finally, under intense pressure the king broke down and signed a new constitution that made him a ceremonial figurehead. The new cabinet included Lorrin Thurston as minister of the interior and fellow conspirator C. W. Ashford in the equally sensitive post of attorney general. The new constitution gave U.S. citizens the right to vote in Hawaiian elections, while a large sector of the ethnic Hawaiian electorate was excluded through rigorous property qualifications and Asians were excluded as aliens. "There is no country where the burden of taxation is less oppressive and in which life and property are more secure than in the Hawaiian Islands," wrote Benjamin Dillingham happily to a friend in England some months later. "The backbone of the whole movement was the money furnished by some of our capitalists," noted the observant Reverend Hyde.[51] To the Hawaiian people, the document so brutally thrust upon Kalakaua has since been known as the "Bayonet Constitution."

The most immediate result of these events was the lightning-like delivery of the Pearl River estuary to the United States, guaranteeing continuation of the Reciprocity Treaty. Once again, the plantation elite had sacrificed a piece of Hawaiian sovereignty (and this time, territorial integrity as well) to maintain its economic links with the continent. The way toward political integration was being paved. But first there would be a fight, for there had been no fundamental reconciliation between the interests of the oligarchy and those of the Hawaiian masses—a fact confirmed by the many embittered protest meetings held in late 1887. As British Commissioner Wodehouse commented, "I think the natives have begun to realize the extent of the change which has just taken place."[52]

5
The Pear Is Ripe

I think that there are only three places that are of value enough to be taken. One is Hawaii. The others are Cuba and Puerto Rico.
—U.S. Secretary of State James Blaine (1889)

If ever there was a movement free from all questionable motives in origins, and from all dishonorable measure in its methods, it was the Hawaiian Revolution of '93.
—Reverend Hyde (1893)

The United States, which had been a predominately agricultural country dependent on British capital and imported goods, was by the 1880s an industrial power second to none with substantial heavy industry and an advanced technological base. The age of the cutthroat robber baron industrialists, who had built huge empires in railroads, steel, oil, and mining, was giving way to the age of the finance capitalist. Wall Street financiers J. P. Morgan and James Stillman coordinated giant monopoly trusts in every major industry in the country. In 1877 the United States had reversed a century-long pattern and become a net exporter of goods. Now U.S. steel was underselling British and continental steel in their home markets. Forty-eight U.S. companies had established themselves in Canada by 1889, the same year in which John D. Rockefeller explained the sudden importance of foreign markets to the powerful new corporate trusts. "Dependent solely on local business," he stated, "we would have failed years ago. We were forced to extend our markets and seek for export trade."[1]

This increasing preoccupation with foreign markets was reinforced by a series of financial panics and economic depressions that struck a rapidly maturing capitalist economy with disturbing frequency in the late nineteenth century. Severe depressions occurred during 1873–78, 1883–85, and 1893–97, leaving in their wake large-scale unemployment, substantial numbers of business and farm failures, and a heritage of political radicalism in the form of

56

Populist, Anarchist, and Socialist movements, all claiming a considerable following among sectors of the working and farming classes. In an effort to bring some degree of coherence to the country's topsy-turvy economic structure, and thus blunt the momentum of agitation against what many in the country regarded as the shameless collusion between Big Business and federal and state governments, Washington policymakers (with some corporate support) opted for federal regulation of various components of the economy, ranging from railroads to banking, as well as severe repression of the working class and its newly formed representatives, the trade unions. During the 1880s and 1890s, these policies were not notable for their success. Working-class agitation in the great industrial cities increased markedly, as did the rage and disillusionment of small farmers in rural areas, who were burdened with rising costs and low prices. William Appleman Williams, in his book on the period, makes the link between these conditions and imperialism: "The economic impact of the depression and its effect in producing a real fear of extensive social unrest or even revolution, had completed the long and gradual acceptance by metropolitan leaders of the traditional farm emphasis on overseas market expansion as the strategic solution to the nation's economic and social problems."[2]

Thus we see the rise of what Gabriel Kolko has called a "foreign policy constituency," oriented toward building the kind of empire that would guarantee U.S. productive surpluses firm market outlets, and including corporate and political figures who were taken with the notion of an imperial America which at one stroke would stabilize the existing economic situation and undermine the growth of an authentically radical movement. Senator John T. Morgan, among others, voiced an expansionist strategy based upon internal economic dilemmas. "Our home market is not equal to the demands of our producing and manufacturing classes and to the capital which is seeking employment. We must enlarge the field of our traffic or stop the business of manufacturing where it is."[3]

U.S. foreign policy faithfully reflected this orientation. In 1889 the United States had strengthened its position in Samoa, sharing the islands with the European powers. Four years later it intervened militarily and diplomatically against Brazilian revolutionaries who were calling a proposed reciprocity treaty exploitative. It

was busy replacing Great Britain as the hegemonic power in
Nicaragua and, in a crucial power confrontation over a Venezuelan
boundary dispute, forced a British retreat there. Clearly a new
imperial power was in the ascendency. The fear of antagonizing
Great Britain was at an end, and the next two decades became an
exercise in foreign aggrandizement for decision-makers in Washington, New York, and other U.S. metropolitan centers.

Imperialism, then, for the elite in the United States at the tail end
of the nineteenth century, was a response to the internal contradictions (and failures) generated by the capitalist system. Rather than
reorganize society in a manner that would reallocate resources on a
different basis (inevitably to their own detriment), rather than re-
distribute national income more equitably to create additional demand within the domestic economy, the elites chose to implement
imperialist policies abroad.

The Hawaiian Islands, as we saw, had been a target area for U.S.
expansion since mid-century. Reciprocity, promoted by U.S.
strategists to tie Hawaii to the United States economically and to
lead to eventual political absorption, had fulfilled its promise. The
Hawaiian Kingdom had become a U.S. economic satellite. For the
years 1887 to 1891, 91.20 percent of all Hawaiian foreign trade was
with the United States; for 1892 to 1896, the figure was 91.92
percent.[4] In dollar figures, this means that of total Hawaiian exports of over $9.1 million in 1894, almost $9 million went to the
United States. Furthermore, the structure of this exchange was
typically dependent in character: raw materials and primary
agricultural products in return for industrial and processed
goods—with sugar far and away the most important export: in
1894 it accounted for over 92 percent of total exports. Remaining
exports were miniscule by comparison: rice $327,400; bananas
$113,000; followed by coffee, hides, tallow, molasses, and goat
skins. The largest import, on the other hand, was iron and steel
manufactures ($405,300 in 1894), followed by manufactured cot-
ton goods ($297,800), chemicals, dyes, and even *refined* sugar; but
large amounts of foodstuffs were also being *imported:* in 1894,
$179,000 worth of wheat flour and $128,000 worth of dairy products were brought in. The allocation of the great bulk of viable
agricultural land to commercial agriculture had clearly undermined the Islands' ability to be self-sufficient in food production.[5]

Thus, although the *Honolulu Star-Bulletin* might assure its readers in 1887, "Let it be remembered that the United States is not an aggressive nation. She has more territory than she can fully occupy for generations to come. . . . She does not cross the seas to enlarge her possessions"[6]—nonetheless, there were powerful interests in the United States determined to gain nothing less than absolute control over the "pearly isles." And indeed, a sustained movement in Washington for the colonization of the Islands began under the auspices of Republican politico James Blaine when he assumed the post of secretary of state in 1889. Blaine, whose expansionist interests extended to the Caribbean as well, had absolutely no reservations about the incorporation of Hawaii, which he was fond of referring to as an "outlying district of California" and "essentially a part of the American system of states, the key to North Pacific trade."[7] His position on annexation was clear:

> There is little doubt that were the Hawaiian Islands by annexation or distinct protection a part of the territory of the Union, their fertile resources for the growth and raising of sugar would not only be controlled by American capital but so profitable a field of labor would attract thither from the United States willing workers. A purely American form of colonization in such a case would meet all the phases of the problem.[8]

These pronouncements were accompanied by a heavy-handed interference in Hawaiian domestic affairs. A comic opera Hawaiian insurrection in July 1889 was routed by government troops abetted by marines from the U.S.S. *Adams* who kept the population under control and distributed ten thousand rounds of ammunition to government forces. Two years later, the U.S.S. *Pensacola* was ordered to proceed to Hawaii "in order to guard American interests in the vicinity."[9]

In Hawaii as well, influential sectors of the oligarchy (now proprietors of *four-fifths* of the arable land in the Islands, holding $23 million of the $33 million invested in sugar plantations) were becoming increasingly taken with the idea of annexation, and the trend was accelerated by the McKinley Tariff of 1891 which allowed *all* sugar into the United States duty free (but provided subsidies for U.S. domestic producers). Almost immediately, economic depression set in, reaching a nadir in the summer of 1892, when sugar prices plummeted to a figure below the cost of production. "The McKinley Tariff has ruined nearly every merchant in the Islands," lamented an official of a leading company involved in recruiting overseas laborers for the plantations; while the U.S. minister to Hawaii informed the secretary of state that the "depreciation of the properties by passage of the McKinley Tariff bills had not been less than $12 million, a large proportion of this loss falling on Americans living here and in California."[10]

Long-time annexationists like Lorrin Thurston were now joined by a number of planters and businessmen who reasoned that the move was imperative if they were to benefit from the $.02 bounty paid to U.S. producers. According to one prominent planter, "If Hawaii is part of the United States, any bonuses to be paid under McKinley's next law to sugar growers will apply to all of its citizens wherever they are."[11] In a dispatch to his superiors in Washington, the U.S. minister to Hawaii informed them that a "consensus of local planters was that a $12.00 per ton bounty will place all the Hawaiian plantations worth maintaining on the road to financial safety and success." He advocated a policy of "wise, bold action if the United States will rescue the property-holders from great losses."[12]

An additional incentive prompting annexationist fever was the obvious threat constituted by the thousands of Asians crowding the plantation camps. In 1890, Asians constituted 32 percent of the population of 89,000. (Hawaiians and part-Hawaiians made up an additional 45 percent and Caucasians the remaining 22 percent.) This, together with Japan's recent military triumph over China and its own military industrial buildup, were beginning to be viewed with alarm by nations with Pacific Rim interests. Yet the sugar interests were enmeshed in a web of contradictions. While the sizeable Asian proletariat was certainly a cause for alarm, it was also recognized that a continued flow of cheap immigrant labor was vital to maintaining the low wages (and hence profitability) of the plantations and mills.

The widespread paranoia about being overwhelmed by a "yellow wave" was expressed in the *Hawaiian Gazette*: "The asiaticizing of the Hawaiian Islands is proceeding at such a rapid rate that those citizens who know what such a course must lead to, may well stand appalled before such a prospect." Or, as the *Advertiser* put it, "It is the white race against the yellow. Nothing but annexation can save these islands." While Thurston, in a pro-annexationist pamphlet, said: "It is no longer a question whether Hawaii shall be controlled by the native Hawaiians or by some foreign people, but the question is—*What foreign people shall control Hawaii?*" The number of Japanese was of special concern, and planter William Alexander warned of a choice between a "Japanized" Hawaii and an American Hawaii: "When the Japanese shall come to form an overwhelming majority of our population, the United States will not be justified in international law in forbidding Japan to take charge of what will virtually be a Japanese colony." The outspoken Reverand J. A. Cruzan wrote bluntly, "Must the White Man go?"[13] These racist messages were as much directed toward whipping up the small shopkeepers and other petty bourgeois elements (who had formed the bulk of the shock troops for the Honolulu Rifles in 1887 and were counted on by the elite as a front-line armed force) as anyone else. Yet they also reflected the planters' deep-seated fear of a swelling Asian proletariat that might one day make common cause with the dispossessed Hawaiians, or even be powerful enough on its own to disrupt the existing social order. No one expressed this dilemma more succinctly than Lorrin Thurston: "Four-fifths of the property of the country is owned by foreigners, while out of an electorate of 15,000 but 4,000 are foreigners—thus placing the natives in overwhelming majority."[14] Thus additional segments of the oligarchy, previously lukewarm to annexation, began to view it as a means of eliminating the dominant Hawaiian-Oriental majority as a political force while keeping immigration flowing unabated. "Alone we are in a great degree helpless. We cannot prevent the tide of immigration," noted W. O. Smith, a sugar planter. "We must make a strong effort for annexation next spring."[15] This was not a situation of complete unanimity, however. Some, like Spreckels and Paul Isenberg, opposed annexation because it would mean the end of the fantastically cheap contract labor system, while others, such as Englishman Theo Davies, supported the Crown on a national basis, fearing the repercussions of annexation on their holdings.

Undaunted by the fact that they only had the support of a majority within the two thousand member U.S. community in Hawaii, the annexationists plunged ahead with their schemes. An Annexationist League, formed during the summer of 1892, laid the groundwork for a projected coup d'état by seeking support in Washington. Secretary of State Blaine and Secretary of War Tracy gave the conspirators every assurance of support. U.S. Minister to Hawaii Stevens, a seventy-three-year-old New England clergyman widely known for his zealous sentiments ("The time is near when we must decide who shall hold these Hawaiian Islands as part of their national territory"),[16] was instructed to aid in the plot.

The death of King Kalakaua in 1891 brought the popular Liliuokalani to the throne. A woman of strong character, acutely sensitive to the long traditions of *Hawaii nei* and the threat to the kingdom's independence, she was determined to preserve Hawaiian sovereignty from outside encroachment. A firm advocate of restoring royal prerogatives at the expense of what she viewed to be an elite-dominated cabinet and legislature, her inclination was thus not to organize the Hawaiian people for an all-out struggle, but rather to attack the institutions of elite control from her position as monarch. She did not take into account that these were times of crises, times when a monarch could no longer hope to maneuver at the top, alternately confronting and allying with the elite, especially in the absence of a solid base of support of her own. Liliuokalani's program (or lack of one), ill-conceived and without broad, popular, *organized* support, rapidly drove the elite into a conspiracy with their continental patrons to topple the monarchy.

The long-awaited crisis erupted on January 14, 1893, when Liliuokalani, in the wake of a series of cabinet shakeups, mounted the throne and read a declaration promulgating a new constitution. It asserted the power of the monarchy over the government and declared that all cabinet ministers would henceforth serve at her pleasure. This was nothing less than a blunt repudiation of the plantation bourgeoisie and the political institutions it had established in the half century since the Bayonet Constitution. That night Thurston's home on Judd Street was the scene of a hasty strategy meeting between Dole, Smith, W. R. Castle, F. W. Wunderburg, and their host. They proclaimed themselves a "Committee of Public Safety," and then went to meet with Minister Stevens, who assured them that "United States troops on board the *Boston* will be ready to land at any moment to prevent the destruction of American life and property . . . and they of course would recognize the existing government whatever it might be."[17] The committee meanwhile organized some one hundred *haoles,* preparing them for immediate action.

The next day Stevens ordered the *Boston*'s commander, Captain Wiltse, to land his troops to "assist in preserving public order"—a phrase somewhat shopworn from being trotted out during nearly every colonial incursion from the Gulf of Suez to the portals of Shanghai. The troops landed on the dock, marched along quiet and peaceful streets, and paused for a short rest at the Alapai estate of Castle and Cooke president J. B. Atherton, then bivouacked in front of the Royal Palace.

Given confidence by this foreign intervention, on the following morning the Committee of Public Safety seized the government buildings and proclaimed the dissolution of the monarchy and the establishment of the Republic of Hawaii. Without active outside support, there is little doubt that their action would have failed pathetically; only the presence of U.S. troops influenced the Queen (who had access to scores of well-armed police and paramilitary troops equipped with field guns, as well as hundreds of supporters calling for arms) to yield. Meanwhile, Minister Stevens, gloating over the success of the operation, wrote home to the secretary of state: "The Hawaiian pear is now fully ripe and this is the golden hour for the United States to pluck it."[18]

During the months that followed, a period in which annexation negotiations were held in Washington between a "Hawaiian" delegation composed of leading planters and commercial men and high-ranking U.S. officials, Minister Stevens placed Hawaii under his protection and U.S. troops occupied key buildings. And well he might. For outside of what Lt. Lucien Young, the officer whose claim to fame was that he had led the *Boston*'s landing party ashore, called "the best citizens and nine-tenths of the property owners of the country,"[19] the government represented a distinct minority. "Eighteen men representing nobody" was one popular comment.

President Harrison drew up an annexation treaty, but the sordidness of the affair left a distinctly bad aftertaste in Washington and considerable opposition in Congress. The seal of doom was placed upon immediate annexation when U.S. government investigator James Blount, appointed to look into the truth of the overthrow, went to Honolulu and, not swayed by the flattery of Island oligarchs ("I was surrounded by persons interested in misleading me," he commented afterward), issued an official report charging the planters with overthrowing the popular sovereign of a nation whose people were deeply opposed to annexation: "The American minister and the revolutionary leaders had determined on annexation to the United States and had agreed on the part each was to act to the very end. . . . The undoubted sentiment of the people is for the Queen, against the Provisional Government and against annexation."[20]

Grover Cleveland, elected president in 1892, less interested in the Pacific and firmly opposed to annexation, allowed the treaty proposal to expire in Congress. "If I were in favor of annexation," he said, "I should oppose taking of the Islands by force and fraud. I think there is such a thing as international morality."[21] Nevertheless, he also refused to dismantle the new regime ensconced in Honolulu, dashing the hopes of the Queen and her many supporters. The annexationist issue remained stalled in Congress, and for the next five years there was a strange limbo in Hawaii.

The composition of the Provisional Government was unabashed in its class basis. The cabinet included such names as Dole, Damon, Smith, and Jones; among the fourteen members of the Advisory Council, the body wielding real political clout, eight were major shareholders in sugar plantations.[22] Short-tempered displays of arbitrary policy-making dominated. Martial law remained in force, habeus corpus was suspended, an Immigration Act restricted entry by "suspicious" aliens, and a Dangerous Persons Act provided a *carte blanche* for the authorities to imprison people on the flimsiest of excuses.[23] Crown lands were opened for sale and lease, with the Queen's choicest lands snapped up by the plantations. The constitution was consciously modeled after the 1891 Mississippi constitution, noted for its effectiveness in disenfranchising black voters, and not only denied the vote to all who were not literate in English or did not possess property worth at least $200, but managed to omit such rights as the right to a trial by jury as well.

Among Hawaiians, the new constitution was greeted with sarcasm, hostility—and plotting. In January 1895 an uncoordinated, poorly planned royalist revolt broke out, but the rebels surrendered after a series of skirmishes around southern Oahu. Immediately afterward, U.S. troops staged highly visible maneuvers in the central Honolulu area for several weeks, in an attempt to intimidate any remaining dissidents.[24] Even this did not satisfy the *Advertiser*, however: "What are we fighting for if not to protect the property of the United States citizens? The American people have $21,700,684 invested in this country—twice as much as any two nations represented in the islands."[25]

In Washington, Thurston and Castle leapfrogged from club to cocktail party to Congressional office, laying out the case for annexation and distributing books and pamphlets extolling the virtues of Hawaii. Thurston's pamphlet pictured Hawaii as a dependent society whose basic institutions and values were largely conditioned by the metropole:

> The general statutes, court procedure and legal methods of Hawaii are based upon—many of them copies of—those in use in the United States. Most of the lawyers and judges are either from the United States or educated therein. The public school system is based upon that of the United States; more than one-half the teachers are American; English is the official language of the schools and courts, the common language of business. The railroad cars, engines, waterworks, water pipes, dynamos, telephones, fire apparatus are all of American make. United States currency is the currency of the country. Government private bonds, notes and mortgages are made payable in United States money.[26]

With the old frontier receding into memory, the Pacific Coast filling up with immigrants, and the export capacity of U.S. industrial and agricultural sectors growing apace, Thurston and Castle found powerful supporters within the marble halls of Congress. President McKinley, whose 1896 election platform included the building of the Panama Canal and expanding national trade in the Pacific, introduced an annexation proposal into the Senate with the highly significant remark that annexation would be the culmination of "seventy years of virtual dependence upon the benevolent protection of the United States. Under such circumstances, annexation is not a change, it is a consummation."[27]

In the debate over annexation that started in 1897 in the Senate, two positions rapidly surfaced. At one pole was a curious coalition of populists, liberals, racists (anxious at the prospect of contaminating Anglo-Saxon America with the likes of "leprous kanakas" and "mongrel senators"), and sugar beet manufacturers, all of whom argued vehemently against it. With the exception of the racially motivated and the sugar beet lobby, the dominant motif was an emphasis on respect for the self-determination of others—which has always been found more in the rhetoric of public life than in the reality of historical experience. These were the people who shrank from the momentous step of committing the nation to the role of overseas imperial power (although they were not adverse to maintaining the status quo, many of them wanting to keep the market for their surplus farm products). Senators Pettigrew, White, Tillman, and others fought an all-out battle on the Senate floor, emphasizing the wishes of the Hawaiian people. "I have talked to everyone who would talk with me," reported Pettigrew of a Hawaiian visit, "and I have failed to find a single native Hawaiian who was not opposed to annexation."[28]

The pro-annexationist side mobilized a wide range of supporters, including military men like Admiral George Balknap, who stated: "We need the group as part and parcel of the United States and should take what is offered to us even at the hazard of war." There was also Lucien Young, the officer on the spot during the overthrow of the monarchy, who claimed that annexation would "give us dominant power over the entire North Pacific." "If I had my way, I would annex those islands tomorrow," wrote Assistant Secretary of the Navy Theodore Roosevelt, who labelled opponents "traitors to the race."[29]

Speaking to a business community increasingly concerned with foreign markets, the *New York Journal of Commerce* declared the coming annexation of "interest to every businessman, for the political change would certainly make a greater opening for American manufactures." The Committee for Interests in China also demanded annexation—"We want a market for our surplus products"—a viewpoint echoed by the *San Francisco Evening Bulletin,* which called Hawaii "the center point of the North Pacific. It is in or near to the direct track of commerce from all Atlantic ports. . . . It is the key to the whole system. In the possession of the United States, it will give us command of the Pacific."[30] During the debate, some senators very explicitly placed Hawaii within the global framework of U.S. capitalist growth, linking Cuba, Hawaii, and the rising interest in the China market. Rabid expansionists like Colorado's Senator Teller (who had once exclaimed, "I am in favor of the annexation of Cuba. I am in favor of the annexation of the great country lying north to us. Mr. President, we want those Islands. We want them because they are a stepping way across the sea. Necessary to our safety, they are necessary to our commerce.")[31] envisioned Hawaii as a strategic American gateway for trans-Pacific expansion.

The sugar-based elite in Hawaii was by now solidly lined up for annexation. As W. O. Smith noted acidly: "The conversion of planters to the cause of annexation has been quite noticeable as of late. The fear of losing the benefits of the Reciprocity Treaty either very soon or later has touched their hearts, or rather their pocketbooks."[32] Yet progress was barely discernible, with fierce opposition blocking the bill in the Senate. The *Advertiser* exhorted its readers to remain firm and "stand by the government you have put into office. There are hardly 2,000 of us able-bodied men who are trying to hold the fort of white civilization here against 80,000 or more who oppose us. We need to make our frontage solid as granite."[33]

Then suddenly came war. The two blasts that demolished the *Maine* in Havana Harbor on February 15, 1898, and provided the pretext for U.S. intervention against Spain were decisive for the annexationist cause. On its way to capture Guam, the crew of the U.S.S. *Charleston* took on supplies and was feted at an enormous picnic by a Hawaiian government only too anxious to stress the Islands' strategic position and loyalty to the American cause. And as the Spanish were defeated at Manila Bay and U.S. troops stormed onto Filipino soil (to "liberate" what had already been liberated by the Filipinos themselves), momentum for annexation gathered force. "The Gibralter of the Pacific," Commodore George Melville called Hawaii. "Bridge the Pacific" headlined the *Philadelphia Press,* "with the Philippines, Guam, the Carolines, a Spanish possession, Samoa and the Hawaiian Islands to complete the chain."[34] Finally, in July 1898, annexationist supporters in the Senate, unable to pass a treaty, managed instead to muster the votes to pass a resolution—the Newlands Resolution—which had the same result. No provision was included to mandate a popular referendum by the people of Hawaii on the subject of their future.

At the formal ceremony incorporating Hawaii into the United States, called by one of the Islands' noted businessmen "this most glorious day in Hawaiian history," there was an eerie lack of Hawaiians in the audience. Invited to play, the Royal Hawaiian Band did not come, while Hawaiians in the National Guard covered their faces as the stars and stripes were hoisted up the pole. According to one observer, Rear Admiral L. A. Beardslee, "The band of Hawaiian damsels who were to have lowered for the last time the Hawaiian flag would not lower it. The band refused to play the *ponoi* and loud weeping was the only music contributed by the natives." While congressmen and military officers attended a splendidly catered annexationist ball and danced with *haole* debutantes in long white dresses, the *Advertiser* trumpeted: "HAWAII BECOMES THE FIRST OUTPOST OF A GREATER AMERICA."[35]

6

Big Five Territory

By 1941, every time a native Hawaiian switched on his lights, turned on the gas or rode on a street car, he paid a tiny tribute into Big Five coffers.

—Alexander MacDonald (1944)

The events surrounding the incorporation of the Hawaiian Islands into the United States' overseas empire provide an essential background for understanding Hawaiian plantation society in its period of maturity. The identity of interests between Island and continental elites that had led to annexation was rigorously maintained. In return for securing Hawaii as a strategic U.S. military and territorial outpost in the Pacific Basin, the plantation ruling class was granted political and economic dominion within the Islands. Annexation afforded Island planters a sizeable annual sugar quota (while a $34 per ton tariff was placed on foreign sugar imports into the United States), and thus ensured the continued viability of large-scale sugar production for export and of the class that controlled the means of production around sugar. But it also perpetuated an acute economic dependence upon the United States and continued the Island elite's subordination to political decisions made by the United States.

The Merchant Street headquarters of the large corporations dominated nearly every aspect of what had become a remarkably concentrated economy. Annexation incited a burst of economic expansion. Thirteen spanking new plantations appeared, fueled by $40 million in new capital investment, the great majority of which continued to be locally generated. Land in sugarcane increased by 128,000 acres between 1900 and 1913.[1] Beginning in 1906, thousands of Filipino men were imported to work in the fields: they formed the labor base for this expansion now that exclusion laws barred Chinese and Japanese. With the opening of the Panama Canal, which significantly augmented the East Coast market for Hawaiian agricultural products, the laying of the trans-Pacific cable that established instant communication links between the Islands and the continent, the widespread introduction of electricity and telephones, and the construction of bigger wharves, Hawaii was drawn more tightly into the world capitalist network. And yet *internally* the elite managed not only to maintain its economic control, but also to deepen and broaden that control through monopoly over the Islands' basic industries and related financial and service institutions, and through the adept use of political power and influence in Hawaii and the metropole. This situation was at variance with the types of dependency in other sugar-producing areas. In Cuba, for example, seven U.S. corporations controlled one-half of all sugar production in 1926 and representatives of U.S. sugar interests were leading figures in public life.[2] The indigenous Cuban bourgeoisie clearly lacked the resources to retain control over their basic economic sector. Direct economic penetration from the center was the consequence.

By 1910 this pattern of tight-knit business direction over Hawaii's economic affairs was firmly established. The elite controlled a diverse empire consisting of plantations, banks, insurance companies, shipping lines, trust companies, railroads, and retail and wholesale outlets. They used a host of methods to ensure its continuance—interlocking directorates, direct stock ownership, holding companies, transportation agreements, family intermarriage, and joint financing. And if stock ownership occasionally gave the appearance of being fairly widely distributed, the reality was one of management and voting control vested in the hands of a minute segment of stockholders, usually acting with the authority of combined family or trust shares behind them.

The Big Five companies (Castle and Cooke, C. Brewer, American Factors, Theo H. Davies, Alexander and Baldwin) continued to be controlled by the long-entrenched *haole* families, still very much in charge of the businesses inherited from their missionary and merchant forefathers. The corporate listings of 1920, to take one year, reveal that two Cookes and one Atherton were directors of the Bank of Hawaii; two Cookes, an Atherton, and a Thurston sat on the Honolulu Rapid Transit Board; American Factors listed a Cooke, an Atherton, a Dillingham, a Frear, and a Wilcox; while an Armstrong, two Athertons, and three Castles graced the Castle and

Cooke board.[3] Decisions were the prerogative of such men, sitting in leisurely ease in their plush offices or in the elegant rooms of the Pacific Club. Stockholder meetings were formalities. At the Castle and Cooke building (until 1938, the company was 58 percent controlled by the Atherton and Castle estates), the Kohala Sugar Company scheduled its annual meeting at 9:30 A.M.; Ewa Plantation followed at 10:00, Wailua Agriculture was at 10:30, and the Helemano Corporation at 11:00.[4] It would be surprising if the handful of men who attended these meetings did not subsequently adjourn to the Pacific Club for drinks at 11:30. Corporate musical chairs. And in 1940 the corporate structure had changed little, the only notable addition being the newly emerged utility companies, which also came under the monopoly umbrella. Given the oligarchy's control over the economy, it was inconceivable that any new technology or industry brought into Hawaii during this period would not be similarly commandeered.

The old missionary firm of Castle and Cooke, with its islands-wide holdings in plantations, warehousing, communications, and finance, was the most eminent of the Big Five. Its situation was enhanced by World War I, when it grabbed the lion's share of the confiscated German-owned Hackfeld and Company (today's American Factors). Two leading luminaries within the Castle and Cooke family, Bank of Hawaii president Clarence Cooke (also a director of Hawaiian Trust, Hawaiian Electric, C. Brewer, Hawaiian Pineapple, and eight sugar companies) and his cousin Frank Cooke Atherton (president of Castle and Cooke, and director of Hawaiian Trust, Hawaiian Pineapple, American Factors, the Bank of Hawaii, the *Honolulu Star-Bulletin,* and seven sugar companies), occupied the pinnacle of the economic hierarchy.[5] Atherton's predecessor, E. D. Tenney, the long-time, autocratic president of Castle and Cooke, performed the versatile feat of presiding over Castle and Cooke, Matson Navigation, the Hawaiian Trust Company, and three plantations, while being on the board of directors of twelve other companies *simultaneously.*[6]

On the island of Kauai, the American Factors (Amfac) land managers, the Rice family, along with the Wilcoxes and Robinsons, were the acknowledged suzerains. The writ of Henry Baldwin ran strongly throughout Maui, while three *kamaaina* families and Amfac controlled the Kona Coast, and East Hawaii was under the

direction of an assortment of Big Five managers. Those presenting
a challenge to the existing power structure were crushed without
hesitation.[7]

The interests of the man who was known to many powerful
metropolitan figures as "Mr. Hawaii"—Walter Francis Dillingham,
who had "worked as best I could as a young fellow toward annexation"—were legion. Inheriting a railroad, some widespread land
holdings, and a wealth of business and political contacts from his
father, Walter soon broadened out into dredging and construction,
turning Kahului and Hilo into active ports. By the early 1920s,
utilizing his old school ties and connections made around the Rac-
quet Club in Washington, Dillingham had "clearly established himself in the eyes of important officials as Hawaii's important
industrialist."[8] He, more than any other member of the Island
elite, benefitted from alliances with elites in the metropole. Indeed,
the spectacular rise of the Dillingham industrial complex (separate
from, yet closely allied to, the Big Five) must be attributed in large
part to the generosity of "Mr. Walter's" Washington patrons. Lav-
ishly entertaining junketing admirals and generals, presidents and
senators at his splendid baroque estate near Diamond Head,
Dillingham obtained lucrative military contracts for numerous
projects in Hawaii and the Pacific, including a series of profitable
contracts around the Pearl Harbor Naval Base. Soon the company's
blue insignia was to be propelled to the furthest reaches of the
great Pacific Ocean.[9]

Dillingham, who in August 1919 had not hesitated to fire seventy
Japanese railway workers, whom he tagged as "agitators," and hire
others in their place, and who never thought twice about using
goon squads to enforce his will, was not a man to tread lightly in
matters that affected his interests. It was Walter (as is revealed in
his remarkable correspondence with Governor Farrington)[10] who
was the *eminence gris* behind a number of the governors of Hawaii.
It was Walter who contemptuously dismissed complaints about civil
rights violations in Hawaii during World War II as "all that sort of
hooey that nobody cared a damn about." And it was Walter who, in
1931, at the height of the nationally publicized Massie rape-murder
case (when the Island elite was frightened by mainland demands to
overhaul the Territorial governing structure), lectured the Chamber of Commerce as to their own class interests: "You businessmen

represented by the Chamber pay 90 percent of the taxes and the time has come for you to demand 90 percent voice in the control of government."[11] Ten days later, after demanding the convening of a special legislative session to establish a police commission and enact a tough new jury law, Walter stormed into the governor's office at the head of a crowd of Big Five executives to receive a response. Melodramatically retrieving the executive order for the new legislative session from his desk drawer, the feckless governor, Lawrence Judd, told his visitors, "Here it is, gentlemen. I signed it yesterday and it goes out today."[12] The first police commission was headed by none other than Dillingham's private secretary.[13]

Among the last of the old *kamaaina* ruling class to accept the passing of a cherished era, Dillingham insisted even in the late 1940s (when president of five companies and director of seventeen more) that nothing had really changed: "We have never given up the leadership and control of the policies in the development of this Territory," he proudly told a Congressional investigating committee.[14] And yet Dillingham was a shrewd capitalist, hatching plans to enhance his family's corporate interests, and remained a man with prominent connections: once, when U.S. president-elect Dwight David Eisenhower arrived in Hawaii and scanned the faces in the waiting crowd, he asked, "Where's Walter?" Nobody asked, "Walter who?"[15] Finally, Dillingham was a man who knew that Hawaii's economic future (and his own) lay elsewhere than in commercial agriculture—in the virtually untouched areas of tourism and land development.

One of the great fears that had haunted the elite after annexation was the prospect of the "ignorant majority"—in Lorrin Thurston's phrase—using legal means to dismantle their carefully constructed economic apparatus. As the first territorial governor, Sanford Dole, so artlessly expressed it: "What if all the natives and the Portuguese can vote without being perfectly responsible simply because they are grown up?"[16] Thurston was most succinct on this same point: "What we desire is some form of territorial government which will give an effective executive, which will not be subject to the whims and caprices and dishonesty of an irresponsible legislative body; as well as maintain government, make revolution impossible, encourage investment of capital and development of resources."[17]

The solution arrived at by Washington and Honolulu, in joint consultation, was to establish an extraordinarily powerful governor, possessing a wide range of administrative and discretionary powers. Control over the governorship thus became one of the keystones of elite control over the entire political process. Officially appointed by the president, territorial governors were in actuality handpicked by the oligarchy. Most, like Dole (1907–13), former president of the Republic of Hawaii; lawyer Walter Frear (1907–13), a thin, goateed man who stepped from the governor's mansion to directorships of Bishop Trust, the Dillingham interests, and the Bishop National Bank; Alexander and Baldwin executive Lawrence Judd (1929–34), who in his autobiography proudly relates how he was literally *ordered* into political life at a meeting presided over by top executives from four of the largest corporations in Hawaii;[18] and Hawaii Sugar Planters' Association labor recruiter Lucius Pinkham (1913–18), who managed to reduce taxes on the plantations by $25 million during his term in office (even though sugar production and profits were higher than ever),[19] were members in good standing of the Island upper class. But even a governor like Wallace Rider Farrington (1918–28), whose background was in education rather than business, was quite amenable to acting in the best interests of the "boys on Merchant Street." As one contemporary critic of the system wrote, "Sugar was so thoroughly king in Hawaii that an appointee for governor (who under the law had to be a bonafide resident of the territory) even if selected from among those having the least direct connections with the dominating sugar interests, would be nevertheless inevitably controlled by those interests."[20]

"In no part of the United States is a single industry so predominant as the sugar industry is in Hawaii," wrote Ray Stannard Baker.[21] A 1905 study elaborated on this: "Directly or indirectly, all individuals in the Territory of Hawaii are ultimately dependent upon the sugar industry. The social, the economic and the political structure of the islands alike are built upon a foundation of sugar."[22] Acting as agents for thirty-six of the thirty-eight sugar plantations, the Big Five openly monopolized the sugar trade. Twenty-nine firms, producing seven out of every eight tons of sugar exported from the Islands, refined, marketed, and distributed their product through the Big Five's wholly owned California and Hawaiian Sugar Company, whose refinery, the largest in the world, was on San Francisco Bay. Such vertical integration made the Big Five almost completely independent of the California-owned sugar refineries and also gave them a dominant share of sugar distribution in vast areas of the western United States.

Although sugar profits varied with the ups and downs of the market price (which was sometimes disturbingly low), there were sufficient years of plenty to offset the lean. In 1925, a bountiful year, Island sugar interests realized $25 million in profits on a $100 million crop. The Hawaiian Agricultural Company made a 30 percent profit in 1915, 67 percent in 1920, and 17 percent in 1925. An even larger Big Five firm, Maui's Hawaiian Commercial and Sugar Company, sprawling out over 35,000 acres and housing 3,200 workers, regularly returned a 20 percent profit to its stock-holders.[23] From 1894 through 1923 Castle and Cooke profits amounted to over $12 million, out of which over $6 million was paid as dividends—average yearly dividends being a most substantial 36.2 percent.[24]

The second keystone of political domination was legislative control. Since the elite was only a small minority of the electorate and could easily be outvoted, it was faced with the continuing problem of establishing an electoral majority. With most Orientals barred from the polls as aliens, the dominant voting bloc was formed by the newly enfranchised Hawaiians. Skillfully using Hawaiian leaders to construct a mass Hawaiian base for legislative domination by the Republican Party, the elite created the vehicle they needed. One such leader, Prince Jonah Kuhio Kalanianaole, was coopted with an offer of the position of Territorial delegate to Congress and vague promises of future benefits for Hawaiians. In Washington he served the plantation interests well for two decades, pleading for sugar quotas and immigration policies; but at home he remained a figurehead. Now and then, in flashes of anger and frustration, he would lash out at the "domination of Hawaii by sugar planters," or in even harsher language would tell a throng of Hawaiians (as at Aala Park in 1912), "Under the political conditions in the territory, a man doesn't own his own soul."[25] Nevertheless, the collaboration continued.

Merchant Street used the "Hawaiian alliance" in a most cynical manner. An excellent example is the Hawaiian Rehabilitation Act, passed by the United States Congress in 1921. The sugar elite's profits depended heavily upon continued access to vast acres of dirt-cheap public lease lands—one plantation, for instance, held ninety-five thousand acres at $.02 an acre per year.[26] With twelve major plantation leaseholds on public land set to expire between 1918 and 1922, and pressure from landless Hawaiians and *haoles* for their repossession and distribution to small farmers, the planters were confronted with a dilemma. The act was thus portrayed as an answer to the condition of thousands of landless Hawaiians occupying hovels and shanties around Honolulu, and it established a Hawaiian Homes Commission to distribute two hundred thousand acres to Hawaiian homesteaders for the creation of small farms. Kuhio, who had promoted the legislation vigorously, hailed it as a "triumph of justice for the Hawaiians."[27]

But a clause was inserted that allowed public lands to be re-leased for indefinite periods and removed all restrictions on the size of a lease. In addition, the sugar planters managed to exclude any of the fertile sugar lands from the distribution process, and nearly all of the alloted acreage was rocky, arid, and sandy. Only 2 percent could be developed at a reasonable cost,[28] and the impoverished Hawaiian homesteaders quickly floundered amidst unsurmountable obstacles. Even those settlements that proved agriculturally sound lacked the essential transportation to markets in the towns. So, not surprisingly, the best homestead lands eventually passed into the control of the large plantations through lease arrangements, while most of the remaining settlements failed, deteriorating with time into rural slums. Moreover, only a small fraction of the Hawaiian population was touched by this "rehabilitation" program, and the great majority were left in a state of permanent economic depression.[29] Once again the elite, able to draw support from allied interests in the metropole, had fortified its economic position,[30] and became the real beneficiary of an act supposedly aimed at ameliorating conditions among the masses.

A political scene that denied participation to entire segments of the populace and coerced others into voting as it wished reduced politics to a charade. Plantation *lunas* escorted their workers to the polls, where they were intimidated into voting "correctly." It was a time when Joseph Cooke could mount a chair at the Republican convention and issue orders to the delegates, many of whom were plantation managers and employees. The Democrats, mainly supported by landless *haoles* but still controlled by plantation interests, likewise had a formidable record of corruption and bossism. During their 1912 convention, Windward Oahu land baron Link McCandless bribed delegates and dominated the floor through the use of strong-armed former policemen.[31] Troublesome independents like Maui contractor Willie Crozier, who spoke for collective bargaining rights for workers and political reforms, were thrown bodily out of the legislature.[32] Legislative bills were drawn up in the downtown offices of corporate attorneys and transmitted to corporate-controlled politicians at Iolani Palace.

Realizing that elections were fundamentally meaningless, the Hawaiian masses enjoyed the *luaus* and the carnival atmosphere around election time, the rhetorical speechmaking and good food and drink, and accepted patronage jobs at low levels of government. Whether Democrats or Republicans were in office they reasoned, real power would still remain the preserve of the elite. As Ray Stannard Baker, one of the leading muckrakers of his day, wrote during a trip to Hawaii in 1911, "Three-quarters of the population of Hawaii have no more to say about the government under which they are living than the old slaves in the South."[33] His sentiments were reiterated twenty-five years later by a hardbitten Hawaiian who had fled to the remote island of Kahoolawe to escape the system: "Whatever the Big Boys want the rest of us will get and like it."[34]

The use of the government apparatus as an instrument of class domination was never more in evidence than during the mature plantation stage of Hawaii's development. The services provided by the Territorial government were legion, and went a long way toward making export crops profitable for their producers. As noted, the government deliberately frustrated land reform in order to continue the policy of huge public land rental by the plantations at nominal rents. It diverted public water to irrigate sugar plantation fields free of charge; it used the police and national guard to break strikes and suppress working-class agitation.

The access of the Island elite to U.S. elites was a further precondition of their survival as a class; that this access continued to be successfully negotiated can be seen from the large quotas of sugar allotted to Hawaiian producers each year. There is a matrix here of reinforcing elements. Control over the basic economic institutions of Hawaiian society reaffirmed the elite's political position, which in turn reinforced its economic domination. Political and economic hegemony *within* Hawaii provided the Island oligarchy with a base from which to deal with elites in Washington, New York, and San Francisco.

The oligarchs ruled with an iron fist, tolerating opposition from neither competitors nor the labor force. Those who challenged the oligarchy's interests were summarily crushed. For instance, the aristocratically aloof James Dole, never on the most intimate terms with the elite, attempted pineapple cultivation around the turn of the century, rapidly expanding it into a big business under the auspices of his Hawaiian Pineapple Company. Profits were comparable to those in sugar: 25 percent in 1920 and 33 percent in 1935. But the onset of the Great Depression, at a time when the company had sixty-five thousand acres planted in pineapple (and heavy outstanding debts), played havoc with its financial position. In 1931, faced with a disintegrating market and a bumper crop rotting in the fields, Dole committed the unpardonable act of abandoning his long-time carrier, the Big Five's Matson Navigation Line, for the cheaper (but overseas-owned) Isthmian Line. Almost immediately, his sources of credit in both Honolulu and San Francisco dried up. Banks were deaf to his pleas for emergency loans. Shortly thereafter, he was forced to concede failure and his company passed into the hands of Castle and Cooke.[35]

Castle and Cooke then resolved to apply the same monopolistic practices it had used so successfully in sugar to pineapple. In conjunction with two other Big Five corporations, the Pineapple Producer Cooperative was formed—a combine which monopolized the world's pineapple trade and determined how much fruit would be produced and who would receive it. By 1940 the Big Five's pineapple holdings had matured into a $50 million business employing thirty-five thousand workers and incorporating the usual techniques of interlocking directorates and secret agreements. Castle and Cooke's Waialua Agricultural Company, for instance, owned enough stock in Hawaiian Pine (36 percent) to draw off over $600,000 a year in dividends.[36]

In the same agrarian context, the oligarchy fought the rise of a strong small-farmer–yeoman class which would demand the kind of drastic land reform that would undermine the plantation estate system. After annexation, the elite had discouraged small farming as an economic alternative—Governor Frear sabotaged land reform measures, as did Governor McCarthy and other Big Five minions. Governor Pinkham classified departure from large plantation agriculture as "absolutely un-American" and praised the existing system as "development on American lines." Although that ersatz reformer, Governor Farrington, announced the existence of "opportunities for citizens of this territory young and old who wished to go into sugar or pineapple cultivation"—adding in his own piece of the Protestant ethic, "The easiest thing in the world is to say it can't be done. Ninety percent of the failures go along that route, all the successes take the other route and do it."[37]—the truth was quite different. As one farmer, an open-faced Swedish immigrant named J. E. Gamielson, had learned.

Gamielson and twenty other small holders were growing sugarcane on homesteads on the Big Island; the Swede's sixty-nine acres were slightly larger than the typical landholding of the group. Around this time—1910—the area's dominant Big Five firm, the Hilo Sugar Company, was conducting a no-holds-barred campaign to drive a small, local, independently owned mill into bankruptcy and, as part of its strategy, persuaded the capital-short homesteaders to sell all their sugar to its refinery at a very good price. However, after delivery of the cane, Hilo Sugar suddenly refused to abide by the original agreement, offering only half the promised price. The homesteaders fell heavily into debt in order to buy needed supplies, and then suddenly, without advance warning, learned that the local Big Five bank refused to extend them additional credit. What ensued was a host of bankruptcies, with the most productive lands absorbed by Hilo Sugar.[38]

This same tale (with some minor variations) could have been told by numerous small farmers. When they applied to the courts for legal redress, they were confronted with Big Five-appointed judges. The local plantation manager himself was, at once, postmaster of the district and commandant of the local police. In testimony before a Congressional investigating committee, Russian-born Nicholas Russet, an Olaa (Big Island) farmer driven to financial disaster by such plantation-bank collusion, blamed the "concentration of economic and political power in the hands of a few" for the failure of small homesteading. "Neither small farming or diversified industries are in the interests of those few," he concluded.[39]

Sugar and pineapple were certainly the principle interests comprising the elite's economic arsenal, but they by no means constituted the entire spectrum of its monopoly control. The Bank of Hawaii, founded a year before annexation by two executives from Castle and Cooke, both prominent conspirators against the Queen, soon held, with the older Bishop First National, a monopoly over the financial and loan business. "Intruders," such as the People's Bank of Hilo and the Bank of Maui, found themselves isolated and unable to forge links with anyone tied to the Big Five—meaning virtually *everyone*. They soon collapsed and were absorbed into the old *kamaaina* financial apparatus. Hawaiian Trust and Bishop Trust handled real estate, stock brokerage, and insurance. Internal transport was under Big Five control as well: Dillingham's Oahu Railway and Land Company was *the* railway on Oahu, while Alexander and Baldwin had *the* rails on Maui and Alexander and Baldwin and American Factors owned *the* Big Island rails. Virtually every sector of economic life was thus subservient to the oligarchy. In 1937 Edward Walker, high sheriff of Hawaii, testified before a Congressional committee on statehood: "Everything that comes into the territory comes through a large corporation. The independent businessman who attempts to enter business here immediately finds that even nationally advertised lines from the mainland are tied up by the Big Five. It is almost impossible to get an independent line of business as they have everything—lumber, paint, right down the line."[40]

Not content with simply directing the Islands' commercial production, the Big Five also oversaw and controlled the movement of goods between the Territory and North America. They came to own the Matson Navigation Company, which had served as their primary carrier of sugar and pineapple since early in the century, thus guaranteeing them a monopoly of their own business. Thanks to the support and patronage of its Merchant Street owner-customers, Matson developed into a leading Pacific shipping line, transporting virtually the entire cargo of freight and passengers moving between the continent and Hawaii.

In their operation of Matson, the Big Five remained faithful to the tradition of refusing to deal with any business enterprise not under their express control. Using every available corporate device to force competition to the wall, Matson bought out rivals like the Los Angeles and Oceanic steamship companies, while the surviving competitor, the Dollar Line, found its rates undercut in a ruthless price war. Finally, reeling from the impact of heavy financial losses, Dollar agreed to terminate regular shipping service to the Islands and kickback 50 percent of its future profits ($1.2 million between 1930 and 1938) from the Hawaiian route to Matson. By the late 1930s the carrier had direct corporate interlocks with *fifty-eight* Big Five-controlled corporations. The transportation monopoly was a fabulously lucrative trump card for the Big Five, which were able to realize enormous profits as commission agents for the steamship companies they "served," while drawing dividends from the same firms.[41]

For people living in Hawaii, monopoly control over shipping and commodity distribution meant high prices and a diminished standard of living. "It does cost more to live in these islands than in almost any other part of the United States," reflected *Crossroads of the Pacific* a dozen years after annexation.[42] To use one example, the Big Five controlled over 90 percent of the retail and wholesale lumber business. In the early 1940s, lumber was priced at $15 a thousand square foot board in California; upon arrival at the Honolulu docks the price had nearly doubled to $28.50; the customer eventually paid $78.[43] Along the way, Matson and Big Five warehousers, wholesalers, and retailers charged exhorbitant markups. This situation was aggravated by the monopoly enjoyed by the Inter-Island Steamship Company—another Big Five company—on internal freight transport within the Islands. Discriminatory pricing and charging what the traffic would bear were their operating principles.[44]

Food prices were equally marked up. In 1930, when *monthly* wages for male plantation workers ranged from approximately $31 for adults to $6 for children, when the cannery paid between $21 and $29 a month, when construction workers received $20 a month and longshoremen between $12 and $14, Honolulu food prices were far higher than anything comparable on the continent— bread was $.10 a pound, eggs were $.78 a dozen, butter was $.58 a pound, and fresh milk was $.20 a quart. The economies of scale and capital investment necessary to further the two-crop export economy precluded the cultivation of vegetables, fruits, and grains, and the building of a local dairy industry. Thus, in a group of islands containing thousands of acres of extremely fertile agricultural land ideally suited for double and triple cropping, and had ample pasturage, eggs, cream, and beans were imported from California, mutton from Australia and New Zealand.[45]

The *kamaaina* elite were in their heyday masters of all they surveyed. Life for what Honolulu writer Donald Blanding called "the select cream, the pale foam on the melting pot" bore a close resemblance to that for other Caucasian ruling classes in the tropics. One recalls the Dutch planters in Java, the French in Indochina, the British gentlemen and ladies of the India of the Raj. Boys and girls might spend their childhoods frolicking with Hawaiian companions in swimming holes and along beaches, but at the age of eleven or twelve, on the verge of adolescence, the law of caste would descend, setting them on the road to their proper station. The young *haole* male went to Yale or Princeton before returning to occupy an office on Bishop Street, or perhaps manage the family plantation or ranch; the girls were expected to make the correct *haole* marriage. The great families lived in splendid Victorian houses overlooking carefully manicured lawns, where they entertained ranking military officers and visiting mainland notables. Appropriately, their favorite sport was polo, the preoccupation of the British rulers of India. An elite which prided itself on prerogatives, it was customary for the curtain of a Maui movie theater to be held until the local plantation manager arrived to claim his seat.[46]

A tightly knit group it was, frequenting the same clubs and vacation retreats, yachting, sailing, golfing, and cruising to Europe together, and living in the same exclusive neighborhoods. Carefully shielded by wealth and the isolation of their class position from harshly critical outsiders and from the resentments and frustrations of the population living under their dominion, they inevitably came to regard themselves as appointed to rule over the "others." The workers may have been a necessary part of the scenery, but they were a people without authentic culture or the mental ability to rule themselves. No one expressed these sentiments more forcefully than sugar planter Royal Mead in 1910: "Up to now, the Asiatic has had only an economic value in the social equation. So far as the institution, laws, customs and language of the permanent population go, his presence is no more felt than is that of the cattle on the range."[47]

Noblesse oblige demanded a certain paternalism, a certain grudging benevolence toward inferiors. Sophie Judd Cooke prided herself on the "domestics who served us well over the years" and on knowing the names of the Japanese chauffeurs, cooks, gardeners, and maids on her Molokai estate.[48] It was a ruling class which retained enough of the missionary spirit to delight in lavishing money upon its favorite charities. There was a year when George P. Cooke donated almost a quarter of his income to various charities; collection plates at the Central Union Church turned up $30,000 on a given Sunday.[49] Yet those same donors recoiled from the idea of voluntarily raising their workers' miserable wages or divesting themselves of ownership of the filthy, falling-down tenement slums in Kakaako. "I have rarely visited a place where there was as much charity and little democracy as in Hawaii," commented Baker in his scathing exposé, written in 1911.[50]

The entire system operated along the racist lines established by the plantation interests in the mid-nineteenth century, when a cultural division of labor had been imposed upon sugar production to facilitate exploitation of (and to divide) the proletariat. A somewhat different cultural division of labor was maintained throughout the pre-Pearl Harbor era: Chinese were found in small businesses, Japanese in small businesses, on small farms, and on plantations, Portuguese were plantation foremen and skilled crafts people, Filipinos were plantation laborers, and Hawaiians were low-level government workers, stevedores, and construction workers. To keep up racial "appearances" and to maintain a loyal *haole* auxiliary, whites were awarded the most prized jobs and paid more for the same labor and the same work.[51] As Koji Ariyoshi, later to make his mark as a radical journalist, noted, "In the various places I worked, even on the waterfront, I had noticed that the *haole* firms did not seem to approve of white laborers working with us. *Haoles* became clerks, watchmen, holding down what appeared to be cleaner jobs."[52] On his first trip to the United States, future governor Lawrence Judd was more than slightly surprised to "see so many light skins on townspeople who were doing all the work, barbering and waiting tables, driving the teams of fine horses and patrolling the police beats."[53] (This did not mean that there were not class distinctions among whites, however. For instance, according to schoolteacher John Reinecke, "I taught for four years at a plantation school in Honokaa and during all that time never once was I invited to the houses of the plantation staff. That was my experience.")

The most ambitious attempt to provide an ideological underpinning for Hawaii's cultural division of labor and for the stark political and economic disenfranchisement of the vast majority of Island people was mounted by S. D. Porteus, director of the Psychological and Psychopathic Clinic at the University of Hawaii and closely linked with the *haole* elite through his wife, a scion of the estate-holding Damon family. A prolonged strike by Japanese and Filipino plantation workers in the 1920s, followed by a tumultuous Filipino strike four years later, were severely repressed by the oligarchy. Porteus provided the repressors with a "scientific" rationalization for their policies and their special prerogatives and privileges, devising, among other things, "racial efficiency indexes" to measure racial intelligence and other characteristics. He characterized the Japanese, for instance, as "intensely race conscious, ready to combine for any purposes of group advancement, aggressive and rather untrustworthy when self-interest is in question."[54] To counter the perceived Japanese threat, he advocated that the "Nordic strongholds in America and Australia must be developed and maintained. To throw them open to the dangers of Japanese penetration, peaceful or otherwise, would be to pursue a policy of race suicide."[55]

The Filipino threat was approached from a rather different perspective. Filipinos were portrayed as a racially inferior, mixed-blood group with a deficient psychological structure, plotting to usurp their betters. The stereotype was equally crude: "Filipinos represent a fine example of a race in an adolescent stage of development. They exhibit all the signs of imbalance and temporary maladjustment that many adolescents show."[56] Such a critique was a convenient rationale for the continued disenfranchisement (and exploitation) of Filipino plantation workers in Hawaii (as well as in the Philippines). Charging that the Filipinos were "improvident and shiftless, highly emotional and impulsive and explosive, of primitive temperament," Porteus drew the inevitable conclusion that they were neither prepared for self-goverance on any level, nor for a responsible role in U.S. society: "It is of our opinion that no matter what labels of citizenship we may put on these people, they remain Filipinos and it will take much more than a knowledge of the three 'R's' to make them Americans."[57]

Porteus' position was—by no coincidence—identical to that of the Hawaiian Sugar Planters' Association, which insisted that an education for non-*haole* working-class children beyond that needed to work efficiently in the fields was not only unnecessary but was a definite *danger* to the system. His advice to the rulers of Hawaii— "The surest way to make a malcontent is to educate him above his intelligence or opportunities"[58]—fell on fertile soil.

The racism of the elite was compatible with its overriding obsession, its determination to maintain absolute control over the working class, especially the plantation workers, who constituted over one-third of all the workers in the Territory. The carrot (paternalism) and the stick (coercion) were employed to achieve this end. Paternalism, in the form of perquisites provided "free" by the plantation—housing, medical care, recreational facilities—was designed to divert the workers' attention from their miserable wages and working conditions and to keep them dependent on plantation resources. Paternalism also allowed the elite to respond to criticism with self-righteous indignation: "I know of no other tropical or semi-tropical country in the world . . . where working and living conditions are as favorable as they are in this country," said Big Five executive Frank Atherton.[39]

Coercion was the other side of the coin. Nine decades of playing race against race, of beatings, shootings, blacklists, and myriad forms of brutalization are summarized in a terse 1939 statement by the U.S. Department of Labor: "Hawaiian management has used every influence at its command to restrict labor organizing."[60] To the planters and their financial allies, a cheap, plentiful, and highly disciplined labor force was the indispensable foundation of their prosperity. Back in 1881 the *Hawaii Planters Monthly* had voiced this continuing planter perspective: "The industrial conditions of these islands require people as laborers accustomed to subordination, to permanency of abode, and to have moderate expectations in regard to livelihood."[61] The commissioner of labor statistics reported in 1916 that the planters "view laborers primarily as instruments of production, their business interests require cheap, not too intelligent, docile, unmarried men."[62]

Coercion was used to prevent plantation workers from organizing for improved conditions. Plans were carefully formulated for dealing with labor trouble and the Employers Industrial Association of Hawaii worked closely with the Honolulu Police Department and U.S. Military Intelligence to smash local strikes. Hawaiian labor history is replete with instances of brutal repression. Scores of organizing drives and protests ended with jail sentences for workers, deportations, beatings, and evictions. In April 1909, when seven thousand Japanese, earning $.69 a day in the fields, walked off the job, Merchant Street attorneys broke into the offices of a Japanese newspaper to dynamite the safe and collect evidence that put the strike leaders in prison for "interfering with plantation operations." One hundred Japanese were arrested. After three months of goon-squad harrassment and court injunctions, the workers, many now sick and destitute, trudged back to work.[63]

In 1920, during the massive Japanese and Filipino strike mentioned earlier, the Big Five whipped up a racist, red-baiting press campaign against the strikers: "IS CONTROL OF THE INDUSTRIALIZATION OF HAWAII TO REMAIN IN THE HANDS OF THE ANGLO-SAXONS OR IS IT TO PASS INTO THOSE OF THE ALIEN JAPANESE?" Thousands of workers and their families were evicted from their corrugated houses on plantation property, made to leave the "flowers and plants carefully nurtured by our own hands." Makeshift camps were strung out along dirt roads from Pearl City to West Honolulu, and in the city itself, amidst a raging influenza epidemic, thousands crowded into tent camps, parks, and temples. As people died ("Their lives went out like candle flames in a gust of wind"), they said, "Don't give up the fight. Fight for the righteous cause." After six months the strike was smashed in what oligarch William R. Castle hailed as "A place to be proud of since America has made it a land of prosperity and happiness and liberty."[64]

In 1924, when thirteen thousand militant Filipino workers, demanding improved conditions, engaged in a series of strike actions, kidnapping and violence were the order of the day. Eventually, a pitched battle flared between armed workers and the police in

Hanapape, Kauai, leaving sixteen workers and four police dead. The planters then imported two National Guard machine-gun squads to break the strike and had sixty strike leaders imprisoned for four years.[65] Six years later, a visiting (and sympathetic) writer noted, "There is no remnant of organization among the plantation workers today and at this time there seems little chance of effective labor action."[66]

In the 1930s, a time when Territorial delegate Joseph Farrington stood on the floor of the U.S. Congress eulogizing Hawaii as the "lighthouse of democracy in the Pacific," labor organizers on the Hawaiian docks were beaten up and deported by thugs personally hired by Big Five lawyer Frank Thompson, and the Honolulu police (besides protecting these thugs) operated as crews to break a 1936 Honolulu-Hilo Inland boatman's strike, reporting to Castle and Cooke managers for orders. On the breezy morning of August 1, 1938, five hundred unarmed, peaceful pickets were fired upon by sixty police protecting a strikebreaking ship in Hilo Harbor. In a torrent of fire and gas bombs, fifty-one were wounded. "They shot us down like a herd of sheep," said union organizer and longshoreman Harry Kamoku. "We didn't have a chance—they just kept pumping buckshot and bullets into our bodies. . . . It was just plain slaughter." Sheriff Henry Martin explained: "The bigshots in Honolulu asked me to give protection to their ships."[67]

In this "lighthouse of democracy," Democratic Party leaders were barred from speaking in large parts of the Islands, and plantation workers were systematically coerced into voting for their bosses' candidates. Those with known pro-union sentiments were blacklisted and prevented from working at all. Repressive legislation written by Hawaii Sugar Planters' Association lawyers—most notably the 1919 Criminal Syndicalism Law, the 1921 Anarchistic Publications Law, and the 1923 Anti-Picketing Law—gave Big Five judges the legal power to imprison trade union organizers and suppress union literature. One 1938 study remarked of these three statutes: "Each one is a potential weapon in restricting the right of labor to organize for security. . . . Labor is denied by these laws the right of organizing openly, of presenting its case before the public and of demonstrating its solidarity in times of crisis."[68]

Under the aegis of former Governor Judd and the Industrial Association of Hawaii (an organization sworn "to check and eradi-

cate communism, radicalism, and all attempts to embarrass, har-
rass, or overthrow our present system of government and
constitutional control"), elaborate dossiers were compiled on corporate employees and suspected labor organizers in an office of the
Castle and Cooke building. In the mid-1930s San Francisco public
relations man Sidney Bowman and his Pan Pacific Company were
hired by the Big Five to foment a propaganda offensive aimed at
inducing yet a greater conformity of ideas. Since the two newspapers and the radio stations had already adopted a self-imposed
censorship, schools and workplaces were inundated with materials
emphasizing the importance of sugar and pineapple to Hawaii's
continued prosperity. Principals and teachers were instructed to
escort their students on carefully planned tours of plantations and
mills, right-wing speakers were regularly introduced into school
assemblies, and informers were placed in teachers' conferences and
even private gatherings.[69]

Thus it was that an inbred clique of autocratic families used its
power to protect and expand its interests at the community's expense. Indeed, during a period when signs like "Mussolini Is Always Right" littered the walls of Italy and jackboots were heard
along the cobbled streets of Germany, it was notable that National
Labor Relations Board representative E. J. Egan could say, with
some credibility, "If there is a truer picture of fascism in the world
today than in the Hawaiian Islands, I do not know a definition of
it."[70] And it is significant that when Hawaiian leader W. A. Kinney
chose to protest the situation, he took his petition to the U.S. Congress. Like many others, Kinney understood that the real font of
elite power in Hawaii lay in the metropole. In his petition he said:
"That it is a system is the trouble. If it were merely a temporary
combination of evil-minded men, their dispersal would be all that
would be required, but what has grown up in Hawaii is akin to the
development of the slave power in the United States."[71]

If Hawaii was a variant of plantation society, it nevertheless
shared the essential characteristics of dependency with such places
as Cuba, Jamaica, and Guyana. Like Cuba, for instance, the Island
political economy "was controlled by a number of organized and
monopolistic groups seeking to maintain themselves through government protection."[72] And Eric Hanley's description of the serious consequences for Guyanese society resulting from the "domi-

nation of King Sugar" could as easily be applied to plantation Hawaii: "It has led to the institutionalization of a system of paternalistic domination, the development of a dependent psychology amongst the population, and the strange combination of cultural assimilation combined with a system of racial and ethnic stratification."[73] Above all, of course, there was a similarity between Hawaii and these Caribbean areas in terms of relationship to the metropole. It was this more than anything else that conditioned the shape and form of their development and their societies.

Hawaii's dependent relationship with the United States extended to such cultural imports as barbershop quartets, silent films, bootleg liquor, flappers, and dance crazes, but its basis continued to be considerably more profound than that and the market for its export crops continued to be almost wholly within the continental United States, so that in 1914 the United States provided the market for over $40.6 million of a grand total of over $42.5 million of Hawaiian exports.[74] (Two decades later, in fiscal 1935, Hawaiian exports to the United States had climbed to over $94.5 million, against exports to *all* foreign nations combined of $1.3 million.)[75] In return Hawaii's imports were also almost entirely from the United States: using 1914 figures again, in that year Hawaii imported $32.1 million worth of goods, $25.8 million of which was from the United States; in 1915 the figures were $69.2 million and $63.5 million.[76]

The breakdown of traded items is also a *déja vu* of the late monarchy period: in fiscal 1913–14, raw and refined sugar accounted for $33.2 million of exports, followed by pineapples at $4.5 million; all remaining items taken together (rice, hides, molasses, coffee, etc.) did not come close to equaling the figure for pineapple. (Again, looking ahead to fiscal 1935, sugar and pineapple exports to the United States together were $89.9 million out of a total figure of $94.5 million.)[77] As for imports in fiscal 1913–14, breadstuffs, cotton clothing, oil, automobiles and parts, nails-spikes-pipes, lumber, tobacco, fertilizers, and dairy and hog products were (in that order) Hawaii's leading imports by dollar volume.[78] These figures reveal a society unable to feed itself or even produce the basic capital goods necessary for its agro-industrial life.

The immense profitability of the mature plantation system for those who controlled it gave them no incentive to diversify. And given the carefully prescribed role which Hawaii played in the international division of labor, any attempt to promote a different sort of economic development would have encountered powerful opposition from entrenched metropolitan industrial interests as well. That Hawaii would remain an area of uneven development was not the concern of the local bourgeoisie—after all, they controlled the basic industries at home and the transportation, merchandising, and distribution of goods from abroad.

Nevertheless, Hawaii, as a dependent economy, was subject to economic fluctuations emanating from the metropole, as evidenced by the rapidly deteriorating position of Hawaiian industries during the most brutal years of the Great Depression in the metropole. The total export value of Hawaiian sugar and molasses in the halcyon year of 1928 was $80.9 million; by 1930 this had plunged precipitously to $56.6 million and in 1934 to $55.3 million.[79] After years of consistently high profits, the Hawaiian Pineapple Company lost $3.9 million in 1931.[80] Despite the fact that more than ten thousand Filipino agricultural workers had been shipped back to the Philippines, the *Honolulu Advertiser* still reported on April 22, 1932: "Unemployment in Honolulu . . . is worse than it has ever been in the history of the Territory."[81]

This vulnerability to developments in the metropole was sharply underscored by events surrounding the Sugar Act of 1934, which in one stroke relegated Hawaii to the category of *foreign* producer of sugar. Not only did Hawaii's sugar interests lose 76,950 tons, or about 3 percent, of their annual sugar quota, but the law stipulated that all sugar in excess of 3 percent of the quota had to be shipped to the continent *unrefined*. The act reflected both the internal needs of the United States and shifting alliances and conditions in the sugar-producing peripheries. Between 1902 and 1930, Cuba was the recipient of approximately 45 percent of the U.S. domestic sugar quota, while Hawaii, the Philippines, and Puerto Rico shared a further 25 percent. This ratio was reversed in 1930, when the three U.S.-controlled areas sharply cut into the Cuban allotment. The result in Cuba was economic ruin, severe depression, and armed uprising. The government was overthrown and the situation threatened to escape U.S. control (as it in fact did a generation later). The 1934 Sugar Act enlarged Cuba's sugar quota once again, and was thus aimed at fortifying the position of the Cuban elite and restabilizing the political situation. It was also a response to the overproduction of sugar for a U.S. domestic market whose buying power had been diminished by the Depression.[82]

Passage of the Sugar Act was significant for another reason. It caused a thoroughly alarmed sugar oligarchy to abandon a generation of fierce opposition and become the principal boosters of statehood. Merchant Street was prepared to risk a popularly elected governor in return for getting two senators who could fight for larger sugar quotas.

The term *limited dependence* might aptly define Hawaiian dependency during the plantation era. It was a dependency characterized (as in the Caribbean and other places) by the subordination of a peripheral economy to decisions in the metropole, by a monoculture economy directed toward the metropole, and by dependence upon metropolitan technology. However, unlike other dependent plantation societies, the plantation elite in Hawaii was able to maintain a certain political and economic authority within the Islands vis-à-vis the metropole. It would take a global war and major economic changes to alter this situation. But what kind of alternative would this be? Would it simply ameliorate some of the society's worst abuses and eyesores, using material goods instead of coercion to manipulate people along carefully preselected parameters, or would it be a dramatic transformation, a fundamental shift in power from one social class to another, with the simultaneous creation of new values and institutions?

The character of the "New Hawaii" that emerged in the generation following World War II would provide an answer. And as in other periods, this character would be decided by the interaction of the forces of international capitalism and those within Hawaii itself. In Part 2, we turn to this period, beginning with an examination of the general dynamic and strategies of international capitalism, in the form of the Pacific Rim strategy.

Part 2

BUILDING THE "NEW HAWAII"

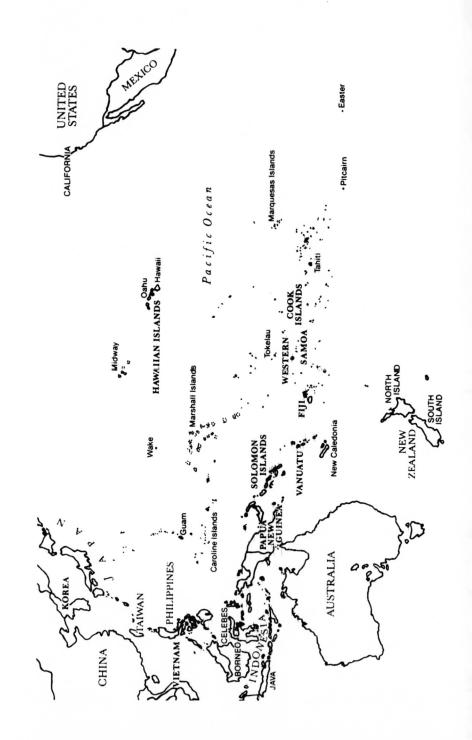

7
The Pacific Rim Strategy

If you go back several thousand years, the Western world revolved around the Mediterranean, then you go back three or four hundred years, it's been the Atlantic. Now it's the Pacific. It's where the population of the world is.
—Thomas Hitch, vice-president, Bank of Hawaii (1971)

When I speak of the Pacific Rim, I am putting the broadest possible construction on the term—the Western coasts of South America and our own continent and extending beyond Australia and the Far East to India. . . . I emphasize that this is largely an underdeveloped area, yet an area rich in an immense variety of resources and potential capabilities. Were we California businessmen to play a more dramatic role in helping trade development in the Pacific Rim, we should have giant, hungry new markets for our products and vast new profit potential for our firms.
—Rudolph Peterson, president, Bank of America; former president, Bank of Hawaii (1968)

In examining the development of a peripheral area like Hawaii over the last generation, we must devote some attention to the internal dynamic of the metropolis that dominates and directs that periphery's political and economic life. This makes particularly good sense for the two-and-one-half decades following 1945, when U.S. power and the expansion of the world capitalist system were nearly synonymous.

The end of World War II found the United States occupying a position of enormous international prestige. The European nations that had dominated the world stage for so long were ravaged by war, their claim to great power status severely eroded. Great Britain and France, although technically among the victors, had emerged from years of fighting with their economies exhausted and their societies wracked by bitter class divisions; they were in no position to assume their old leadership role in world politics. Germany was devastated and divided, its cities razed, its formidable industrial apparatus in ruins. The greatest Asian industrial and military power, Japan, was occupied by U.S. armies and ruled by a U.S. proconsul more absolute than the Tokugawa Shogun. And even the Soviet Union, whose industrial and military power had so convincingly driven the Nazi tide back into the heart of Central Europe, had achieved an essentially Pyrrhic victory: 20 million Soviet citizens were dead, factories, mines, dams, and farms were wrecked. Facing a monumental task of reconstruction, the Soviet Union was in no position to mount a challenge to U.S. global hegemony. In the United States itself the war had succeeded in accomplishing what seven years of New Deal economic strategies had failed to: it had mobilized the full capacity of an awesome productive apparatus and had laid the basis for the consumer economy of the next generation—for the sharp increase in per capita consumption, the unprecedented rise in almost every important sector of productive capacity, and a series of striking technological innovations. It was this revitalization of the U.S. economy, the harnessing of the nation's huge natural resources and technological, military, and industrial power, in conjunction with the demise of Western Europe as the arbiter of global affairs, that gave the United States the unique opportunity to restructure the postwar world.

What this meant in practice was that for the quarter-century after 1945 the world capitalist system functioned under the guidance of U.S. elites and that U.S. interests took precedence in the international decision-making process. This led to the continuing integration of world capitalism under U.S. control, to the establishment of the U.S. dollar as the world's currency, to U.S. corporate penetration of the Western European economies as a quid pro quo for U.S. financial support in restoring France, Great Britain, West Germany, Italy, Belgium, Holland, to U.S. domination over such international economic institutions as the World Bank and the International Monetary Fund, and of course to U.S. political and military leadership in the confrontation with the noncapitalist world. It enabled a sustained capitalist expansion that only came to a halt in the wake of the Vietnam war, when the internal contradictions of this type of development began to be revealed. It was, in short, the age of Pax Americana.

This momentous postwar expansion was accompanied by a series of transformations in the dynamics of capitalism. For one thing, there was an enormous growth in the role of the state (which paralleled, and often exceeded, private sector growth). At almost every level, from military procurement to sustain powerful "defense" contractors, to opening foreign markets through "aid" or political manipulation, the state came to buttress and even administer the affairs of the capitalist system.

These years also were the "age of the multinationals," multinational corporations being a logical outgrowth of a long train of events in the evolution of capitalism that led from the small eighteenth-century workshop to the nineteenth-century factory producing for a regional market to the national corporation of the early twentieth century. After 1945 it became imperative for many of the largest U.S., European, and Japanese domestic corporations to expand overseas in order to sustain (and increase) their share of the market vis-à-vis their competitors and retain attractive profit margins to secure future financing. Thus throughout this period U.S. direct investment abroad grew by about 10 percent annually, or twice as fast as the U.S. economy as a whole: between 1951 and 1976 the book value (always understated) of U.S. investment abroad rose from $16.8 billion to $80.3 billion.[1] Companies such as U.S. Steel, IBM, Coca Cola, Honeywell, Ford, Colgate-Palmolive, and Standard Oil came to draw in excess of one-half of their profits through their foreign operations. The major U.S. banks found themselves in a similar situation: by 1973, the seven largest took 40 percent of their total profits from abroad.[2]

Today, multinational corporations clearly dominate global economic markets and national destinies alike. Their profit needs directly conflict with the needs of the host countries, especially in the Third World, for genuine development. Outside companies command the most vital economic sectors of the host nation, those areas with the greatest potential to diffuse benefits throughout the economy; other options are foreclosed. Real decision-making is transferred from the host country to corporate headquarters overseas. Ultimately, the host country suffers from growing social inequality, increased unemployment and underemployment, and escalating class tensions.

No study of the dynamics of contemporary Hawaii can ignore

the impact of the multinational corporation. In this chapter, we are approaching their role in molding Island development through an analysis of their general strategies within the area dubbed the Pacific Rim. Discussing Hawaii in the context of the "Pacific Rim strategy" will provide a coherent framework in which to understand an entire generation of change.

In our own time, we have witnessed bank presidents, corporate executives, business magazines, and politicians exhorting U.S. businesses to find salvation in the markets and resources of the Pacific Rim. None of this was terribly new, of course. These ideas had been anticipated by a host of businessmen and politicians as early as the late nineteenth century. When the U.S. Navy was seizing the Philippines and Hawaii and grabbing a slice of the China market, Theodore Roosevelt (who considered the Pacific an "ocean of destiny")[3] was heard to intone that the "Pacific era is destined to be the greatest of all."[4] And noted social commentator Brooks Adams expressed that rather odd mixture of economic and strategic determinism and Social Darwinism that so characterized the U.S. imperialist position at the turn of the century when he remarked: "Our geographic position, our wealth and our energy preeminently fits us to enter upon the development of Eastern Asia and to reduce it to part of our own economic system."[5]

Yet until the outbreak of the Great Pacific War in 1941, U.S. interests in the Pacific were minor, representing only a tiny fraction of aggregate U.S. investment abroad and involving the participation of only a handful of leading corporations. The United States continued to maintain its economic linkages with the advanced capitalist powers of Western Europe. On the eve of Pearl Harbor, Atlantic parameters still largely defined U.S. economic interests overseas, although certainly decision-making elites within the United States continued to recognize the Pacific's long-term economic and strategic significance.

The outcome of World War II transformed the political and economic configuration of the Pacific Basin beyond recognition. It led to the virtual elimination of a European colonial presence, and terminated Japan's own grandiose designs for imperial hegemony. And if the United States after 1945 enjoyed a near monopoly of political, economic, and ideological authority throughout much of

Western Europe, the vacuum of power bequeathed by the war made its situation in the Pacific even more favorable. With a divided China caught up in civil war, a conquered Japan, and a devastated, politically cautious Soviet Union, the Pacific quickly became, in the words of a number of high-ranking U.S. officials, an "American lake."[6] Militarily secure, Washington adopted the official U.S. navy position—"maintain strategic control over the Pacific"—and established a Pacific-wide security zone consisting of thirty-three bases in twenty-two locations, from the Aleutians to Australia. U.S. corporations began to capture (and create) new markets, and to use new sources of cheap raw materials and labor. Although exploitation of Pacific resources had occurred for half a millenium, and had intensified with the development of the world capitalist system, it still lacked the comprehensive and systematic character it took on after World War II. Now Pacific Basin oil, rubber, hardwoods, copper, tin, uranium, etc., together with factory girls assembling electrical components in Penang and Taiwan and hundreds of millions of eager consumers from Seoul to Sumatra formed an indispensable link in the chain of world capitalism. After 1945, a capitalism undergoing an unprecedented expansion in its productive and distributive capacity, and consequently in dire need of huge new resource inputs and markets, found it imperative to integrate the Pacific Basin into the world economy to an extent unimaginable before the war. This marked not only one of the great watersheds in the history of the Pacific and its peoples, but also presented a severe challenge to the forces of international capitalism: the failure of the advanced capitalist world to continue to command the resources of the Pacific on its own terms in the 1980s and 1990s will have the most dire consequences for its survival.

U.S. corporations formed the leading wedge of the penetration of international capital into the Pacific. After some initial hesitation, they recognized the commercial opportunities presented by an area of 14.1 million square miles, containing two-thirds of the world's population, and began to respond to what one corporate executive called the "challenges and opportunities offered by this last great frontier."[7] And the magnitude of this response was impressive: U.S. direct investment in Asia rose from $1 billion in 1950 to $5.56 billion in 1970 and $11.4 billion in 1976; in Oceania it had reached $3.49 billion by 1970. Profits were substantial—25.5 percent in Asia (outside of Japan), and 11.3 percent in Japan itself—and provided the impetus for even greater capital penetration.[8]

The Pacific Rim strategy was thus developed over a number of years, and was only enunciated when already well in effect. It is the strategy for sustained corporate profitability (and thus survival) as applied to the special historical, socioeconomic, and political circumstances of the Pacific Rim nations. The central theme it shares with multinational corporate strategies elsewhere is the implementation of a division of labor whereby some nations are frozen into the role of raw material suppliers and cheap manufacturing units for the benefit of other nations. Pacific Rim corporate strategists are fond of assuring everyone that not only is the "Pacific division of labor" eminently desirable from a developmental point of view, but that it is quite definitely in the interests of *all* concerned. Herbert Cornuelle, president of the Dillingham Corporation—a company involved in at least a dozen Pacific Rim nations—is explicit:

> Resource endowments among the Pacific nations beg for development and trade patterns diametrically opposed to the classic Atlantic example. That new pattern must encourage each Pacific location to nurture its comparative advantage, whether in agriculture, industry, or in recreational capabilities. Only such a division of labor along the lines of natural competitive advantage, with specialization in those activities for which nations' natural and human resources are best suited, will permit the underdeveloped areas of the Pacific Rim to achieve their full measure of attainment.[9]

And what institutions are to implement this new pattern? Cornuelle is equally explicit about this: "Only the multinational conglomerate," he says, "is in a position to fully utilize the diverse resources spread among the nations of the Pacific."[10]

The Pacific Rim strategy is not confined to the United States alone: the phoenix-like resurgence of Japan from the ashes of 1945 enabled it to become a junior partner with the United States in the Pacific. Faced with an ascendent Communist Party in China and rising currents of communism and nationalism throughout Southeast Asia, decision-makers in Washington were prepared as early as 1947 to reestablish Japan as the dominant industrial-economic power in Asia. U.S. policymakers further recognized that if Japan was to be maintained within the U.S. (i.e., capitalist) orbit, and the attraction of Moscow and Peking minimized, then it would be necessary to create a viable economy that would provide an adequate standard of living for the Japanese people, and thus to provide Japan with sufficient raw materials and markets in Asia for this to happen. They knew that the severe economic crisis of the 1930s, largely caused by the closing of traditional Japanese export markets by the Great Depression, had been a major factor in precipitating Japan's policy of imperialism, and thus of bringing on war with the United States. A 1952 analysis by the influential Institute of Pacific Relations is clear on this point:

> There can be little question that . . . the best area for Japanese economic expansion is in Southeast Asia, with its demands for capital and consumer goods, its raw materials and [Thai] rice surplus. . . . It would seem that Japan be encouraged to develop trading outlets there in the interest of the overall structure of Pacific security. Japan herself has shown keen interest in these trade possibilities, especially in Thailand, Malaysia, Indonesia and India.[11]

Thus the United States actively encouraged the emergence of Japan as the "workshop of the American lake."[12] Official policy during the later years of the U.S. occupation was to promote the revival of Japanese light and heavy industry (a project that was greatly facilitated by the Korean war) and close off commercial relations between Japan and the United States' own Pacific Rim clients (Taiwan, South Korea, the Philippines, South Vietnam, Thailand, etc.). The huge Japanese industrial cartels (*zaibatsu*), targeted for dismemberment in the early days of the occupation, came to be viewed as the most likely vehicles for reestablishing Japanese export capacity. Even the $400 million the United States lavished on a bankrupt France, to underwrite a hopeless colonial war in Indochina, was justified by President Eisenhower as necessary to maintain Southeast Asia markets and resources for Japanese industries.

All this hinged, of course, on maintaining Japan as a *junior* partner, which in the end proved impossible. As Peter Wiley has put it, "If the United States can continue to keep Japan in the position of junior partner while countering the threat of revolutionary nationalism, it can gain control over the Pacific and organize its markets in a way that would not be conceivable in Western Europe."[13] But Japan, with a highly literate, skilled, and disciplined labor force, and a great fund of technical knowledge and export experience, rapidly moved from its initial industrial buildup in the early 1950s to the economic miracle of the 1960s and 1970s. Export supremacy and productivity became twin national obsessions. By 1968, after a decade of unsurpassed growth, Japan had become the world's third industrial power and the leading producer of ships, cameras, radios, and steel. Japanese exporters had captured markets on every continent, even in the United States and Western Europe.

At the same time, however, rapidly rising wages (due to high production and a critical labor shortage) and the adoption of import substitution programs by countries inundated by Japanese goods, forced Japanese corporations to begin a program of large-scale direct investment abroad—a strategy identical to that pursued by their European and American competitors. Nippon Mining, Hitachi, Matsushita, Toyota, Toshiba, and Teijin were only a few of the scores of Japanese corporations that proceeded to establish production facilities throughout Asia. Japanese trading companies, acting as coordinators of the overseas investment process, created links with local "intermediaries" (inevitably either local comprador capitalists or the bureaucratic-military bourgeoisie) in the Asian-Pacific nations, who facilitated the Japanese entrance into the local economy. By 1975, Japanese companies not only provided a substantial proportion of the imports taken in by Pacific Rim countries, but they had gained considerable dominion over their key industries as well: from Korea to Indonesia, essential economic sectors—including oil, timber, rubber, light manufacturing, and mineral extraction—fell under Japanese ownership or control.

What this great overseas expansion has engendered is a stark new vulnerability to any political change in Asia or the Pacific that might deprive Japanese capital of its essential resources. This vulnerability promises to intensify as competition drives Japanese transnationals to structure the Pacific division of labor even more tightly and to further subordinate the economies of the Pacific Rim to Japanese needs.

The Pacific Rim strategy—in its U.S. and Japanese aspects—is the framework within which Hawaii's development over the past generation has taken place. But although multinational capital has been a prime actor in Hawaii, it has by no means monopolized the stage. Certain critical forces and structures within the Islands have played roles, and the drama of their transformation and interaction with outsiders will be our focus here. In chapters 8, 9, and 10 we will examine the transformation of the Big Five into distinctive multinational corporations under overseas control, the emergence of the post-World War II political elite, and its integration into an enlarged bourgeoisie. Then, in chapter 11, we will look at the result of these processes, Hawaii's tourism society.

8

The Great Corporate Transformation

We're not involved in a social exercise. We are responsible to stock-holders, 80 percent of whom are overseas. We have to put our money into what gives us our greatest returns.

> —Malcolm MacNaughton,
> chairman of the board,
> Castle and Cooke (1974)

It's very simple. A corporation is in business for one thing only and that's to make a profit. If we get fuzzy in our thinking about that, we're in serious trouble.

> —Herbert Cornuelle,
> president, Dillingham Corporation (1975)

On the evening of May 12, 1954, two rather aged men who sym-bolized the old and new capitalism in Hawaii met and clashed in the unlikeliest of places, a zoning hearing in Oahu's Waianae High School. One was Walter Dillingham, now eighty-four years old, an honored member of the *kamaaina* elite and still every inch the formidable patriarch. This man, for decades the real power behind the governor's office and a corporate magnate with a broad range of diverse interests, could not accept the arrival of a new economic era in Hawaii, or of the powerful forces it brought with it, forces that threatened to diminish his own role in the locus of political and economic power.

His antagonist, Henry John Kaiser, represented expanding mainland capital anxious to cash in on the Islands' emergence as a tourism center. Kaiser was the legendary "master builder," a man who had translated a ferocious capacity for work, great organiza-tional ability, influence at top levels of government, and a flair for self-promotion into one of the great American success stories. His saga had moved in stages from roadbuilding on the West Coast in the 1920s to construction of the massive Western dams in the 1930s to national prominence as the "production genius" who turned out

104

Liberty ships for the U.S. merchant fleet during World War II. By 1953, when Kaiser journeyed out to Hawaii for a vacation and then decided to "retire" in the Islands, he was overlord of a vast complex of business interests that included aluminum, steel, engineering, construction, cement, automobile, and chemical industries worth upward of $1 billion and accounting for $600 million in annual sales—figures greater than those of the Big Five–Dillingham complex combined. If the *kamaaina* elite were big fish in a lake, then Kaiser was a mighty fish in an ocean.

Kaiser immediately recognized Hawaii's fantastic potential for tourism: "If the legislature will cooperate, we can do something that will make Hawaii world famous and bring more tourists than you could dream of," he stated. And he was determined to stake out an early claim: "I have missed the tourist boom in Florida and California. I'm not going to miss it here." By 1955, after only one short year of residence, Henry J., as he was known to his associates, was already the biggest landowner in Waikiki and was nonchalantly talking about investing $20 million in resort development and constructing a $50 million island off Waikiki—astronomical amounts for the time. A year later he was buying up local radio and television stations, building the Hawaiian Village Hotel, and laying plans for a massive 6,000-acre Southern California-style residential development on the flanks of the Koko Head Crater.

Mr. Walter and Henry J. were not strangers. Both were past masters of the art of using personal salesmanship and political contacts to wring enormously profitable contracts out of Washington, and during the war companies they controlled had worked together on major contracting jobs in the Pacific. They had a friendly, if casual, personal relationship. Yet by 1954 they were competitors, engaged in a bitter struggle over control of Hawaii's resources. The immediate issue was Kaiser's plan to build a $13.5 million cement plant for his Permanente Company in the Waianae area of Oahu. This was strongly opposed by the Dillingham interests, which had fond hopes of monopolizing the cement business (sure to boom in the tourism–land development construction rush) through Walter's own Hawaiian Cement Company. Ben Dillingham—Walter's son and a power in the Republican Party—had thrown down the gauntlet early in the meeting by arguing that it would be improper to grant Kaiser the rezoning he needed to build the plant without first receiving approval from the City Planning

Commission (where the Dillinghams exercised considerable influence). Kaiser then stood up and delivered a prepared address attacking the Dillinghams for sending agents into the Waianae area to stir up resentment against his plant. He minced no words: "The Dillingham proposal is a red herring for the purpose of indefinitely delaying our cement plant and getting it studied to death." Ben, clearly out of his depth and easily rattled, fired an angry salvo at Kaiser: "He has rushed down here to tell the people he's God's gift to Waianae."[1]

Then the old patriarch rose ponderously and picked up the microphone: "I don't think it's a very nice thing for a visitor to Hawaii, no matter how many millions he's spent here, to attack a son of mine and of Hawaii." This rather whining performance did little to win the crowd over to Dillingham's side. Indeed, the crowd was solidly pro-Kaiser, mistakenly believing that if the rezoning was granted, a Kaiser hospital or clinic would immediately follow. "We are a working-class people in this area. We haven't had proper medical care," explained one local resident.[2] The Waianae District Council, immediately after the meeting, voted a resolution supporting Kaiser.

The Dillingham defeat showed the growing power of "outside" interests, but it was not devastating for the company's fortunes, not only because in the boomtime Hawaiian economy of 1955–74 there was ample room to accommodate everybody, but because Dillingham and the Big Five companies were able to adopt new strategies in time to survive and to some extent flourish.

The first disturbing signs that the days of King Sugar would not last forever had come from Washington, in the form of the Sugar acts of 1934 and 1937. As a result of the 1934 law, Hawaii's annual sugar quota was reduced by 76,950 tons and the Territory relegated to the status of a secondary producer for the U.S. market (in the same category as foreign producers). When the law was revised three years later, Hawaiian sugar planters were once again included in the domestic production category, but the quota remained well below the pre-1934 figure. Moreover, there was a new system of crop restrictions and compliance payments that the plantation owners objected to. After holding extensive talks with Big Five officials throughout the Islands. an observer noted their dissatisfaction: "Compliance with the terms of the Sugar Act has in innumerable details proved expensive and onerous."[3]

The foundations of the old sugar economy were also being undermined from other directions. Beet sugar was now grown in almost half the states of the union and was increasingly competitive with cane sugar. And in Hawaii itself, the organization of the plantations and mills in 1946 by the International Longshoremen's and Warehousemen's Union (ILWU) struck a blow at a major source of profitability—absolute control over labor conditions and wages. Hawaii's sugar workers could henceforth claim wages and benefits far exceeding those of their counterparts in Louisiana, Texas, the Caribbean, and the Philippines.

By the early 1950s these factors combined with declining sugar consumption and prices—a glut on the world market kept sugar prices under $.05 a pound for much of the 1950s and 1960s—to deliver the Hawaiian sugar industry into one of the bleakest periods in its history. In 1953 seven of eighteen plantations, including many of the largest, paid no dividends at all.[4] C. Brewer's president admitted, "The future still poses serious challenges for us. The rate of return over many years on capital invested in our plantations judged by any standards has been far from adequate."[5] In 1958 the situation had improved only marginally and a new C. Brewer president, Boyd MacNaughton, again expressed displeasure at recent earnings: "These earnings are well below a satisfactory profit margin in light of the capital requirements and the risks of our enterprises."[6]

If sugar was stagnating in Hawaii, the situation in the pineapple industry, which lacked the benefits of an annual quota or a controlled market and was also considerably more vulnerable to foreign competition, was critical. Agribusiness multinationals like Libby and Del Monte had already established themselves in nonunion, cheap-labor, cheap-land areas in the Caribbean and Asia and were making deep inroads into the one-time Dole monopoly on the sweet fruit—production of Taiwan pack pineapple, for instance, jumped from 70,000 cases in 1946 to 2 million cases in 1961.[7] The unionized workforce in Hawaii was in a position to use its power to win demands for improved wages and benefits—in 1958 a strike shut down the entire pineapple industry for months—something pineapple workers in Taiwan, Mexico, Malaysia, and South Africa could not do. The result was a sharp differential between the labor costs of Hawaiian and foreign pineapple, which left the Island industry at a competitive disadvantage in the world market. As *Hawaii Business* remarked, "No matter how you slice it, labor costs are the focal point of the pineapple industry's anxieties."[8] With Dole's share of the world pineapple market falling—from over 75 percent in 1950 to slightly over 50 percent by the mid-1960s—a powerful impetus existed for the transfer of Hawaii pineapple operations abroad. As Dole president Herbert Cornuelle noted, "The basic decision is comparing Hawaii with elsewhere, that is, comparing Dole's local costs, yields and so forth with those projected for any foreign project."[9]

It had become apparent to the "boys on Merchant Street," as they were called, that the plantation system that had sustained their class for four generations was beyond salvage. Their choice now lay in expanding into new industries and geographic areas, with a radical restructuring of their corporate apparatus to meet the demands of a wholly new era of capitalism, or in allowing their attachment to the past to lead them into an irretrievable decline. And despite a lingering attachment to the accoutrements of aristocracy, the *kamaaina* elite did indeed proceed to transform their corporate organizations and reorient themselves toward new production and new markets, using the profits derived from their domination of Island financial institutions and industries to do so.

The reorganization of the two major Island banks, the Bank of Hawaii and the First Hawaiian Bank, provides a good illustration of this process. In the mid-1950s high-powered mainland executives such as Rudolph Peterson (who came to the presidency of the Bank of Hawaii from one at TransAmerica) were brought in to hold key management positions. They almost immediately began to adopt the most sophisticated overseas banking techniques and technology. The relatively relaxed atmosphere of plantation banking soon gave way to an emphasis on operations efficiency and maximizing business. And, in a major historical departure from a century of Big Five banking practice, they began to encourage outside capital to play a role in Hawaii. "The whole philosophy of the bank has changed," noted one contemporary report on the Bank of Hawaii. "It goes to the people. It is aggressive. The bank studies where to lend its money. A definite schedule is set up and customers are contacted regularly." A top banker commented: "It changes the whole philosophy of banking operations here. We must hustle. In fact, we are forced to hustle."[10]

This aggressiveness was reinforced by the new technology from the mainland—electronic bookkeeping, drive-in banking, closed-circuit television—whose cost put the banks in the position of having to expand. As banker Dan Dorman remarked, "All of this automation equipment is very expensive and we'll have to keep it busy to pay off. That's why we will be interested in developing new kinds of businesses. We'll be going out and selling bank services more and more."[11] From the banks' viewpoint, the results of this program were impressive. Between 1954 and 1959 the Bank of Hawaii doubled its profits and increased its deposits by over 60 percent; Peterson's performance, in fact, led to his going on to become president of the mammoth Bank of America.

Once the basic reorganization was completed, both the Bank of Hawaii and First Hawaiian began to adopt their own version of the Pacific Rim strategy. By the early 1960s the Bank of Hawaii was involved in "third-country financing for Pacific Basin imports" and was playing a middleman role in various international deals. Its executives were promoting Hawaii's role as the "Switzerland of the Pacific," picturing the Islands as "a training ground for Japanese businessmen entering the United States market."[12] As the 1960s wore on, the bank committed increasing resources to the Pacific and also helped overseas investors enter into the Hawaiian tourism-land development sectors. As its own advertising put it, "Through its activities, the bank discovers business and investment opportunities for local firms in Pacific Basin countries and helps finance their ventures. It also brings opportunities in Hawaii to the attention of Far Eastern and 'Down Under' investors and businessmen."[13] By the early 1970s, with seventy-one branches spread throughout the Pacific Rim, the bank was advertising itself as the "Bank of the Pacific."[14] First Hawaiian had also gone multinational, establishing branch offices in Guam, Tonga, Micronesia, and many other places, and Vice-President Thomas Hitch noted, "The biggest part of our lending experience in recent years has been in the international field, much of it in the Pacific."[15]

Multinationalization fever was equally prevalent among the Big Five–Dillingham corporations, but it took place more gradually, and the process can be broken into closely interrelated stages: internal corporate consolidation, rapid expansion into overseas areas, a shift from local to mainland (and foreign) corporate control, and a greater emphasis on profitability with an accompanying ruthlessness and arrogance in pursuing corporate objectives. For purposes of analysis it is easier to discuss them separately.

The first, the process of internal corporate consolidation, occurred under the direction of new corporate managers, such as Malcolm MacNaughton and Herbert Cornuelle. They implemented a thoroughgoing reappraisal of existing assets and streamlined corporate structures. In the initial stage, unprofitable properties or holdings that did not fit into future expansion programs were sold off to obtain liquid capital. Thus Dillingham sold its Oahu Railway holdings, along with a number of real estate parcels. Castle and Cooke sold its holdings in Theo Davies, Amfac, Hawaiian Airlines, and Honolulu Iron Works and, along with three other Big Five corporations, sold all of its stock in Matson Navigation to Alexander and Baldwin. Meanwhile, Theo Davies disposed of its wholesale drug, dry goods, and hardware interests, and Amfac, soured by low profits, sold its materials supply business as well as substantial holdings in Hawaiian Western Steel, Oahu Transport, and the Princeville Ranch.[16] Unprofitable plantations and mills were closed, and more profitable agricultural units transformed into wholly owned subsidiaries. Amfac, for example, which owned less than one-third of the Oahu Sugar Company in 1958, had 100 percent stock control three years later. Similarly, after an intricate series of stock exchanges, Dole Pineapple became a subsidiary of Castle and Cooke. What was important here was that the Big Five concerns, hitherto holding part of each other's companies, untangled themselves, and the old *kamaaina* complex fragmented, once again becoming a number of individual companies. The Big Five gained the flexibility it needed in order to gradually liquidate commercial agriculture in Hawaii, while maintaining its grip on hundreds of thousands of choice acres for future land development.

Finally, there was a restructuring of the various corporate bureaucracies to bring them in line with the most up-to-date managerial thinking on the mainland. Dillingham's 1961 merging of the Oahu Railway and Land Company with Hawaiian Dredging and Construction to form the Dillingham Corporation (Dilco), and its establishment of divisional management groups in construction, property management, and transportation was typical. Other firms built similar structures and introduced cost-benefit analyses, combined with sophisticated managerial techniques. The comparatively loosely knit corporate structure of the plantation era was replaced by a standard U.S. capitalist bureaucracy with the flexibility and concentration of resources to take the multinational route.

Then, beginning in the late 1950s and continuing over the next two decades, the Big Five and Dillingham, in possession of corporate structures geared for international activities and under great internal pressure to raise their profit rates, went overseas. When the president of Castle and Cooke commented in 1961 that "We consider our growth and development to lie outside of this state,"[17] he was simply echoing the plans of a score of Hawaii corporate executives. For the most part, this monumental move would be in two directions: eastward to tap the markets and advanced technology of the United States and the cheap labor and fertile lands of Latin America, and westward to the equally plentiful land and labor of Southeast Asia and the resources and markets of Oceania. Some companies—notably Castle and Cooke, Amfac, and the banks—were more successful at this, but all made it a major part of their new strategy.

Dilco quickly established itself in a myriad of activities, specializing in building physical infrastructure for the exploitation of Pacific Rim resources, as well as luxury facilities for the affluent classes. In the process, the company gained control of more than thirty companies, from California construction firms to Australian shipyards, and became a leading international contractor. Dilco has constructed California shopping centers, bank buildings, condominiums, and luxury subdivisions; it has built pulp mills and terminals in Canada, highways in Fiji, condominiums in Singapore, hotels in the Philippines, office buildings in New Zealand, petroleum docks in Southeast Asia and Latin America, and naval bases in Guam and Thailand. It quarries rock and lays pipelines in New Guinea, prospects for minerals in Australia (where it also is one of that nation's leading construction firms and owns a ranch twice the size of Oahu), has drilled for oil in Saudi Arabia and mined argonite in the Bahamas. Its fleet of 100 tugs and 150 barges is one of the largest of its kind in the world. Thus by the mid-1970s Dilco was a Hawaiian corporation in name only: less than 25 percent of its revenues were generated in Hawaii and less than 20 percent of its more than twelve thousand employees were Island based;[18] revenues from U.S. mainland subsidiaries were 2.5 times those from the Islands.[19]

Dillingham executives regard such phenomenal expansion—despite intermittent financial problems—as a proven formula for profitable operations. As the *Dillingham Quarterly* informed its readers, "We are in the businesses that are going to have a growing part in the next ten years in the development of the Pacific";[20] and a corporation pronouncement noted confidently, "We believe we are in the right markets with the right people at the right time, in the right parts of the world."[21]

Much the same forces were at work at Castle and Cooke. As one journalist has said of the company's empire, "Its corporate dimensions extend across Hawaii and the mainland, with extensions into Alaska, Central and South America, the Philippines, Thailand, Malaysia and Japan."[22] In the late 1950s, this old missionary firm, under the whip of hard-driving managers imported from the mainland, consolidated Dole Pineapple and the recently acquired Columbia River Packers (subsequently reorganized as Bumble Bee Sea Foods) to form the core of a multinational agribusiness network. Castle and Cooke's initial objective was to regain the share of the pineapple market that had been captured by multinational competitors in the Third World, and in 1963 it began a massive transfer of pineapple production to the Philippines, where it established a 20,000-acre plantation on Mindanao. This, the largest pineapple complex in the world, was an attempt by the Castle and Cooke management to erase the historic gains made by Hawaiian workers, to turn the clock back, to reestablish plantation Hawaii society (circa 1930) in the Philippines. As President Malcom MacNaughton explained, "Dole wants to compete in this expanding market. We believe the Philippines venture will make it possible not only in the Far East, but in Europe and elsewhere."[23] The company also bought the largest producer of bananas in the world, the Standard Steamship and Fruit Company, which owned 194,000 acres in Central and South America as well as important vegetable agribusiness interests in California and mushrooms in Brazil. Castle and Cooke's agribusiness activities now account for over 75 percent of its revenues. Moreover, the company's multinationalization extends beyond agriculture to glass manufacture in the Philippines, pipe manufacture in Thailand, real estate in California, and rock quarrying in Singapore. Those in command retain full confidence in policies that have transformed a Hawaii plantation holding company, with revenues of about $10 million annually in 1947, to a billion dollar giant stretched across five continents: "Today in Honduras, Thailand, Malaysia, and Singapore, we have majority ownership positions in a broad range of industrial activities. We plan to expand significantly this type of investment because the profit margins are excellent and the growth greater than the developed countries such as Japan and the United States."[24]

Amfac followed much the same route. Amfac's interests have expanded mainly in the United States. Its growth has been meteoric: from a $100-million Hawaiian plantation agency with some tourist and retail holdings in 1967, it grew into a multinational with annual sales of $1.4 billion in 1977. In a November 1974 interview, then company Vice-President Lawrence Gay reported: "We've changed from a company in 1967 almost completely Hawaiian—98 percent of our income was here. Then we decided we had the resources to be bigger and these were small islands. If we were going to grow, we were going to have problems. Developments forced us to shift growth emphasis to the mainland." Thus between 1968 and 1973 Amfac went on a spree of corporate acquisition, taking over *fifty* corporations, including the Fred Harvey restaurant chain, a Utah drugstore chain, a Washington state meat-packing plant, and Lamb Wesson frozen foods. Amfac has over one hundred subsidiaries in seventeen states and three foreign countries. It sells insurance, owns cocktail lounges, beauty shops, and mortgage-leasing firms on the Pacific Coast, as well as shopping centers and hotels in Kansas. According to *Hawaii Business,* "Around three-fourths of Amfac's revenues and at least that amount of its profits now originate from its diverse mainland operations."[25] In fact, mainland holdings are so extensive that corporate headquarters of the Asset Management Division were finally moved to San Francisco in 1982—the first Big Five company to make such a move—and the rest of the company is in the process of following. (The future may see increasing Amfac penetration of the Pacific, however, where the company already has sizeable Australian interests.) As for C. Brewer, the oldest of the Big Five, it has specialized in the export of agricultural technology, expertise, and capital to more than sixty nations. Using Brewer Agronomics as the vehicle to effect this expansion, the company established huge sugar, rice, macadamia nut, and spice plantations in sixty nations, from Indonesia to Guatemala to Iran, and acquired facilities in Oregon and Midwest feed lots—until the fall of the Shah in 1979 led to its collapse as a viable subsidiary and its sale to a Middle East buyer.

Even the two smallest Big Five corporations have expanded overseas, although both still draw the bulk of their revenues from traditional Hawaiian industries and are in considerable financial difficulty. Theo Davies holds a myriad of appliance and light manufacturing companies in the Philippines, while Alexander and Baldwin owns the largest processing company for tropical hardwoods in Southeast Asia, with 250,000 acres of timber in Indonesia and factories in Taiwan, Singapore, Hong Kong, and Malaysia. As Alexander and Baldwin President Lawrence Pricher noted, "Geographically, we seek investments in the Pacific Basin—from East Asia to the Western edge of the Western hemisphere."[26]

The move overseas—profitable as it has been—has exacted a bitter price from the once haughty local oligarchy, which has lost control of companies that had been treated as family heirlooms for generations. Inevitably drawn to major overseas capital markets to finance their expansion, *kamaaina* executives soon found overseas financial institutions exercising crucial leverage over corporate policies. Thus Amfac's decision to place its stock on the board of the New York Stock Exchange was vital to its meteoric rise, because it enabled the firm's management to secure huge sums of money to acquire promising companies across the globe. A 1971–72 public offering of 1.2 million new Amfac shares, for example, brought in $37 million of immediately usable capital.[27] As Amfac grew, its access to overseas capital became still easier: "A company's ability to raise funds increases geometrically with size," noted an Amfac vice-president.

At the same time, the number and composition of its stockholders obviously changed dramatically. In 1948 Amfac had only 2,160 stockholders; twenty-five years later there were over 11,000.[28] As recently as 1967, three-quarters of them resided in Hawaii; today three-quarters reside overseas. In 1973 the board of directors included the chairman of the board of the Bank of California, a Chicago banker, an Atlanta businessman, the chairman of the board of Western Airlines, the director of the Fireman's Fund Insurance Company, and other powerful mainland business figures. Moreover, Gulf and Western, a multibillion-dollar conglomerate, purchased a one-fifth share of Amfac in the mid-1970s, chiefly attracted by the corporation's huge landholdings in Hawaii and the high profitability of the Islands' tourism industry: "The real frosting on the cake, however," noted a *Forbes* article on the Gulf and Western purchase, "is those thousands of Hawaiian acres washed by the waves of the Pacific, drenched with sunshine and covered with fat, white beaches."[29]

The Amfac scenario has been repeated in the other Big Five companies and Dilco: overseas financing of the multinationalization process has meant overseas control over the corporations themselves. For Dilco, a clear majority of the stockholders reside on the mainland and the board of directors includes the president of Southern California Edison, a director of the Bank of America, a New England investment banker, and a California business executive; for Castle and Cooke, 80 percent of its stockholders are overseas. C. Brewer and Theo Davies are now completely controlled by overseas conglomerates—Brewer by International Utilities, a Delaware-based holding company which purchased a 54 percent interest in the Hawaiian firm in 1969 and has been steadily moving toward absorbing it completely, and Theo Davies by the multibillion-dollar Hong Kong-based conglomerate Jardine-Mathiesson.

For the Big Five and Dilco, multinationalization has meant an intense preoccupation with profitability. Their overseas stockholders and financial creditors will not settle for less than a solid annual return on their investments. As Malcolm MacNaughton has explained, "We expect to average an increase of about 15 percent a year in earnings from operations. This means doubling profits every five years."[30] For C. Brewer, a statement by Chairman John Seabrook—who oversees a business empire of thirty subsidiaries on four continents—in a 1971 speech in Montreal puts his point of view bluntly: "Some companies have an emotional attachment to the businesses they are in, but at International Utilities our only attachment is to our shareholders' needs."[31]

In an intensely competitive global capitalist arena, the drive to increase profits is inevitably accompanied by an increased ruthlessness toward both human beings and their environment. Like multinationals throughout the world, the Big Five and Dilco are in the position of being everywhere without being responsible to anyone. They have huge interests in Hawaii, in Southeast Asia, in Latin America, and on the mainland United States, and yet manage to remain unaccountable. They will close down agricultural operations that no longer fit into the "profit picture," leaving thousands unemployed and entire communities devastated. They will bribe Central American generals and Asian politicians to let them continue their lucrative "turnkey" operations, which contribute nothing to the genuine development of the host country. And they have no loyalty to, or respect for, the people who create their profits.

Thus in 1974, when Honduras, Nicaragua, and Costa Rica announced their intention to place a $1 per crate tax on exported bananas, Castle and Cooke's Standard Steamship and Fruit Company reacted violently, calling the tax "illegal and uneconomic" and threatening to move its operations out of the region. "If necessary," Malcolm MacNaughton said, "there are areas of the world other than Central America where bananas can be successfully grown." In addition, "Standard Fruit first ceased the production and export of bananas in Costa Rica and Honduras, putting thousands of people out of work and letting thousands of crates of fruit rot on the docks. The company threatened that it would stop all of its activities in these countries and refused to pay the tax."[32] The company also tried to undermine the governments—Panama accused Castle and Cooke of plotting to assassinate the country's president and overthrow the governments of Costa Rica and Honduras.[33]

A description of Dilco's depredations against people and environment could fill tomes. In California, where the corporation has evicted thousands of poor people from central city areas in order to construct luxury apartment houses and office buildings for the affluent, the Mobile Country Club Estates is a case in point. In 1969, 479 people, mostly old and on limited incomes, were informed of their eviction from a San Jose trailer park to make way for a Dilco hotel-office building complex. Feeling relocation would be very costly, the residents (with the support of some outsiders) confronted Dillingham and local politicians with the demand that the developer foot the bill. One resident who had lived in the trailer park for eight years and been promised a seventy-five-year lease, commented bitterly, "Dillinger used to steal from the rich and give to the poor; Dillingham steals from the poor and gives to the rich." The *San Jose Maverick,* which led opposition to the evictions, editorialized: "Let's show these few who have the money that we can also talk loud. Let's stop this thief who thinks he can play God with people's lives."[34] These San Jose residents won their claim, a "kindness" not shared by thousands of other Dillingham evictees.

Dillingham has also been cited by conservationists for destroying reefs and fish life in the course of argonite mining in the Bahamas and for illegally converting a bird refuge at its luxurious Tahoe Keys residential development on the California-Nevada border into a sailing lagoon without government permission. Indeed, a Pacific Studies Center examination of Dillingham's activities concluded with the devastating indictment: "Dillingham thrives on war, racism, and human misery."[35]

Hawaii-based multinationals have found it to their advantage to cultivate close relationships with a host of dictators and to locate their overseas operations in some of the world's most oppressive countries. Malcolm MacNaughton, a confidant of Ferdinand Marcos, was on hand when martial law was declared in the Philippines and is a fervent supporter of Marcos's "New Society." The Phillipines government is willing to shoot or arrest labor organizers in the Dolefil plantation fields and arbitrarily violates the constitution by giving overseas companies a wide range of land and investment concessions. Likewise, when ex-dictator Anastazio Somoza of Nicaragua came to Hawaii for a vacation, it was MacNaughton who escorted him around the plush local spots, while C. Brewer executive Wayne Richardson used to sit in his office in front of a prominently placed picture of the Shah and Empress of Iran and referred to the Iranian monarch as "one of the finest leaders in the world. He has run toward success in developing Iran at a pace no one else can match."[36]

Like multinationals everywhere, the Island-headquartered corporations have been a primary force in establishing an international division of labor that supports dependency and underdevelopment. Big Five agribusiness activities in the Third World—pineapple in the Philippines and Thailand, coffee and spices in Guatemala, mushrooms in Brazil, bananas in Central

America—as well as Dilco's construction of infrastructure for the extraction of minerals in Australia, Alexander and Baldwin's ownership of tropical hardwood factories in Southeast Asia, and Theo Davies and Castle and Cooke's control over light manufacturing in Southeast Asia serve to inhibit the growth of locally centered, diversified, mutually reinforcing economic structures characteristic of developed economies. This, indeed, may be the harshest legacy of Hawaii's multinationals to the people of the Pacific and beyond.

Although Hawaii plays a major role as a base for capital penetration of the Pacific Rim, it is even more important as a site for such penetration by the overseas multinationals. For John Seabrook, in his office in Philadelphia, for Jardine-Mathiesson executives on the upper floors of their office building in Hong Kong, for the banking and insurance executives who own and finance Big Five–Dilco activities, their Island holdings are a major corporate asset to be exploited for maximum profitability. In practice, this means that the same ruthlessness in pursuit of profits that is the trademark of their overseas operations is applied to Hawaiian activities. As a Big Five executive admits, "It seems that these old firms are now being guided less by a fatherly concern for Hawaii than by the standards of mainland business—stockholders, price-earnings ratios, and growth."[37] This has led them to collaborate with mainland capital in ruthlessly imposing a tourism society on Hawaiians. The closing of marginally profitable plantations, leaving economically and psychologically shattered communities, is but one aspect of this process.

In January 1970 C. Brewer closed down its Kilauea, Kaui, sugar plantation. One laid-off worker, Philip Panquiles (with a family of nine to support), noted sadly, "I drove truck, hauling sugar for twenty-seven years. It's terrible to be without work." Another resident commented, "Now even the chicken fights have stopped because the man who kept the chickens has left." When Castle and Cooke announced its intention to terminate 108 years of sugar production at its Kohala plantation in 1981, a local woman described her reaction: "For me, when I heard the news, I went home and I sat down, so stunned I didn't know what to do. I wanted to cry—but, do you know, it was too strong, the feeling I had. Even beyond crying. Kohala is such a pleasant place to be. Good air, no crowding. . . . North Kohala seemed a very special, very precious place, and a place of promise. . . . Can a corporation arbitrarily decide the fate of a community? Whose responsibility in our modern industrial society, is people?"[38]

For the newly multinationalized *kamaaina* companies, tourism-land development is to form the base of their economic operations in Hawaii. At a November 1977 news conference in New York City, Castle and Cooke president Donald Kirchoff told the press, "Don't quote me back home but . . . we're going to become strictly a tourist center."[39] Throughout much of the 1950s, 1960s, and 1970s, Island hotels were near or at the top of the U.S. industry in occupancy and profit ratios. Taking 1969 as an example, hotels in Hawaii had the comparatively high occupancy rate of 75.6 percent and profit ratios after taxes of 27.5 percent—as compared to the national average of 19.8 percent. According to state statistics released in 1973, the profit ratio for Hawaiian domestic corporations (in relation to taxability) taken as an aggregate was 6.5 percent, yet in finance and insurance (both intimately related to tourism–land development), the figure was 17.45 percent, in real estate it was 20.48 percent, and in services it was 13.26 percent. Overseas corporations engaged in real estate reported profits of 105 percent![40]

In 1960, Lowell Dillingham, another of Walter's sons, told an interviewer from a national magazine: "We've all missed the boat in land development. Local managed interests could have done the developing that mainlanders and the *huis* [locally based developer groups] are doing. The Big Five have plenty of land, but they've been so busy trying to keep the sugar industry in a profitable position they haven't had time or effort or money for much else."[41] Within a few years, however, the advent of new Big Five ownership and management committed to a buildup of the tourism-land development sector made these words obsolete. By 1967, in fact, Dillingham himself was proclaiming that "these islands may together build such a combined visitor recreation facility as the world has never seen with a multiplicity of resort complexes throughout"[42]— a scenario that could only be realized with the massive involvement of the Big Five and their related estates. A C. Brewer president, sent to Hawaii by International Utilities to drive up Brewer's dismal balance sheet, remarked, "Our job is to make the best profits we can from our assets, and for us that means land,"[43] and a Brewer divisional executive described the firm as "a real estate corporation whose goal is to get the maximum return from all its properties."[44] Brewer subsequently built several resorts on the Big Island. Meanwhile, Castle and Cooke built a large subdivision, Mililani Town, in central Oahu and planned to transform its wholly owned 90,000-acre pineapple fiefdom, the island of Lanai, into a resort area. And the president of Amfac announced, "We've got lots of land and we're going to have lots of hotels in Hawaii and in the Pacific." By the middle 1960s Amfac was beginning to construct a sprawling series of resorts along the coast of Kaanapali in Maui and on Kauai. Despite their huge land holdings, their dynamic new managers, and their intensely ambitious development blueprints, they still found themselves unable to proceed without involving outsiders. Lacking the financial resources and technical and managerial expertise to develop and sustain a series of large resort-residential complexes oriented to an international clientele, they turned to some of the most formidable multinational investors and developers in North America and Japan. Large investors and developers, sensing the enormous profits to be made in resort and second-home development in the Islands, were only too eager to enter the scene.

Collaboration, hammered out in negotiations between Hawaii-based firms and outsiders, took on a multitude of forms. There were joint ventures (e.g., Dilco and American Airlines in the Ala Moana Hotel project); there were outright sales or leases of land to overseas interests (e.g., Amfac's sale of Princeville, Kauai, ranch land to the Consolidated Oil and Gas Company of Colorado and Laurence Rockefeller's purchase of land from the Parker Ranch to build the Mauna Kea Beach Hotel on the Big Island); and there were complicated agreements in which partners were assigned specialized roles, as in the Kapalua resort complex on Maui, where Maui Land and Pineapple provided the land, Rockefeller interests the managerial expertise, and the Bank of America and the Bank of Hawaii the financing.

In all cases, however, these were deals in which land-rich, capital-poor Hawaii-based corporations provided land (and local political influence) to capital-rich but Hawaii-land-poor overseas corporations that could also provide resort development–management expertise. And they had the effect of reducing the Big Five, Campbell and Bishop estates, and the big ranches, to an intermediary role in the development of Hawaii, utterly at the mercy of investment decisions made in the metropolitan centers. A good illustration of this was provided by the 1977 appearance of Phillip Spaulding, Jr., president of Molokai Ranch, before the board of directors of the Louisiana Land and Exploration Company in New Orleans to ask for a $2 million commitment for a joint project. Molokai Ranch had sold Louisiana Land and Exploration thousands of acres for its Kaluakoi resort complex and had a "working agreement" with the firm. While Spaulding waited to present his case, he became aware that the other item on the agenda was the question of the company's investing *$446 million* in a new oil and gas venture. A bit chastened by the extent of his "partner's" financial power, Spaulding remarked, "When I heard about that other item on the board's agenda, I suddenly realized what a drop in the bucket Kaluakoi was to Louisiana Land."[45]

This situation is representative. The relationship between Molokai Ranch and Louisiana Land, between the Parker Ranch and Laurence Rockefeller, Signal Oil, or Boise Cascade, between Maui Land and Pineapple and the Bank of America, between Ulupalakua Ranch and Seibu, and between Campbell Estate and Prudential Life Insurance is hardly equal. The huge overseas multinationals inevitably become dominant in the relationship, controlling management and financing, and mapping out programs for expansion, from the home office in the United States or Japan.

Thus the transformation of the old *kamaaina* corporate complex in Hawaii from local sugar agencies to medium-sized transnational corporations with far-reaching interests has *not*—contrary to prevailing wisdom—acted as a force for genuine economic development and political liberation in Hawaii. Instead, as Laura Brown, and Walter Cohen argue, "Multinationalization has led either to outright acquisition by outside interests or to a greater dependence on more dominant centers of international trade and investment."[46] Like the cooptation of radical labor leaders and the postwar political elite, to which we now turn, the multinationalization of the long dominant economic forces in Hawaii was a decisive step toward the integration of the Islands into the Pacific division of labor as a dependent tourism-land development economy.

9

The Era of Consensus

We've had a rich man's club in the legislature for fifty-four years.
Now it's going to be a people's club and with a few easy motions we
are going to wipe out some of those laws from the books.
—Vincent Esposito,
Territorial legislator, 1954

It was during the administrations of William Quinn (1957–63) and
John Burns (1963–73), and due to their development policies, that
the contemporary political economy of Hawaii was created. By
the late 1950s a series of elements—the increasing importance of
the Pacific Rim to the U.S. economy, Hawaii's potential role as a
U.S. showcase in the area, and a shift in congressional opinion—
had made statehood a virtual certainty. Quinn, a youthful Big Five
lawyer, was appointed to the governorship by powerful Republicans in Washington who regarded Samuel King, his predecessor,
as too old, tired, and lacking in the leadership qualities necessary to
implement the modernization of Hawaii's governmental structure
along the lines of a mid-twentieth century U.S. state. Quinn, a
vigorous thirty-eight years old at the time of his appointment, was
perceived by Washington (and by the corporate elite in Hawaii as
well) to be of a different stamp, far more attuned to the necessity of
a greatly expanded role for the state government in Hawaii's economic transformation. A thriving tourism industry required far
greater governmental support and financial outlays than did the
old plantation system, including airports, roads, sewerage facilities,
new beaches, promotional activities, and a rationalized governmental bureaucracy capable of implementing all of these.

Thus Quinn's first priority was to streamline the rather cumber-
some Territorial bureaucracy in order to make it a more efficient
instrument of capitalist accumulation. By 1959 an unwieldy assortment of bureaus and commissions had been consolidated into sixteen departments—a "revolution in government," as Quinn called

it—and Quinn was ready to begin building the physical infrastructure that would lay the basis for the new economy. In 1960, shortly after statehood, he proposed a massive Capital Improvements Budget (CIP), including $23 million for road and harbor projects and for a new Kona airport—"to allow the Kailua area to develop fully as a major visitor destination." A 1961 speech to the legislature provides an insight into how far the state was now prepared to go to underwrite the costs of tourism development:

> During these first years of statehood we made great strides developing the economy of the state. Water development, transportation, and land development projects have moved forward at an accelerated pace. We cannot afford to slacken our pace, if we are to achieve our desired goals. May I point out, however, that development of water alone will not speed development of an area. We must also have roads, harbors, airports and other facilities to serve the people of the area and visitors to our shores. We must move forward in balance.[1]

Quinn's unprecedented use of governmental funds (his program called for the expenditure of $260 million in CIP monies over a six-year period)[2] to construct a sizeable infrastructure was an essential precondition for Hawaii's incorporation within the Pacific division of labor as a tourism center. What was being created here was an infrastructure in the broadest sense of the term. In Joyce Kolko's words, "An infrastructure means more than transportation, ports, power supplies and the like. It also means an economic environment, a framework of fiscal and monetary policies conducive to 'development' along essentially unquestioned and preconceived paths."[3]

The manner in which these infrastructural funds were obtained served to further integrate Hawaii into the dominant sectors of metropolitan capitalism, the beginning of a process that saw a growing dependence on overseas bankers, merchant brokers, and money markets. Quinn and other state officials, as well as executives in the private sector, made trips to the mainland to sell Hawaii. In 1960, for instance, a committee composed of the president of Dole Pineapple, executives from the Bank of Hawaii, the First Hawaiian Bank, and Hawaiian Electric, and five state legislators traveled to New York, Chicago, San Francisco, and Dallas to impress upon mainland financial interests the attractiveness of Hawaiian state bond issues and private securities. A year later Quinn, the mayor of Honolulu, and leading bank executives did the same thing with a group of prominent San Francisco bonds and security analysts. The large mainland banks were soon snapping up substantial bond issues—in November 1961 a Chase Manhattan Bank syndicate purchased $10 million worth of Hawaii state bonds; in May 1962 Wells Fargo bought another $10 million. The remaining funds were garnered by means of one of the highest per capita state tax rates: by 1960 Hawaii had the fifth highest taxes in the United States, a pattern that has been maintained.[4]

This huge state spending on a tourism–land development infrastructure, accompanied by the banks' solicitation of large mainland investments, led to massive sums of overseas capital entering Hawaii. Even the utilities—traditionally locally financed and owned—began to seek mainland capital for expansion: the president of Hawaiian Electric announced in 1961 that his firm would alter its historic pattern of financing to "seek a minimum of $10 million of new money annually from outside."[5] Mainland life insurance companies began to play an increasingly significant role in the Islands' economy: by the end of 1963 giants like Equitable (with $46 million invested in Hawaii), Prudential ($44 million), John Hancock ($53 million), New York Life ($25 million), and Occidental Life ($25 million) had substantial holdings in the tourism-land development sector. Profitable opportunities abounded in an economy whose growth in 1959 and 1960 was a striking 12 to 13 percent per year, and in which tourism increased by over 41 percent in 1959 and 22 percent in 1960. As the decade began, a San Francisco stock brokerage firm was describing Hawaii "as a magnet for mainland capital in the sixties. Roughly one-third of Hawaii's total economy may be considered strongly dynamic, promising well above average growth in the sixties."[6]

The Quinn administration's attitude toward land reform proved another enduring element of the "New Hawaii" developmental model. Land concentration had grown to an unprecedented degree: by 1960 less than one hundred owners held half of all of Hawaii's land. Land once again became a political issue, and Quinn and his cohorts were anxious to defuse the growing demand for redistribution of corporate holdings. Quinn had not, after all, been placed in the governorship to implement land distribution programs that might limit the economic options of Hawaii's power structure. Thus intent on preserving the status quo, Quinn attempted to divert the attention (and wrath) of Hawaii's landless majority from the estate and Big Five-controlled acreage by simply denying the need for large-scale reform. Instead he claimed that "The real issue is not to just break up land ownership in large quantities for the sake of breaking it up. The real issue is to make homesites available"[7]—which could be done with state-owned lands.

During the 1959 election campaign, in what was both a clever political maneuver and a further device for mystifying the land-reform situation, Quinn promised to implement a so-called Second Mahele, making this one of the Republican Party's major campaign planks. Under this proposal, 175,000 acres of state land were to be sold to families at a cost of between $1 and $1,000 an acre (with a limit of ten acres per family), depending on quality and location. Of course, prime agricultural land owned by the state but under lease to Big Five plantations (for nominal rents) was pointedly excluded: "State lands essential to our major agricultural industries should continue to be devoted to these uses," Quinn noted.[8] Even so, after the election was safely over the Second Mahele quickly went the way of most election promises.

In what was something of a departure from previous Republican practice, Quinn adopted a policy of filling key state boards and high bureaucratic positions with a "judicious mixture" of representatives of both the older Big Five complex and the newer Asian land development capital—a further reflection of their coincidence of interests. His 1961 appointments to the State Land Use Commission, charged with ensuring orderly growth and protecting the Islands' rural areas from overdevelopment, were indicative of this: they included the former president of the Chinese Chamber of Commerce, the manager of the largest ranch in Hawaii, a Dole land manager, the owner of a meat processing firm, a sugar company manager, and a Dilco executive.[9]

The "New Hawaii" economic model was based from its beginnings on the utter primacy of tourism, since outside investors would only direct their funds to this profitable sector, while government capital resources had to be focussed on infrastructural activities aimed at attracting these same investors. Yet even the model's most ardent advocates (Quinn, and later Burns and Ariyoshi) could not accept such a dependence, especially in the face of the historic vulnerability of tourism to economic downturn (and memories of its virtual collapse in Hawaii in the 1930s). Thus although his administration used virtually every resource at its command to promote the growth of a massive tourism industry, Quinn himself still voiced a certain uneasiness about tourism's future as the primary foundation for the Islands' economy: "We've known for a long time that we're perched precariously on four major pillars," he said once. And on another occasion, "We have placed enough emphasis on the tourist industry; it is a very sensitive industry, a luxury industry. We still have to depend on our long-range interests, on stable agricultural industries, not on these fast-buck operations."[10]

Quinn—and his successors—then took a further step, and denied the necessary dominance of tourism in the model, stressing instead Hawaii's ability to build a "diversified," balanced, economic structure. Quinn emphasized the immense opportunities that awaited Hawaiian industrial and financial interests in the Pacific, which if exploited would allow Hawaii to reverse its subordinate relationship to the advanced capitalist centers and assume a dominant role vis-à-vis Micronesia or the Philippines. "Hawaii's special role in the Pacific" was then touted for almost a generation—in politicians' speeches, newspaper editorials, and at businessmen's luncheons. The new governor touched upon this theme at his inauguration in 1957: "In the immediate future, I shall dedicate myself to the full realization of our destiny as the focal point of the Pacific. For with this realization will come great industrial and commercial development."[11] His most concentrated effort toward making it a reality was his channeling of large funds into the University of Hawaii budget, in a program aimed at transforming what had been essentially a mediocre "pineapple college" into a major state university that could conduct scientific research and development and provide vital support systems for economic and cultural penetration of the Pacific Basin. In 1959 and 1960 business and engineering schools, an economic research center, and a statistical center were established on the Manoa campus. In 1961 and 1962 twenty-six academic departments were added to the existing thirty-four, and a host of new buildings were constructed. And in 1961

Quinn abruptly replaced the entire University of Hawaii Board of Regents, naming Herbert Cornuelle, president of Dole and one of the most Pacific-expansion-oriented young executives in Hawaii, the new chairman, and choosing for the other regents those he felt would favor a "New Hawaii."[12]

None of this could have been done without the collaboration of the Democratic Party politicians who controlled the Hawaii legislature and who greeted the Quinn program with rapture and enthusiasm. The Oahu Democratic County Committee at one point even tried to claim credit for it: "It is encouraging to note that a Republican governor appears willing to adopt and use the long-range development program which we Democrats labored to produce."[13] With hotels studding the Waikiki horizon, Boeing 707s disgorging tourists from half-a-dozen different directions, land values constantly rising, high rates of employment, massive capital improvement, and a construction boom on nearly every island, the Democrats were confident that the foundations of a solidly prosperous society were being laid. Yet at the start of the same decade a different Democratic Party had had a different vision. What had happened?

On the morning of April 30, 1950, at its annual convention, the Democratic Party of the Territory of Hawaii split. The long dominant conservative wing, scandalized by the seating of a group of delegates belonging to the International Longshoremen's and Warehousemen's Union who had just been indicted for refusing to testify about their association with the Communist Party, walked down the steps of Honolulu's Kalakaua School and opened their own caucus near the Ala Wai canal.

"This is the new Democratic Party. It is the party the Republicans are beginning to fear," boomed Vincent Esposito, the convention keynote speaker, trying to calm the two hundred somewhat shaken men and women of the Democratic "left wing" who had remained in their seats. Esposito then proceeded to enunciate the broad principles of the political program formulated by these predominately youthful party members, a program committed to substantial reform of Hawaii's grossly inequitable social system:

> I'll tell you what the Democrats can do. They will change the tax system and make a real American progressive tax based on the ability

to pay. . . . On land, we will make available this land at auction in small parcels so that farms can be built up all over this beautiful land and people can own their own homes, grow their own vegetables and live as free Americans: "You, the Democratic Party, are the hope, the courage and the heart of a strong America."[14]

The Democratic Party's prospects seemed to justify Esposito's rather picturesque rhetoric. True, the Republicans still controlled the Territorial legislature, but the Democrats had made sweeping advances, reemerging as a formidable rival to the GOP's half-century of political monopoly. The Democrats felt it was only a matter of time before they would mount the steps to Iolani Palace and political power in Hawaii. Indeed, a solid majority of Hawaii's electorate—long under the rule of the Big Five's Republican Party—looked eagerly to the popular young Democrats for real change. The political vacuum was about to be filled by those now in the school.

And indeed, many of the faces in the crowd that morning belonged to men and women who would become Hawaii's political stars and superstars in the following generation. The majority were Asian-Americans, sons and daughters of plantation workers, and they were confident as never before that the caste restrictions of the prewar era would be swept away and that the Democratic Party would be their vehicle for finding a place in the sun.

The Asian population in Hawaii—whose ancestors had come from frugal, commercially minded societies with a work ethic enforced by heavy population pressure on scarce land resources—had, over the course of a century, assimilated the capitalist value system far more easily than had the Hawaiians. Within about twenty years after the first Chinese had disembarked, coolie-peddlars were appearing in Honolulu and the ubiquitous *pake* store was becoming a fixture at plantation crossroads. Aspiring Asian entrepreneurs found those few niches deemed not worth taking by the Merchant Street monopolies, and went into barbering, fishing, taro and hog raising, small restaurants, drugstores, laundries, and gas stations. Usually family-centered and miniscule in size and capitalization, these enterprises nevertheless provided the second generation with the accumulated capital and business expertise to move into more profitable investments (especially in land—always a prized commodity in land-short Asia), when an expanding

Hawaiian economy created such opportunities during and after World War II.

A handful became wealthy. Chun Hoon, for instance, was a one-time contract laborer who abandoned the plantation to hawk eggs on the streets of Honolulu and slowly built up a thriving grocery trade, winning a series of military contracts to deliver groceries. Wilfred Tsukiyama rose from humble beginnings to become a judge and legislator, a loyal Republican who was rewarded financially and politically for his unswerving cooperation with the elite. These local Horatio Alger stories were celebrated by the oligarchy—it could have been you, was the implied moral, if only you had shown the ambition and drive of these people.

By the early 1940s, as war threatened to envelop the Pacific, it was obvious that the Chinese businesspeople and lawyers on Smith Street and the young Japanese filling the classrooms of McKinley, Hilo, and Baldwin high schools and the University of Hawaii were increasingly impatient with a racist system that circumscribed their social, economic, and political roles. By 1945 the twenty-five hundred young Hawaiian Japanese who had formed the core of the 442nd Regimental Combat Team—the most highly decorated combat unit in the U.S. army—and the hundreds of thousands who drew inspiration and meaning from the unit's gritty determination in the fierce battles across the hills and valleys of Italy and France were convinced that the war had vindicated their claim to equality and to a major voice in Hawaii's future. The conversation between wounded veterans—and future Democratic Party luminaries—Dan Inouye, grandson of a plantation worker, and Sakae Takahashi, a Hanapepe teacher, lying in a Jersey City hospital room, expressed sentiments widely felt throughout Hawaii:

Takahashi: Most of all I want to know why there has to be a limit to our hopes.

Inouye: Who says there's a limit?

Takahashi: Suppose you wanted to join the Pacific Club. Could you?

Inouye: Big deal.

Takahashi: Suppose you wanted to be governor of Hawaii.

Inouye: We ought to have that right. What I'm interested in is tomorrow. I want my kids to have an even break. I demand it.[15]

And many years later, Dan Aoki reflected on the thoughts of the returnees:

> Would they have to go back to the plantations and work for a dollar a day? Would they have to go back and work for the big corporations and be paid on a dual scale—large salaries for the *haoles* from the mainland and only a fraction as much for them because they were Orientals from Hawaii. . . . Is this what would be in store for them—nothing better?[16]

Sakae Takahashi similarly articulated the objectives of his generation: "Sound and efficient state government to protect and uphold the rights and liberties and dignity of the individual." All these future political leaders shared an ideological orientation and vision of the future; and all were, in the tradition of other ethnic groups, prepared to use access to the political apparatus as a means of individual social mobility and material enhancement.

Writers on the rise of the Asian political elite have emphasized the importance of a public educational system that taught young students such as Inouye and Takahashi the ideals of liberal thought as being basic to their decision to demand equal rights. We are told, for instance, how McKinley High School Principal Miles Carey encouraged young Dan Inouye: "In a few years, by the time this war is over, your people will have as much opportunity as any white man in these islands."[17] But this is entirely too superficial an analysis. It fails to look at the real content of the educational perspective promoted by Carey and other educators, a perspective which, no matter how liberal, infused the young Asians with an individualistically oriented competitive world view exalting middle-class materialistic goals and equating success with wealth, status, and power—an education for selfishness and self-aggrandizement in the traditional American sense. It succeeded only too well in training a generation that thought first of "making it" and second, if at all, of what was happening to the society around them as they enriched themselves. The returning 442nd Regiment soldiers thus used the educational system, an expanding economy, and their own growing political influence to enter the bourgeoisie—taking their place as lawyers and doctors, in the swollen upper reaches of government bureaucracies, in insurance and real estate companies. And they entered the Democratic Party in large numbers.

The November 1954 election gave the Democratic Party decisive command over both houses of the legislature and was hailed by many as a "revolution by ballot," with the Democrats promising "a new era of justice and fairness to all the people of this territory"[18]—including a strong government that would grant equality of opportunity regardless of race. As John Burns put it, "We are going to change things in line with the platform. We have an outright mandate from the people to change the way of life down here."[19]

What they were not demanding is equally important, however. Unlike their contemporaries, the ILWU organizers, they had not developed a class analysis that argued that reforms might mitigate the worst abuses of capitalism, but that without the overthrow of the system of private profit, private ownership of the means of production, and political domination of the ruling class, there would in the long run only be the worst sort of regression. The postwar Asian political elite, despite its working-class background and the sufferings of the prewar years, never questioned the morality or viability of capitalism, especially a capitalism that had sufficient resiliency to provide them with the kind of wealth and position they could not have even imagined achieving during their younger, leaner days. Indeed, their incredible success—within a decade of the end of the war they had mostly graduated from law school, entered politics, taken control of both the Democratic Party and the legislature—guaranteed that they would never question the system that had been so generous to them. As one-time Democratic Party leader Thomas Gill, who knew the postwar political elite from their humblest beginnings, noted, "Making the old order over became less important than simply making it."[20] And the abandonment of even mild reforms and a cascade of corruption, petty graft, influence peddling, land speculation, and favoritism in awards of government contracts began with the Democratic Party takeover of the legislature in 1955. It is thus not surprising that even during this euphoric period, when populist legislators were calling for the break-up of the great landed estates and their distribution to the landless, and for the creation of an equitable taxation system, there were voices in the party leadership counseling compromise. Dan Inouye, for example, warned his colleagues that "Too drastic a change would shake up our economy too badly. Our economy at present is dependent on some of our biggest boys on Merchant Street, you might say. The legislature will not work hand-in-hand with them, but will keep their position in mind."[21]

Given this attitude among influential Democrats, and the ability of Governor Samuel King—closely attuned to Big Five interests— to veto any legislation that might unduly disturb the Islands' status quo, Merchant Street remained confident that time, greed, and a fierce desire for "respectability" would reconcile the "young Turks of '55" to the existing order. This confidence has not been misplaced. And indeed, the new political elite's attraction to personal wealth and status, its lack of a clear critique of capitalism, the absence of a solid base to hold it accountable for its actions—all made it easy to understand how the new politicians could, within a brief ten years, end any serious discussion about the restructuring of Hawaiian society to accommodate the vast majority of landless citizens and enter a period of political opportunism and collusion with powerful corporate interests. "You can work up a real appetite in 52 years," commented one Democrat after the 1954 election,[22] in anticipation of the patronage available to a party which had languished for decades in the political desert. In retrospect, this statement seems like sheer prophecy.

The link between the politicians and the land developers through the former's personal investment in speculative properties was key to this transformation—average land values multiplied seventeen times between 1950 and 1975, and in some areas multiplied *fifty* times. George Cooper, in his meticulously documented study of this process, writes: "It is simply no exaggeration to say that almost every political figure to emerge out of the Democratic revolution, or at least, most of his or her close advisors, invested in the boom by the 1970s. Every key institution of political power was dominated by or contained many who were investors."[23] Controlling the political levers of power, they forced the big landed estates to grant their *huis* development rights and to hire them as lawyers to secure rezoning agreements and "smooth" the political process.

A case from 1954 illustrates how this process worked. It involved a prominent Democratic politician, Mitsuyuki Kido, a key figure in nearly a score of land development *huis* in the 1950s, 1960s, and 1970s, and William Vanatta, a leading developer and future Democratic candidate for mayor of Honolulu. Kido, as a member of the

Oahu County Board of Supervisors (now the City Council) had just granted a special waiver to Vanatta's Hawaii Land Development Company, allowing the firm to construct a new residential development in Kaneohe without the legally required reservoir. This act of "generosity" saved the developer some $100,000. During the minor rumpus that followed the disclosure that some of Kido's family had invested in the project, Kido made a remarkable statement justifying his role:

> Mr. Vanatta told me that the Kaneohe Ranch and Kaneohe Development Company was interested in getting a group to develop some home lots in Kaneohe and that he was going to get a few of his relatives to join in this venture. He asked me if I would be interested in getting a few of my friends into the deal. I asked him how much it would take and he said that the original capital was going to be very nominal and if things worked properly, there might be a fairly good profit. I said I would consult a few of my friends and let him know. Subsequently I talked to my brother-in-law and sister-in-law. The only thing I want to say is there was no conflict of interest on my part. I'm a real estate developer and promoter and investment counselor and I have advised many friends and relatives, including these two, to go into many other real estate deals.[24]

Multiply this incident five-hundred fold, and understand the value system that informs the statement, and you will gain insight into the workings of the entrepreneur-politician class of the 1950s.

The class composition of successive legislatures provides an index to the new elite's progressive dependence on an expanding economic environment of land development and tourism. The 1957 legislature included two business executives, four small businessmen, eight attorneys, one sugar company clerk, one investment salesman, one airline salesperson, and one court practitioner. This pattern was repeated in the Senate, which included seven attorneys, one hotel owner, one industrial relations manager, one real estate broker, one editor, and two small businessmen.[25]

What made the political coalition lined up behind the "New Hawaii" model invincible was the inclusion of the International Longshoremen's and Warehousemen's Union (ILWU). The ILWU arose during the labor wars of the 1930s, the high-water mark of U.S. working-class militancy and solidarity. Its crucible, the fierce

1934 San Francisco waterfront strike, was the scene of bitterly
fought battles between dockworkers and police that left two workers dead and hundreds in jail, and culminated in a general strike
that closed down the city. Out of conflicts such as these emerged a
tough cadre of organizers ready to take on even that most forbid-
den of places, the Hawaiian Islands.

In 1936 a tall young sailor from the mainland named Jack Hall
began organizing the sugar plantations of Kauai and publishing a
labor newsletter. Hall and his ILWU comrades—including Frank
Thompson, Robert McElrath, Newton Miyagi, "Major" Okada,
Carl Damaso, and Dave Thompson—were ideally suited to provide
leadership in the struggle for unionization. They had the tenacity,
courage, and dedication to build union strength in the face of
constant harrassment and bullying by the Big Five-controlled
police and courts.

The backgrounds and theoretical perspectives of the ILWU core
group were key to their success. These men were no strangers to
the unemployment, bread lines, and job shape-ups of the Great
Depression; nor were they immune to the widespread disillusionment with the failure of capitalism. As Harry Bridges, the fiery
ILWU president, was fond of saying, "Capitalism means the exploitation of a lot of people for profit. I haven't much use for it."
Indeed, the young ILWU organizers had imbibed much of the
revolutionary outlook of Marxism, and many were partisans and
members of the Communist Party of the United States, which was
at the center of organizing heavy industry in the 1930s. This provided them with a collective outlook that transcended capitalism
and embraced the concept of a socialist workers' state—they believed that the collapse of the existing system must inevitably bring
the working class to power, and thus that they were building not
merely a new union, but a new society as well. It was this vision that
sustained them through long years of lockouts, police violence,
arrests, government investigations, and attempts on every side to
break the union.

And they succeeded, as no one in Hawaii had before, in subor-
dinating the intense local ethnic divisions to the unity of a multi-
ethnic union. No longer could the Big Five play the different races
off against each other or manipulate long-nurtured prejudices to
undermine labor organization. "The Union, to be successful, was

compelled to forge an interracial solidarity which is unique in America," recalled Jack Hall years later. "In Hawaii, only an interracial statewide union could cope with the Big Five."[26]

ILWU leaders recognized early on that the Big Five's tightknit, integrated monopoly over nearly every facet of the Islands' economy demanded a parallel union structure, so that when oligarchy and union reached the point of confrontation, workers on plantations, in canneries, warehouses, and docks could be mobilized in support. Inch by inch, the union consolidated its position, aided by a well-conceived program of political education promoting working-class unity against Big Business. Just before the end of the war, the parallel structure was finally cemented in place: the union had the support of workers in every strategic Hawaiian industry.

Then came the first of a series of confrontations, this one in the sugar industry, as ILWU demands for recognition, wage increases, and shorter hours clashed with the determination of the Big Five to smash the union. In 1946, twenty-eight thousand workers downed their tools, closing thirty-three of thirty-four plantations in the Islands. After seventy-nine tumultuous days, filled with arrests of picketers, court injunctions, and media denunciations of union leaders, came victory for the ILWU. Union leaders were exultant. Bridges declared, "This victory makes Hawaii part of the United States for all Hawaiians, especially the workers. It is no longer a feudal colony." "The victory is a tremendous one," commented Hall. "The interracial unity and determination of the workers to end for all time dictatorial control over their lives and to guide their own destinies is the outstanding feature of the strike."[27]

Three years later there was a second great confrontation, the dock strike of 1949. Refusal to consider ILWU demands for parity wages with West Coast stevedores (who were earning $.32 more an hour) brought two thousand longshoremen out on strike. This was the most prolonged and militant strike in Hawaii's history, replete with wholesale arrests of striking workers and the press barraging the public with cries of "excessive" union power and of the "public interest" being flouted. Newspaper editors charged that the strike had been initiated by Communist leaders in order to cripple the Hawaiian economy and weaken the United States. Through a long summer and an even leaner fall, the rank and file held fast, and hundreds of picketers clashed with the police when the government attempted to charter a new company to break the strike. The ILWU's only allies were their fellow workers on the West Coast— primarily ILWU longshoremen and warehousemen—who refused to handle any cargo from the Islands and immobilized the Big Five sugar refinery in California. At one point, desperate to break the blockade, the Big Five arranged to have sixty tons of sugar unloaded at the remote Oregon town of Dalles, only to have two hundred and fifty Portland dock workers burst into the town, seize the waterfront, and pitch the unloaded cargo back into the holds of the ships. "The record is all too clear. Our friends have been few and we are doubly grateful for their assistance," Jack Hall observed three years after the great strike, "but by and large, we came over the rough and rocky road on our own steam, on our own strength. The employers, the press, the government have always been against us in our past struggles, just as they are today."[28] Finally, in October 1949, with 400,000 tons of sugar stacked up in Hawaiian warehouses and business losses mounting to well over $100 million, the oligarchy finally agreed to meet the union's demand for a substantial wage increase.

The implications of the six month dock strike were profound: the local working class, in an event unique to its long history of exploitation and powerlessness, had demonstrated that it could totally undermine the economy. The ILWU, with the firm support of the great majority of workers in Hawaii's basic industries, had become a powerful force in the economic and political life of the Islands. Some even called it the "Big Sixth." At the ILWU convention in Honolulu in April 1951, the general tone was one of anger and radicalism; the image projected was that of a tough, resourceful trade union, proud of its self-reliance, struggling against an oppressive system, beseiged by its enemies, yet winning victory after victory through class solidarity.

In retrospect, however, this was the last hurrah of radicalism. Over the next few years, the pressures brought to bear on the union proved overwhelming. A skillfully manipulated anti-Communism was of course the most powerful weapon: the Big Five had begun a well-financed campaign of red baiting against the union leadership as early as 1947, and a year later a U.S. Senate Committee ostensibly studying statehood charged that "international revolutionary Communism has a firm grip on the economic, political, and social life of the territory. . . . . Communism in Hawaii operates chiefly through the ILWU and has persistently sabotaged the economy." The senators even bruited about the fantastic charge that Harry Bridges "is the unseen Communist dictator in Hawaii."[29] In April 1950 the House Un-American Activities Committee conducted hearings on Communist influence in the Islands. Thirty-nine witnesses (subsequently labelled the "reluctant thirty-nine") refused to appear and were cited for contempt of Congress. Within a year, the full onset of McCarthyism and the nationwide plunge into anti-Communist hysteria created a still more favorable atmosphere for persecution. Early in the morning of August 28, 1951, the police walked into the homes of ILWU Regional Director Jack Hall and a number of others closely allied with the union, arresting them on a federal warrant charging the advocacy of the violent overthrow of the U.S. government. After a trial lasting seven and a half stormy months, the accused were found guilty, sentenced to five years in prison, and given heavy fines. The sentence was later overruled by an appellate court, but the possibility of having to serve time hung over the seven until 1958. Dr. Willis Butler, who watched his friend Hall slowly wither and retreat under this fierce repression, has remarked, "There is absolutely no doubt about it. It was the Smith Act trial which crushed Jack and the whole ILWU—years of fabricated charges, weary courtroom sessions and personal harrassment. They were never the same again."

The attack on the ILWU in Hawaii was only a small part of a nationwide campaign. The U.S. government repeatedly attempted to deport Bridges back to his native Australia, even charging the veteran labor leader with obstructing shipments to the Korean war front. A concerted program to crush the union culminated in the passage of the Communist Control Act of 1954, which deprived "Communist-dominated" trade unions of their collective bargaining rights. The labor movement it had done so much to build also turned against it, and the ILWU and other leftist trade unions were expelled from the Congress of Industrial Organizations (CIO).

There were other factors in the union's decline that were specific to Hawaii. For one, the Big Five began to transfer its agribusiness industries to low-wage Third World areas, severely undercutting the union's bargaining position. Indeed, the runaway shop and automation became the Big Five's answer to unionization of the fields, mills, and docks. The ILWU found itself increasingly unable to counter this attack on its main souce of strength, its membership.

Not surprisingly, then, the union turned desperately and uncertainly to the tourism industry as a source of new membership, and soon became one of the strongest proponents of huge public funding of the tourism infrastructure—Jack Hall even assumed the role of vice-president of the Hawaii Visitors' Bureau. It lost its radical aura, and entered an era of "friendly cooperation and collaboration" with the bourgeoisie. In the face of advanced capitalism's seeming ability to generate an unprecedented assortment of commodities and experiences, in Hawaii as elsewhere, both the leadership and the membership abandoned their faith in socialism and endorsed captalism's program. Decision-making authority within the union came to be concentrated in a small group at the top, and rank and file members were discouraged from promoting reforms or taking initiative. Union officials became ever more divorced from the class they had been born into; they lived in middle-class neighborhoods and even engaged in land speculation. They became, in short, comfortably assimilated into the existing order, and ceased to think seriously of restructuring it.

The first manifestations of this transformation appeared as early as 1952, when union demands were suddenly surprisingly modest. Strikes and job actions were dramatically reduced, Hall speaking of the "tremendous progress in union-plantation relations." ILWU Education Director Robert McElrath's radio program began to play down class struggle and preach acceptance of capitalism as a rational system that worked. There was a growing tone of complacency (amounting to smugness), a feeling that the labor movement had accomplished its essential objectives, that the great struggles were now history, the account closed. "The old conditions have been swept away," announced McElrath. "A new era has arrived in which the freedoms and rights of individuals are respected." In the late 1950s Hall was serving on Territorial boards, and a plantation manager lectured an ILWU convention on how to "obtain genuine respectability."

The ILWU's position in the Territorial political arena also changed. During the early postwar period the union had made an all-out effort to control the Democratic Party, but, wary of close entanglements with Democratic politicians, had maintained a sense of distance and kept its own counsel. By the mid-1950s, however, the union leadership was making some definitive moves toward *full* integration with the Democrats and unqualified endorsement of party programs and candidates—calling it the "party of the people" at the very time it was increasingly controlled by the newly *arriviste* professional–land developer–administrative petty bourgeoisie on the make toward higher status and financial power. The stage was set for the complete transformation of the ILWU from a force for political change to a mainstay of the status quo.

10
If the Price Is Right...

In the early 1950s, we were on the outs. We wanted our share. Burns told us to do it through politics. He was absolutely correct. Local boys got a good share.

—Mike Tokunaga,
aide to Governor Burns (1979)

In the past, we have moved from a feudal society to a society in which very possibly the dignity of all persons is held at the highest level anywhere in the world.

—Governor George Ariyoshi (1982)

The 1962 election witnessed the defeat of Quinn by John Burns, a veteran Democratic politician who had been a principle lobbyist in Congress for the passage of the statehood bill three years earlier. On December 4, 1962, Burns was inaugurated governor of Hawaii, but the change was hard to discern. As the *Honolulu Star-Bulletin* mused, "Many of the programs Governor Burns outlined might have been taken from the radio scripts of his predecessor."[1] Burns' policies echoed those of Quinn: "I am pledged to the people of Hawaii to work for a more favorable climate for business, to encourage small business, to utilize the available offices of government for meeting the needs of business, and to remove illegal barriers to their rapid growth."[2] In retrospect, the fact that the forces that dominated the Burns coalition (the land-developer bourgeoisie, the ILWU and government workers' unions, the monopoly corporations, and upper levels of the state bureaucracy) were firmly attached to the existing model made it clear that change would be marginal at most. What change did occur was in the realm of quantity, not in quality or structure.

The differences between Quinn and Burns were primarily the result of the time period in which each functioned: Quinn in a transitional period from a still relatively insular, plantation-dominated capitalism to a more mature tourism–land development

economy; Burns in the context of a model at its full maturity, a
more complex situation that demanded continued public expenditure to attract investors, as well as programs to stabilize a society
increasingly rent by social and economic contradictions. He was
helped immeasurably by the fact that the heyday of his governorship was concurrent with a great period of global capitalist expansion, so that the model, for all its inadequacies, was able to generate
high rates of economic growth, bringing with it high levels of investment, employment, and state revenues.

Although fond of populist rhetoric ("People born with silver
spoons in their mouths don't know that the people can think"), the
shrewdly opportunistic Burns remained a conservative politician
whose commitment to the interests of the bourgeoisie was strong
enough to convince land developer Clarence Ching to be his
finance manager and corporate plutocrat Lowell Dillingham to be
his biggest financial backer. Like Quinn, Burns journeyed to the
U.S. mainland to meet with business and financial representatives
of some of the largest corporations, and his administration was
equally successful in attracting huge sums of capital to Hawaii. As
he reported in a 1964 statement (which also spoke volumes about
the values taking precedence in the development process):

> The measure of the strength of our economy and the character of our
> society may be found, however, not so much in the claims we make,
> but with demonstrations of confidence which others have in our state.
> An expression of this confidence is the fact that foreign and mainland
> investments in Hawaii have increased from approximately $900 mil-
> lion in 1959 to an estimated total of more than $1.5 billion today . . .
> this increase is a great compliment to our economy and a significant
> indication of our growth potential.[3]

The primary vehicle for attracting this kind of capital inflow
remained the socialization of infrastructural costs through massive
public expenditures. Immediately upon taking office, Burns proposed a $490 million, six-year CIP budget financed from bonds,
cash, and federal funds, with the emphasis on communications,
transportation, and recreational facilities and the opening of Windward Oahu to intensive suburban development.[4] Large construction projects were begun, including Magic Island, the Lunalilo
freeway, the Honolulu airport, the Kahaluu airport, the Hana Belt

Road, Volcano roads, Lihue airport, and the widening of Kuhio beach. Mainland banks continued to provide much of the capital: in October 1963, for instance, a Bank of America consortium purchased $39.6 million worth of state bonds, while a Chase Manhattan syndicate snapped up $15 million of a subsequent issue.[5] Between 1958 and 1968, the state's outstanding public bonds increased sharply, from $212 million to $528.9 million,[6] while an average of $48 million in bonds was sold annually between 1960 and 1967.[7] The state government was continuing to mortgage its future to the dominant financial institutions in the United States.

These policies continued to find favor with the land developer elite and the Big Five–Dillingham–estate interests, all of which quickly transferred their allegiance from the hapless Republicans to the Democrats. As *Pacific Business News* commented approvingly in 1965, "It is fair to say that the large companies have found it to their advantage to live harmoniously with the Burns administration."[8] Indeed, Burns regarded a strong business input as basic to decision making in his administration: his handpicked director of the state Department of Planning and Economic Development, Shelly Mark (later a Bank of Honolulu director), defined a "healthy business climate" as an "environment providing rules under which the business community can play a leading part in partnership with government, labor, and citizens at large."[9] And such cooperation with large corporate interests extended to foreign capital. The governor—who had said that "The state welcomes and will continue to welcome Japanese interests in Hawaii, including investments"— sent a number of official delegations to Japan to solicit investments and helped set up the $1 million Hawaii exhibit at the Osaka World's Fair. Major Japanese investors received assurances of state support and cooperation at every level.

As with the Quinn government, the composition of key government boards and commissions continued to reflect the state's commitment to the virtually unlimited expansion of the tourism–land development sector. While Burns was obligated by the nature of his political alliances to appoint more union officials to certain strategic state boards, these were still dominated by representatives of Big Five capital and land development entrepreneurs. For example, when it came time to appoint a State Land Use Commission in 1963, Burns chose a Big Island ranch manager, the manager of a

Kona hotel, a Maui real estate man and insurance salesman, an Oahu sugar company manager, a poultry farmer, a state functionary, and one conservationist-photographer.[10] This board and its successors indiscriminately rezoned thousands of acres (including some of the most fertile agricultural land) for development and were wracked by constant scandals involving personal and institutional conflicts of interest. One example must suffice to show how these deals worked: at one point in the early 1970s Alex Napier, a member of the State Land Use Commission and a Kahau Ranch executive, had some of his ranch land upgraded just before being sold, increasing its value *116 times*. Meanwhile, another member, C. E. Burns, a vice-president of Amfac, was voting on the rezoning of large Amfac properties on Kauai and Hawaii, and a third member, Shiro Nishimura, was reaping $575,000 in profits from land speculation on land he had helped rezone in Kalaheo.[11]

Burns also continued and expanded Quinn's emphasis on Hawaii's role in the Pacific Basin. In a 1964 speech he proclaimed: "I believe that today we have a great destiny. We are the people who are going to bridge East and West. This is going to become an outstanding educational and cultural center. It follows from this . . . that it will become an economic and political center."[12] One year later he was telling *Time* magazine that the "world is moving toward a new era—the Pacific era," and was vowing to make Hawaii the "hub of the Pacific."[13] Hawaii would become a focal point for the export of capital and technology and "a center for stimulating exchanges between peoples of the Pacific Basin, for providing services that would facilitate that exchange, and attract future Pacific traders to come to Hawaii for negotiations."[14] In this vision of the future, Hawaii would emerge as a sophisticated economic entrepot and diversified manufacturing center, the headquarters for numerous major corporations engaged in Pacific Basin activities and a model society for the developing nations of the area. This vision was echoed by other Hawaiian leaders, especially the bankers, and a special task force of local "dignitaries," set up to study "Hawaii and the Pacific in the Year 2000," pictured the Islands as a major Pacific financial and exporting center: "We would emerge as the 'Geneva of the Pacific,' playing an intermediate role between the financial markets of Tokyo, Hong Kong, Singapore, and New York, San Francisco, and Montreal."[15]

Burns' administration devoted considerable energy and funds to trying to make this vision a reality—including building up the Hawaii International Services Agency, whose seminars were designed to encourage mainland and Japanese corporate officials to locate their regional headquarters in Hawaii and whose other objectives including assisting Island firms in finding opportunities for investment abroad. But Burns, like Quinn, focussed on the University of Hawaii as the primary vehicle. He insisted that the university "be a center of learning for the entire Pacific Ocean area," and finalized the transformation of the Manoa campus into a major state university with fully equipped facilities and a specialization in those areas (oceanography, agriculture, international business and tourism, research and development, Asian studies) considered to hold special promise for Hawaii's expansion into the Pacific world. Large amounts of money were appropriated for this purpose: the university's 1959–60 operating budget of $4 million had expanded to $41 million only a decade later—a rise of 742.5 percent, the greatest increase for any state university in the United States during this period.[16]

Cornuelle and Burns imported big-time administrator Thomas Hamilton, president of the State University of New York, to oversee the transformation of the university. Hamilton was presumed to have the necessary administrative ability, contacts in Washington and elsewhere, and energy to consolidate the modernization program. During his five-year term in office, he established and strengthened a Tourism Industry Management School—which provided hotels with both cheap student labor and graduates able to fill supervisory and middle management positions—a greatly expanded business school, oriented toward serving multinational corporations in the Pacific Basin, and Asian-Pacific social science and language programs whose objective was to produce trained personnel for U.S. corporate and governmental penetration of the Pacific.

Hawaii's position as the major staging area for U.S. military activities against Indochina and the massive military presence of Pearl Harbor, Hickam Airforce Base, and Schofield Barracks (on Oahu), encouraged Burns and Hamilton to build a military research and development complex as well. Between 1966 and 1970 the university engaged in over one hundred contracts with the U.S.

military, worth over $20 million. A dozen academic departments, eighty-seven professors, and hundreds of assistants conducted research for such projects as the $140,000 polytoxin research project (conducted with the Army's Edgewood Arsenal), a $76,000 jungle defoliation research project, and an $80,000 study of soil-applied herbicides for tropical vegetation control. In 1969 deadly anthrax germ warfare agents were tested at the university's agricultural experimentation station, while research findings from the Tropical Agriculture and Soil Science Agronomy departments on defoliation and rice disease went to the U.S. Army's Chemical and Biological Warfare Center in Maryland. As for the Hawaii Institute of Geophysics, according to an official state publication, "Many of their research activities are connected with the Navy's oceanographic research programs and anti-submarine activities."[17] There were also alliances with major war corporations, such as the one signed with Ling-Temco-Voight in 1965.

After Hamilton's rather sudden resignation in 1968, the result of pressures generated by strong faculty-student support for a left-wing political science professor he had fired, he received lucrative corporate sinecures from a grateful bourgeoisie: he became president of the Hawaii Visitors' Bureau (and thus leading front man for the tourism industry), advisor to the Bishop Estate, and a director of Hawaiian Telephone and Hawaii Thrift and Loan. His successors—former U.S. ambassador to NATO and head of the U.S. Mutual Security Agency Harlan Cleveland, and Fujio Matsuda, one of Hawaii's "floating population" of corporate-governmental bureaucrats and director of half-a-dozen tourism–land development-related companies, including United Airlines—pursued identical policies, albeit under the more constricted financial conditions of the crisis-ridden 1970s and 1980s.

An important component of the University of Hawaii complex and perhaps the most widely publicized symbol of Hawaii's "special role in the Pacific" is the East-West Center. Despite the glowing one-world rhetoric that surrounded the 'Center's founding—Vice-President Lyndon Johnson announced, "The University is here to serve Hawaii, but the Center is here to serve the world."[18]—it was clearly envisioned, both in Washington and Honolulu, as a weapon in the cold war rivalry between the United States and the so-called Eastern bloc for influence in Asia and the Pacific. The U.S. Senate

Appropriations Committee report of February 1961 specifically referred to the Center as "an institution which offers a unique opportunity in the battle for men's minds,"[19] while the *Honolulu Star-Bulletin* called the Friendship University in Moscow the "Communist rival of the East-West Center."[20] The web of corporate ties represented on the Center's first national consultative group (the presidents of the Ford and Asia foundations, Rockefeller representatives, and California industrialist Edwin Pauley) and also by the local bourgeois members of the Friends of the East-West Center (Chinn Ho, the president of Hawaiian Airlines, the director of the Hawaiian Sugar Planters' Association, and the editor of the *Honolulu Advertiser*) provided an early and clear indication that this was an institution concerned with far more than simply the professed goals of "cultural harmony, interchange, and understanding."[21]

Indeed, the Center was created in the belief that the thousands of Asian and Pacific students who would experience a taste of American life and receive American educations in an American environment would inevitably develop strong attachments to the values and aspirations of American capitalist society. As they then began to assume key positions in their own countries, this orientation would greatly facilitate U.S. corporate and cultural penetration, and the Pacific Rim strategy in general. John Witeck, a former grantee and one of the most knowledgeable and outspoken critics of the Center, has noted: "I once felt the Center was merely an escape, a victim of circumstance, a tragedy of unachievable idealism, an apathetic or frightened eye in the hurricane's center. Now, I am convinced, it is both victim and executioner, both product as well as implementer of cultural and economic imperialism, a true cult of imperialism."[22]

Witeck's argument is buttressed by the revelations in 1967 that the Center had coordinated grants for sixty-five Indonesian military officers who were undergoing "small-arms training" courses on Oahu in 1962 and 1965, just before the military coup that destroyed the Indonesian Communist Party and left over half a million people dead, and also by the reorientation of the Center after 1970 to "problem solving institutes" under the guidance of such "intellectuals" as Michael Pierce, who made the easy transition from Rand Corporation expert making an "evaluation of the pacification program in Vietnam" to the post of assistant director of the Institute of Technology and Development.[23]

The Quinn-Burns model assumed that Hawaii could break out of its historic dependence upon monoculture-type industries tied to the United States market by integrating completely with the most advanced sectors of the global capitalist economy and exchanging Hawaii's traditional role as a backward periphery for a dynamic role as a core to a developing Pacific. Yet despite protestations to the contrary—the Burns administration even flew in twenty-four business writers from major magazines to spread "news about the diversification of economy and not tourism"[24]—the spectacular growth of tourism was the *only real basis* for the Islands' "economic miracle." Between 1963 and 1973 the number of arriving tourists increased from 429,140 to 2,630,140, while the number of hotel rooms jumped from 12,460 at the time of Burns' inauguration to over 43,000 when he left office.[25] Meanwhile, the much heralded "industrialization of Hawaii" stagnated: indeed, manufacturing employment actually declined during the Burns' period, from 25,000 to 21,400.[26] *Pacific Business News* editor George Mason was one of a growing number who were voicing concern about the emergence of what he described as a "booming but lopsided economy" dominated by tourism: "Take away tourism—or even eliminate its growth—and where would we be? . . . Hawaii's economy has become so heavily dependent on transient people and transient activities that we have become inured to the possibility of setbacks from purely outside influences."[27]

By the end of the 1960s the contradictions of this development model were beginning to come home to roost. Ugly subdivisions and condominiums sprawled across hillsides and valleys, traffic jams, pollution, housing crises, welfarism, crime, and personal and familial disintegration rapidly undermined the distinctive Island character, and a widespread malaise developed. Residents found themselves burdened with a cost of living 20 to 25 percent higher than that of the mainland, a situation not helped by the high taxes noted earlier. A bare third of Hawaii's families were obtaining sufficient incomes to live at what they called a "moderate standard of living."[28]

None of this seemed to overly concern Burns or the little circle around him, and their main response was to escalate their rhetoric to new heights of euphoria: "Our horizons are limited only by our vision and by the depth of our desire to see the highest goals," was Burns' message to one group, while he told another that Hawaii was in the process of building the "era of the Pacific which will rival the culture and the civilization of any that we have henceforth known or that we have dreamed about." Shelly Mark, Burns' chief economic planner, proved equally adept at this sort of hyperbole when he described Waikiki as "a world wonder, a true hospitality industry, a meeting of persons in a recognized climate of mutual respect and honor, in which hosts and guests share the finer gifts."[29]

The Burns period witnessed the much deeper involvement of the Democratic Party politicians, who despite their factional infighting and cliques now had deep vested interests in the "New Hawaii." Particularly relevant were the increasing numbers involved in land development. As Thomas Creighton has noted of the 1969–70 legislature, "A majority of its members were in some way professionally concerned with the income to be derived from real estate, directly as developers, indirectly as attorneys, insurance brokers, consultants to developers, or managers or salesmen of developers' land."[30] A clear majority identified themselves as businessmen or listed their primary economic activity as business. Both the older Big Five-related capital and the newer land development–financial interests were represented, and both were committed to an expansive tourism–land development model of economic development. In the House, such key members as Wilfred Soares (director of marketing and sales for Amfac Properties), Toshio Serizawa (district manager of Hawaiian Airlines), Frank Judd (formerly labor relations director for Dole Pineapple), and Joseph Garcia (superintendent of a C. Brewer plantation) had close ties with the traditionally dominant capitalist interests, while Hiram Fong, Jr. (director of Market City Corporation), Stuart Ho (director of Capital Investments of Hawaii and Ilikai Inc.), Robert Taira (vice-president of City Mill Company), Monoru Ianaba (branch manager of the Great Hawaiian Financial Company), and others like them represented the relatively newer land development-based capital.[31]

In the Senate, fifteen of the twenty members had strong business backgrounds, including Toshio Ansai (personnel director for the Wailuku Sugar Company), William Hill (director of C. Brewer and president of Hilo Light and Power), Hebden Porteus (former Alexander and Baldwin legal manager and Damon Estate trustee), Kenneth Brown (director of American Factors and chairman of four other companies), and Wadsworth Yee (president of the Grand Pacific Life Insurance Company and a bank director).

House committees were key to the legislative dominance of the land development interests, and strategic committees were securely in their grip. Again using 1969–70 as an example, the chairman of the Committee of Economic Development was a retail executive, the vice-chairman an airlines district manager, and members included the vice-president of the First National Bank of Hawaii, a real estate lawyer, an investment company president, a finance company director, a Big Five manager, and the owner of a large landscaping firm. The Finance Committee, vitally important because of its budgetary powers, included the same landscape company owner, a businessman, three real estate men, one sugarcane grower, one bank executive, and two insurance agents. The Tourism Committee's lineup was three businessmen, three real estate men, and one trade union official.

In the Senate, the Committee of Economic Development, Tourism, and Transportation included an electric company superintendent and pineapple grower, two real estate developers, a bank director, a finance company director, Wadsworth Yee, Kenneth Brown, and Toshio Ansai. The Utilities Committee's chairman was a gas company and bank director, its vice-chairman an electric company superintendent, and its other members were the president of a utility company and two businessmen—and it was charged with regulating the "public interest"!

The 1969–70 legislature has been described in detail not because it was an aberration, but because it was typical of every Hawaiian legislature for a generation. Indeed, in the 1970s those with ties to tourism–land development interests were joined by a whole new passel of recently elected businessmen-politicians. Those few Democrats who had retained a measure of their reformist zeal were bitterly critical of what was happening, but there was little they could do but resign. Maui political maverick Nadao Yoshinaga (himself a real estate salesman) did this in 1961, charging the party leadership with "political irresponsibility." "They showed they do not have the interests of the people at heart," he said. "Their being Democrats disgusts me. I feel that the Democrats in the legislature . . . are beginning to regard the legislature as a purely political field for personal advancement."[32]

Marching in lock step with the Democratic politicians were their close associates in the local land development bourgeoisie. Chinn Ho, to name the most prominent member of this new social stratum, was a shrewd land speculator who turned inside information into a series of speculative windfalls on Oahu during and after World War II and then expanded into tourism and land development in the 1950s and 1960s. By the late 1960s Ho—now a legendary figure in the Islands and with a personal fortune estimated at over $20 million and interests spread across the Pacific (Hong Kong hotels, California subdivisions, newspapers in Hawaii and Guam, and so on)—had acquired the status of senior business leader. His advice was solicited by government officials and his presence required on numerous state commissions concerned with Hawaii's economic development. For Ho, as for his colleagues, access to governmental machinery provided by his allies in the Democratic Party meant pro-development legislation, state and county subsidies to tourism and land development, favorable rezoning, and lucrative government contracts, all indispensable components of his financial success. Therefore, over the years, he and his fellow developers cultivated the closest ties possible with the new political elite and contrived to involve them in their investment *huis.* For Ho, "social progress" and "democracy" were synonymous with the utilization of the political process for capital accumulation. As he put it, "The elections of 1954 and 1956 saw the political party which had dominated Hawaii for over fifty years give way almost completely to its opposition which represented forces for liberalization and general social progress. Hawaii had finally become democratized." Herbert Horita, Hawaii's leading developer (who was grinding out $160 million a year in residential and hotel construction by the end of the 1970s) publically acknowledged the importance of politics to his financial success: "We used the political vehicle to create reforms and laws to change the regulations, laws and business principles so we had our own power structure."[33]

And there was land developer Clarence Ching, a prime beneficiary of favorable rezoning who sold $60 million in residential construction in the Salt Lake area of Oahu (in the process filling in the island's only natural lake to build an exclusive golf course for business executives from Japan) and plunked down $1 million to secure a nonrefundable option on the purchase of the Kuilima Hotel. Ching, who at one point served as John Burns' campaign finance manager, was gifted at garnering large contributions from fellow land developers, tourism companies, banks, and architectural and engineering firms.

The control of state politics extended in all directions. Elected officials had strong vested interests in the expansion of the land-development–tourism model of development, and moved back and forth between elected office and business with aplomb. Neil Blaisdell, mayor of Honolulu from 1964 to 1968, was a former Big Five corporation official who, when he failed in his bid for re-election, became the director of state and community affairs for Western Airlines. His successor as mayor, Frank Fasi, had made his fortune in the construction supply business, and although he ranted against "fast buck developers" during his campaign, he also accepted $8,000 from Clarence Ching as a "contribution." The mayor of the Big Island, Herbert Matayoshi, had been president of Hilo Investors, while his counterpart on Maui, Elmer Cravalho, held directorships in Maui Factors, the Pacific Guardian Life Insurance Company, and the Central Pacific Bank.[34] During the mid-1970s, two of the most strategic state government departments, the Department of Planning and Economic Development and the Department of Land and Natural Resources, were headed by former Castle and Cooke executives. Thus a "floating population" of bureaucrats and lawyers moved easily from the boardrooms atop the Financial Plaza to the chambers of state, city, and county departments and commissions three blocks away: people like power broker Matsuo Takabuki, kingpin of the Honolulu City Council from 1953 to 1968, key advisor to Governor Burns, and lawyer for Chinn Ho and the Campbell Estates; Liberty Bank vice-president Sunao Miyabara, who headed the Honolulu Redevelopment Agency and the Hawaiian Housing Authority, both key to land policy and implementation; Hideto Kono, assistant to the president of the Dole Corporation, president of Castle and Cooke East Asia, chief counsel to the Joint Legislative Reorganization Committee, and then director of the Department of Planning and Economic Development; John Henry Felix, vice-president of Roy Kelley Hotels, president of World Wide Factors, and director of the Honolulu National Bank, as well as chairman of the Honolulu City and County Planning Commission and the Honolulu Redevelopment Agency, and at one point executive assistant to the governor.

The extent to which political and economic power had become identical was revealed in mid-1970, when Burns' long-time political antagonist, Lieutenant-Governor Tom Gill—a liberal reformer highly critical of the transformation of the Democratic Party into a tool of unscrupulous land developers and financiers—mounted a vigorous primary challenge. The class forces behind Burns mobilized in desperation. Not that Gill was a great radical—he went out of his way to assure businessmen that he supported "a free competitive economy where private interest is properly balanced by the public good. Every constructive businessman should have a decent chance to make his way"—but he did represent a threat to the *complete* control which the elite exercised over the governmental structure.[35] It was feared that he would end the most glaring aspects of governmental collusion with land speculators, developers, and the tourism interests, and initiate some modest programs of public housing and even land reform. Access to, and the ability to manipulate, the political apparatus had become *so critical* to the profitability of many corporations that any departure from the status quo was seen as a threat. Thus they were determined to maintain Burns in office, regardless of cost.

On July 30, 1970, with Burns trailing Gill rather badly in the polls, over two hundred and fifty contractors and developers were brought together by Burns' top managers and exhorted to pledge substantial campaign contributions. Shortly thereafter Department of Transportation Director Fujio Matsuda presided over a meeting attended by representatives of firms with state contracts in which demands were made for large contributions in return for guarantees of future contracts.[36] Almost immediately huge sums of money, unprecedented in Hawaiian politics, began flowing into Burns' coffers. Dilco was one of the leading contributors: using a variety of devices, it siphoned between $150,000 and $300,000 into Burns' campaign chest. As Lowell Dillingham explained, "Burns is best for the interests of the state and the Dillingham Corporation. I think executives of this company have an obligation to contribute to good politicians its *kokua* in the interests of the company."[37] (Indeed, during Burns' tenure Dilco had received lucrative roles in virtually every major construction contract awarded by the state, from the Lunalilo freeway to the Honolulu airport to state office buildings. Furthermore, during the closing moments of the 1969 legislative session, Burns had personally intervened to secure passage of a resolution authorizing high-rise, high-density construction in the Kewalo Basin area of Honolulu, where Dilco was planning a major resort complex.)

In all Burns spent $700,000 on the primary campaign alone (and $1 million during the primary and general elections together), more than all the other candidates from both parties combined. In fact, the cost of the governor's massive television blitz (which was generally regarded as decisive to his victory) was substantially greater than Gill's entire campaign budget of $205,000. What a striking contrast with Burns' 1948 electoral bid for Territorial delegate, when he had spent less than $1,000 and walked the streets in a threadbare suit.[38]

In 1970, as in other years, ILWU support was to prove an essential component of Burns' success at the polls. As the years rolled on into the 1960s, the "historic compromise" had magnified in scope and depth. Having abandoned its strategy of mobilizing a militant, politically conscious working class to do battle on political and work-related issues and become one of the prime components of the Democratic Party machine, the union had forfeited its ability to articulate a position independent of the bourgeois elements controlling the party—or even to mount a left opposition within the councils of Democratic politics. Burns, a conservative with strong ties to big capital, received ILWU endorsement as "a man of all the people and a man of his word," and was elected governor three times with strong ILWU support. As a quid pro quo, ILWU officials were appointed to state commissions at all levels. Easily the most strategic ILWU appointee was International representative Eddie Tangen, who was chairman of the State Land Use Commission from 1969-77. In this position he treated the command as a personal fief, granting land developers and financial interests what they wanted most of all, the rezoning of land for resort and residential development—a job he did with a ruthlessness that earned him a citation by the State Ethics Commission for unethical practices in securing privately negotiated concessions from sugar companies in return for rezoning their lands.

Although the quid pro quo was supposedly a concession to the ILWU, ultimately all the wheeling and dealing was in vain. Al-

liances with the local bourgeoisie destroyed the political independence of the union and its effectiveness in defending the interests
of the workers. While the corporations used ILWU political muscle
in the U.S. Congress and the state legislature to gain continued
agribusiness subsidies and to allow continued polluting, they nevertheless mechanized the fields and docks, dismissed thousands of
workers, and set their own timetable for diversifying out of Island
agriculture and into international activities—with nary a harsh
word from the union. By 1982, when Amfac's Puna Sugar announced its closing, throwing five hundred workers onto an already severely depressed labor market, ILWU spokesmen actually
praised Amfac for its "open position" in the current sugar crisis,
and for trying to meet its responsibilities to Hawaii, the workers,
and their families.

No one personifies the tragedy of the ILWU more clearly than
Jack Hall, whose great leadership abilities were channeled into the
narrow confines of conservative (and increasingly autocratic) trade
unionism. When he died in 1971, his once powerful body worn
down by years of illness, hard drinking, and deep disillusionment
at the corruption and demoralization he saw enveloping the union
along the U.S. West Coast and Hawaii, the oligarchy that had once
feared and hated him provided front-page treatment—a tribute
reserved for a successful man who had made his mark upon the
world: "Although at times accused of being a Communist . . . Mr.
Hall long before his death was recognized as a respectable community leader, working in a variety of civic programs with some of the
same businessmen he at one time counted among his bitterest
enemies." The vice-president of the First Hawaiian Bank further
eulogized him: "During his last years in Hawaii, he took the position that government, business, and labor working together will
best solve the social problems that arise from our ever changing
economy." But a close friend had a very different epitaph: "Jack
Hall was a prisoner of his illnesses, his image, his corrupt subordi-
nates. He died a defeated man."[39]

For the people of Hawaii, the disintegration of the ILWU as a
force committed to the powerful socialist ideals of economic justice,
mass democracy, and workers' power was a tragedy of the first
order. The integration of the union into the framework of the
political-corporate apparatus that controlled Hawaii after the
1950s provided the bourgeoisie with an invaluable instrument to

use in its creation of the new economy of resorts, condominiums, subdivisions, and international investments. In the absence of a viable organization actively defending the interests of the working class (and dispossessed in general), the local and international bourgeoisie could proceed to integrate the Hawaiian Islands into the Pacific division of labor and construct the "New Hawaii" in their own image. This they have done.

The 1970 election left the "New Hawaii" model as once again the "only ball game in town." When Burns fell critically ill in 1973, Lieutenant-Governor George Ariyoshi (former director of the First Hawaiian Bank, the Honolulu Gas Company, and Hawaiian Guaranty and Insurance Company, and a loyal Democrat who had faithfully served the party leadership for two decades) was catapulted into the governorship. Neither Ariyoshi's corporate ties, his loyalty to the party directorate, his ideological baggage, nor his family connections (his brother was one of Oahu's larger condominium developers) argued for any dramatic break with the Quinn-Burns model, and in fact the changes that did transpire were largely in the realm of rhetoric. But this was necessary if the model was to continue in effect, for Ariyoshi's terms were—unlike Burns'—spent in the midst of an escalating worldwide capitalist crisis, compounded by monetary, energy, and stagflationary dilemmas in the advanced nations that proved equally traumatic to the Hawaiian economy, tied as it is to these centers. High rates of growth, high levels of investment, employment, and state revenues abruptly gave way to serious joblessness and dependence on welfare. The average rate of growth of the economy fell from 7 percent in the 1950s, 1960s, and 1970s to less than 1 percent in 1974. A state commission established to investigate unemployment reported: "Since 1971, a general lack of new jobs has kept unemployment high in Hawaii. No annual unemployment rate has been less than 6 percent and the welfare rolls have continued to climb."[40] In mid-1976, with *official* unemployment rates at over 9 percent, more than 2,000 unemployed workers exhausted their benefits each month and the coffers of the State Unemployment Insurance Trust Fund emptied. The construction industry, Hawaii's third largest, had 29,000 on-site construction workers in 1974 and only 19,000 two years later.

The impact on the state treasury was severe. As a government report stated, "Hawaii's cost of $78.2 million for regular and special unemployment insurance benefits in calendar year 1975 was twice the combined total for 1971."[41] Welfare costs were also spiraling: by 1976, the economic crisis had resulted in an annual state welfare bill of $190 million and a caseload of 122,064—15 percent of Hawaii's population. The state's sources of revenue were undermined as tens of millions of dollars of expected tax monies failed to materialize. This in turn intensified an already existing fiscal crisis whose origins lay in the continuing usurpation of state revenues by the tourism–land development interests, and in the state's massive borrowing—by 1976, the state of Hawaii had an indebtedness in financing capital improvements of $900 million, and debt service costs had increased from $35 million a year in 1971 to $92 million in 1976.[42] By 1982 Hawaii ranked seventh in the nation in per capita debt.[43]

Yet massive borrowing *had* to continue ($275 million, for instance, during the 1975-76 fiscal year) for not only did the massive CIP budget erect the infrastructure necessary to keeping Hawaii "attractive" to overseas investors in the tourism–land development sector, but it also guaranteed continued accumulation of capital for the construction trade bourgeoisie (contractors, architectural and engineering firms, etc.) close to the Burns-Ariyoshi machine and employment for many potentially volatile construction workers who would otherwise have been on the public rolls. Indeed, when State Budget and Finance Director (now Mayor of Honolulu) Eileen Anderson defended huge state borrowings in 1977 with the statement that "To take any other course would be disastrous. We must continue to help the construction industry," she was merely admitting the limited options available to the state.[44]

All evidence indicates that this pattern will only intensify, for the massive multinational corporate enclave resort complexes now being planned from Princeville, Kauai, to the Big Island's Anaehoomalu Bay demand even greater infrastructural services than did the more concentrated Waikiki area. Moreover, it has become increasingly difficult to attract resort financing from overseas. As *Hawaii Business* noted in 1977, "Hotels have not been a particularly attractive investment for developers, with better returns possible in other forms of investment. Financing will likely continue to be the biggest deterrent to an expanding visitor industry in the years ahead."[45] This places Hawaii in the position of having to compete for investment funds against tourism centers in the Caribbean, Mexico, and the Pacific, and gives the outside investor tremendous leverage in pressuring the state to socialize a wide range of costs that would otherwise cut private profit margins.

This expanded role for the state does not make the politicians and bureaucrats who command the top rungs of Hawaii's political structure uncomfortable. For instance, Richard Wakatsuki, Democratic leader in the House, noted in 1977 that "a healthy and viable tourism industry is a must for the survival of our economy," and argued for a new state commitment to underwriting the accumulation of capital: "We must become . . . a provider of cheaper money to our major employers who wish to extend their operations through investments in capital goods and facilities, thereby creating jobs."[46] Meanwhile, State Senator Francis Wong, hotel owner, member of a dozen *huis*, and chairman of the Senate Committee on Economic Development, was introducing bills to grant tax incentives, the use of state lands, and waivers of environmental standards to new investors. "We must find new ways to attract new equity and mortgage capital to Hawaii," he said. "We must eliminate government red tape and make Hawaii more attractive for investment capital."[47] Clearly, Wong and Wakatsuki represent a significant segment of the land speculators, developers, real estate brokers, attorneys, construction interests, Big Five and estate development subsidiaries, insurance agents, and so on, who control Hawaii's politics and are prepared to place the state and county treasuries even more completely at the disposal of international capital. Not only the state's interests but their own personal interests depend upon an infinite expansion of tourism–land development in Hawaii.

The appropriation of state revenues by international and local capital requires that the state maintain exceptionally high taxes and reduce social welfare programs.[48] Unlike in the 1960s, when state resources could accommodate both needs, it has since been impossible to continue to do so. Thus in the 1970s and 1980s Hawaii's elites have been relentless in their demands for a "ceiling" on state spending. John Bellinger, president of the First Hawaiian Bank, is one of those most attuned to using terminology like "fiscal responsibility" as a cover for governmental attacks on the working class:

"One of our overriding concerns will have to be fiscal responsibility. To be sure, fiscal responsibility is always an imperative, but it's more urgent now in 1977 when the boom economy that came with statehood is no longer with us. . . . The conflict between the demand for services and the availability of funds is a critical situation for the government."[49]

In practice, this has entailed a direct assault on the living standards of the poor. In 1974 Ariyoshi called the state legislature into special session for the pupose of enacting legislation forcing general assistance welfare recipients to work for a part of their check. By 1976, 2,976 recipients found themselves working in parks, schools, and other state facilities with none of the monetary or fringe benefits of unionized state workers doing the same jobs, and without any job security.[50] The state also enacted a partial flat grant law, which immediately reduced welfare payments to two-thirds of the state's recipients, and laws denying unemployment compensation to workers who had either quit or been fired from their jobs. Even the University of Hawaii, that once sacred cow, was held to a "no-growth" budget: by 1976, Hawaii ranked forty-sixth among fifty states in terms of the percentage of general state revenues allotted to higher education.

Ariyoshi also had to confront the fruits of a generation of large-scale evictions that had made land available to the tourism–land development interests but had evoked strong resistance from small farmers and urban dwellers alike and had left tremendous bitterness in their wake. From the time in April 1971 when a group of young people occupied Oahu's Kalama Valley in support of farmers and workers being evicted by Bishop Estate, to the huge protests against the TH-3 highway, designed to fully open Winward Oahu to land development, to the massive defiance against court eviction orders by residents of the Waiahole and Waikane valleys, resistance to corporate expropriation of living places has increased. As a Waimanalo resident who was being evicted from her home said, "Our community is fed up, not only with the state's disregard of our lifestyle and community, not only with its not providing us with good alternatives, but also with its unresponsiveness to our questions and demands. . . . This island is just drowning in hi-rises and yet we have a housing crisis. Yet our own government is kicking us out of our homes. . . . And our representatives who should be fighting for us are apparently too busy to care."[51] The late George Helm, one of the leaders of a group struggling to reclaim Kahoolawe Island from the U.S. Navy, spoke for many when he remarked, "People call me radical, okay, so I say call me radical but I refuse to sit on my *okole*, remaining idle while these politicians make whores out of my culture for the sake of the bucks. And it's about time we get down and say wait now."[52]

Living in a new and much more alarming era, the Ariyoshi administration could no longer indulge the illusions that had been so carefully nurtured during the Quinn-Burns period. A generation of massive state intervention had not only failed to resolve the essential contradictions of a dependent economy—unemployment, housing, and so on—but had in fact increased and intensified them. It was clear that, far from evolving into the "hub of the Pacific," Hawaii was simply an escape mecca for millions of North Americans and Japanese.

Faced with rising antagonism at the grassroots against tourism and land development, the Democratic Party leadership sought to solve these problems by finding a *rhetoric* appropriate to the situation. This first became apparent during the 1974 election campaign (Ariyoshi had barely won the nomination—he received only 36 percent of the primary vote against two "anti-machine" candidates), when issues like "selective growth" and the need to regain "control" over Hawaii's economy were repeated in the governor's speeches. "Our economy is very fragile," he said. "We have very little control over those federal and tourism dollars. Consequently, we feel the need to create an economy over which we will have a greater degree of control."[53] A related theme was the identification of in-migrants as the source of social problems and a threat to the well-being of the society: "The problem of excessive population seems to be central to nearly every problem in our state; too many people means too few jobs and too much competition for them; too many people means too little land for agriculture and parks and scenic vistas."[54] All this of course allowed the governor to disclaim responsibility for the crisis. Ariyoshi also spoke of the "financial crunch" and "heartbreakingly high unemployment" in his 1977 State of the State speech: "There is no reason why we must endure what . . . an unregulated future holds for us. We must shape our future, not have it thrust upon us by forces over which we have little or no control."[55]

Despite the rhetoric, the policies pursued by the Ariyoshi administration have been almost identical to those of the Quinn-Burns era. The state has continued to provide heavy political and financial support for a tourism infrastructure (including the $80 million reef runway at Honolulu airport and the $35 million Hilo airport), and has supported the construction of the TH-3 highway and the efforts of developers such as Joe Pao to conduct large-scale evictions in rural areas. In short, state policies have only served to reinforce the "lack of control" the governor promised to fight; the gap between rhetoric and reality has become a chasm. While Ariyoshi was proclaiming that "We can't depend on the growth of the visitor industry. We must have diversification,"[56] his lieutenant governor was assuring Big Island tourism interests: "I've talked with the governor and he agrees that tourist-related projects should have first priority. More importantly, perhaps, he has indicated also that he will move to release the appropriate funds at the earliest possible date if they are tourist oriented."[57]

Yet despite his clear failure to provide leadership or programs of any value, Ariyoshi was reelected in 1978 and again in 1982. The basis of these successes was the clever manipulation of huge campaign contributions ($1.6 million in 1978 and $2.1 million in 1982) that were used to build him a positive public image, the ethnic loyalties of Japanese voters, and low taxes on the upper middle class. Moreover, his opponents—inevitably Frank Fasi and D. G. Anderson) were themselves shadow imitations of Ariyoshi, utterly lacking in any viable alternative program. Politics in Hawaii, as shown by the 1982 election, had degenerated to the point where the most critical issues of the time were ignored. It was a politics of irrelevance.

One can evaluate the historic role of the political elites that have governed Hawaii for the last generation on the basis of their own platforms and promises. The 1952 Democratic Party stated that "it is essential to a healthy island economy to have fee simple ownership of house-sites and small farms" and pledged "to enact laws which will make land available for purchase in fee simple for home construction and for small farming and ranching."[58] Given the immense concentration of land under the control of the Big Five and the estates, the implementation of this program would have required far-reaching land reform and land redistribution policies. This was never done, and land concentration during the last twenty years has actually *increased.* As a consequence, Hawaii still has by far the lowest percentage of homeowners of any state in the union and a noticeable scarcity of small farms and ranches. Indeed, one must travel to the Philippines, Guatemala, or another such underdeveloped country to find a landholding situation similar to that of Hawaii—where C. Brewer (249,000 acres), the Parker Ranch (262,000 acres), Castle and Cooke (145,000 acres), Amfac (65,000 acres), and a handful of other corporations, estates, and ranches monopolize nearly all privately held land. The Bishop Estate, presided over by a mixture of Big Five and land development corporate executives (and sometimes called "Hawaii's second government"), owns more than 17 percent of the privately owned land in the Islands.

The significance of all this should be obvious by now: control over the land has given the old *kamaaina* corporations and the new mainland investors tremendous power to define the contours of contemporary Hawaiian life. On a group of islands where the seven largest landholders control 30 percent of the total land (over 1 million acres), they can readily manipulate the developmental process in their own interests, particularly when these same landholders are closely linked with powerful financial and land development corporations inside and outside Hawaii.

So it is the relationships between the local landed estates and overseas capital, rather than "planning" on the part of state and city governments, that is key. The State Department of Planning and Economic Development may emphasize that "adequate planning is necessary to protecting and managing Hawaii's scarce environmental resources. . . . It should be able to allocate scarce resources according to society's goals,"[59] but the department's own economist, Richard Joun, acknowledges, "If money is to be made, they'll put these hotels up anywhere. The important economic decisions are made in the boardrooms of the Big Five and then transmitted along proper channels."[60] The *Pacific Business News* adds that "investment decisions determine the shape of things far more than planning decisions."[61] Ultimately, the failure to dismantle the enormous oligarchical land baronies has meant doom for economic or political democracy.

Tax equity was the other keystone of the Democratic Party reform program. The 1954 platform pledged to "thoroughly revise Hawaii's antique tax laws . . . and to shift the tax burden from those least able to pay to those who are most able to pay."[62] In a study done some twenty years later, two University of Hawaii economists concluded that the poor in the Islands carried the heaviest percentage of the tax burden: individuals with an adjusted gross income of less than $3,000 were paying an average of 15.85 percent of their incomes, while those in the over-$25,000 per year category were paying 11.26 percent. Moreover, regressive sales taxes accounted for $175 million in state revenues in 1970, as compared to $112 million taken in through personal income taxes.[63] A political elite, now comfortably ensconced in the bourgeoisie and laying claim to substantial incomes, was refusing to enact tax legislation that would affect their class adversely.

The 1952 Democratic platform also committed the party to "encourage the overall economic development of these Islands through intelligent and comprehensive economic research and planning."[64] However, given the investment orientation of local and overseas capital and the personal drive of the political elite to participate in the boom, the project of constructing a multifaceted, diversified economy floundered and then ground to a halt. Hawaii neither became the "trade center of the Pacific hemisphere" nor experienced the "major breakthrough in manufacturing" predicted by banker James Shoemaker.[65] By 1978 employment in diversified manufacturing accounted for only 6.5 percent of the state's workforce, while the great bulk of new jobs was concentrated in service-related sectors (i.e., tourism).[66]

Democratic Party platforms in the late 1940s and early 1950s had promised to use the state sector to bring about full employment, and John Burns had stated in 1966 that his administration would "assure a job for every citizen who is willing and able to work."[67] Yet the reality is that between 1947 and 1974, the workforce in Hawaii doubled while the number of unemployed *quadrupled*.[68] And the years since 1974 have seen substantially higher levels of unemployment.

There is a dialectic here. The integration of the old political elite into the land-development bourgeoisie during the 1950s and 1960s was a direct result of the role accorded Hawaii within the Pacific division of labor. Moreover, the consolidation of the elite not only guaranteed that Hawaii would remain within the confines of the role prescribed for it, as a tourism–land development economy dependent upon advanced capital centers, but also that this role would be constantly broadened and deepened. The political elite, now a privileged class, could not represent both the popular classes *and* the interests of local and transnational capital, and it inevitably adopted policies that turned the government apparatus into an instrument of capital accumulation by the international bourgeoisie. The politics of complicity and self-enrichment have directly intensified Hawaii's historic dependency.

A fitting epitaph to the "revolutionaries of '55" was unwittingly supplied by long-time Democratic Party functionary (and assistant to Burns and Ariyoshi) Dan Aoki. In 1976, when confronted by irate Waiahole-Waikane residents demanding to know why a Democratic politician had been able to purchase land in their valleys while they were being evicted, Aoki replied, "In our fine society, everything and anything is for sale if the price is right." Whereupon one resident exclaimed, "You're not a right-hand man, you're a horse's ass."[69]

11

A Tourism Society

As as the years go by tourism will continue to grow stronger and
stronger, providing ever greater benefits for those of us who live in
the Islands.
— James Morita, president of the
Hawaii Visitors' Bureau (1964)

Life today is sickening; youths go to school and learn what the *haoles*
did and what the *haoles* taught the Hawaiians. People read the papers
and read who built this, and who broke that, to build something called
"Progress." . . . Nowadays, it's the tourists who are important.
— Sixteen-year-old Hawaiian girl (1972)

Hawaii, like dozens of other island and coastal places in the Caribbean, the Indian Ocean, and the Mediterranean, is a society economically dependent on tourism. Now, a generation after these
tourism societies began to appear, we can see how they share a
common fabric of dependency and underdevelopment. Their relationship to the metropole, from whence the tourists come, is key
here. Through their apparatus of airlines, banks, travel agencies,
tour wholesalers, international financial institutions, and so on, the
tourist-generating regions in the advanced capitalist world organize the tourism industry: they dominate the financing and construction of the tourism plant, market and promote the tourism
product, deliver the clientele to their resort niches, escort them
around their destination, and return them to the metropole.
Further, not only do the countries receiving droves of tourists lack
control over the principle institutions and agencies of the tourism
industry, but the internal linkages necessary to make tourism an
instrument of local development are equally absent. Indeed, in the
face of vertically integrated multinational corporate tourism, the
only role available to the tourist-receiving nations is to provide
land, cheap labor, and governmental subsidies to the tourism de-

velopers from the metropole. As Herbert Hiller, former president of the Caribbean Tourism Association and author of a book on the effects of tourism, has put it, "If tourism is supposed to help development, then no one has told tourism about it."

As is the pattern elsewhere, overseas ownership and control of Hawaii's tourism industry has intensified during the past two decades. The immense profitability of the hotel sector in the 1945–60 period was the stimulus for this takeover. Occupancy rates in Waikiki between 1946 and 1954 averaged a most respectable 83 percent, and between 1955 and 1960 averaged 75–80 percent.[1] This placed Hawaiian hotels among the most profitable in the U.S. industry. What made investments in the Hawaii hotel plant even more attractive was the fact that the highest occupancy rates were usually recorded in the largest, most modern and luxurious hotels—exactly the kind that the big outside investor intended to develop.

The emerging postwar giants of international tourism rushed in to fill the "vacuum." First came Sheraton, which purchased a string of hotels from Matson Navigation. Sheraton's president noted, "I don't know whether it will be a Hawaiian corporation, or California or Delaware. It's up to the lawyers to figure out what is most advantageous."[2] Hilton, Hyatt, Inter-Continental, Holiday Inns, Western International, and Ramada Inns followed soon after. Vertically linked national and multinational corporations came to dominate the industry, making it increasingly difficult for independent local establishments to compete, and by 1975 the hotel chains controlled 75 percent of the larger (over 100-room) hotels in the Islands and 60 percent of the entire room plant. Hotels also steadily increased in size: average room capacity in Waikiki was 28 in 1946 and 129 in 1976. Small locally owned guest establishments could not compete against such hotels as Pan American Airways' 600-room Maui Inter-Continental (whose general manager once remarked, "We market through Honolulu and mainland sales offices, as well as in-house at our other hotels, especially in Australia, New Zealand, and Japan.)"[3]

In 1971, a group of Hawaii-born students on the mainland voiced their apprehension about overseas economic control in the Islands. They saw tourism, logically enough, as the trojan horse within the gates: "The resort development industry is the grossest example of mainland economic encroachment. If the present trend continues, most of the major hotels and resort areas will be under mainland control."[4] By the end of the decade, their fears were realized. A 1981 survey of the major hotel operators in Hawaii revealed that at least six of the Islands' top ten hotel operators were overseas based;[5] one of the remaining four is a subsidiary of a predominantly mainland-owned Big Five corporation, and all are dependent on overseas capital for financing.

This pattern has been accentuated by the enormous cost of building hotels—the president of the Hyatt Corporation has commented that "hotels are too expensive for mere mortals to build"—and the reluctance of major financial institutions to invest money with any but the largest and best known hotel operators and developers, i.e., Rock Resorts, Hyatt, Hilton, Holiday Inns, etc.[6] Lacking the resources to construct and manage modern resort complexes, the principle corporations and banks in Hawaii turned to agreements and "partnerships" with major overseas interests. According to one government report:

> Even Alexander and Baldwin viewed Wailea as too massive a project to undertake themselves and thus entered into a development partnership with Northwestern Mutual Life Insurance Company.
>
> The unavailability of financing precludes all but the most substantial and venturesome of developers from participating in resort development projects. The equity required in the beginning of resort development and the futuristic nature of returns cause this to occur.[7]

Overhead costs are also enormous, and new hotels must be of truly monumental size and feature a wide range of shops and restaurants to generate adequate returns. Built during the early 1970s, the 1800-room Sheraton Waikiki cost $45 million and was financed by a Bank of Hawaii-organized consortium. More recently, the 10-story Biltmore (a giant in the 1950s) was dynamited to make way for a $67-million Hyatt Regency, with 1260 rooms on twin 40-story towers, 5 restaurants, 5 cocktail lounges, and 70 shops. Financing for the Hyatt was also secured by the Bank of Hawaii, which organized a consortium consisting of some of the largest financial institutions in the United States, including Bank of America and the Wells Fargo Bank. The fact that the Hyatt chain operates fifty-one hotels around the world and is controlled by the powerful Pritzker family of Chicago (steel, manufacturing, lumber, real estate, and magazines) was decisive in securing financing. Opening on Maui in the early 1980s were an $80 million Hyatt and $60 million Marriott.

As the recent development of Maui indicates, the trend is away from a historic concentration on Waikiki and toward developing "destination resorts," a combination of hotels, which provide the initial attraction for affluent visitors, and land development schemes, where people are persuaded to purchase condominium units, townhouses, and single family homes in areas adjacent to the resort. Rather than the hotel being the centerpiece, it is used by the developer as a draw for the really lucrative business in land and housing units. Indeed, when one destination resort developer, Consolidated Oil and Gas Company of Colorado, committed the cardinal error of building residential housing at its Princeville, Kauai, complex in advance of the hotel, land sales stagnated. Once the hotel opened, the market for Princeville's townhouses immediately improved.

By the late 1970s there were eleven major destination resort schemes in the planning or construction stages, valued at over $2 billion and including 18,000 hotel rooms and 33,000 residential units—tourism on a monumental scale. Amfac was ushering in Hyatt, Sheraton, and Marriott to build a complex with 7,000 rooms, 1,800 condominium units, 200 single-family units, and 100 shops at Kaanapali, Maui. Over on the Big Island, Boise Cascade's 32,000 acres were planned for 3,000 hotel rooms and almost 11,000 residential units. Not far away, Signal Oil was busily constructing a "leisure community" of 2,400 hotel units and 800 "ranchettes" on 8,000 acres. At Wailea, Maui, Alexander and Baldwin and the Northwestern Mutual Life Insurance Company were transforming a 1,500-acre parcel of great natural beauty along the coast where Inter-Continental and Western International had already opened hotels into another huge resort-residential complex, and it was expected that the permanent residential population would eventually number well over 10,000. Wailea had the usual amenities offered by destination resorts: 5 beaches, 2 18-hole golf courses, tennis courts, and a shopping center. At Kapalua, also on Maui, a "leisure community" that includes a 196-room hotel, 2 golf courses, a tennis club, 3 beaches, restaurants, shops, and condominiums. Maui Land and Pineapple, Laurence Rockefeller, and the Bank of America are the principle interests involved. Louisiana Land's Kaluakoi development, on land purchased from Molokai Ranch, is huge by any standards of resort development: 3,600 hotel units, 3,400 villa and cottage units, and 6,606 townhouse and house units.[8]

Land speculation periodically grips the destination resorts, driving land prices to levels far beyond the means of even well-off locals. Intense speculation pushed the price of Kaanapali Whaler one-bedroom condominium units up from $86,000 in 1975 to $534,000 four years later. At Kapalua Bay Villas, condominium apartments increased in price from $135,000 to $500,000 between 1976 and 1979. Between 1978 and 1980 oceanfront condominium units at Popiu, Kauai, doubled in price. Wailea, Maui, has become the most notorious destination resort for this sort of rampant speculation. In 1979, when Wailea units were being auctioned off to a host of overseas speculators, *Hawaii Business* described the frenzied scene thus: "Some [of the auction winners] never got as far as the table where they were to sign up and plunk down their deposits, but openly hawked their winning numbers to others in the audience whose names hadn't been drawn. One winner reportedly sold his chance to buy a choice unit for a cool $40,000."[9] The president of the Maui County Board of Realtors commented, "In certain ways, the condominium prices are incredible. There's a lot of cash coming into the Islands. This has an impact. For example, Wailea has drastically affected the prices of the residential project just above it." And a Kona realtor said: "Condominiums are running wild. It's like the Alaska Gold Rush. . . . Prices have escalated so fast it's impossible to keep track of the Kona market."

Such massive speculation (tied to high interest rates and building costs) has driven at least 95 percent of the locals out of the housing market. To quote *Hawaii Business*, "It has now become virtually impossible for most local residents to purchase a house." By 1981 the average single family residence was priced at $169,107, or *triple* the national average. On Oahu one-third of all families are paying over 35 percent of their income in rent; moderately-priced rental units are rare indeed. And embittered locals realize only too well that their housing needs take last priority. A National Institute of Health team studying "ethnic Hawaiians" found them "serious about their fight and struggle over the absorption of their land. They expressed a willingness to fight by any means necessary. There is most definitely a strong potential for violence."

The full implications of the destination resort type of tourist development need further study, but there is evidence enough to draw some conclusions. For one thing, the destination resort experience is overseas-dominated in the extreme. There is absolutely no place in the destination resort scheme for the small, low key, locally controlled hotel. From airline counter to hotel to rent-a-car, the tourism monopolies are in control. They package the tours and furnish the airplanes, accommodations, and ground transportation. The food the guests eat, the beds they sleep in, and the sports equipment they use do not originate in Hawaii, but are imported from the metropole—as are those who manage the hotels and restaurants. Hawaii provides only cheap labor to clean the rooms, kitchens, and gardens, to carry the bags, and to drive the tour buses; and the sea and sky and sun and land . . .

The destination resort literally engulfs the area where it is located. Thirty thousand residents are projected for Kaluakoi's Molokai project, on an island with five thousand inhabitants, and Castle and Cooke plans to triple Lanai's population. What choice do the local residents have but to become a service class at the beck and call of far more affluent outsiders with a different lifestyle? For one thing, local developmental alternatives are severely limited. As a Maui farmer angrily lectured state officials at a meeting on economic growth:

> Right now we're importing about three-quarters of our fruits and vegetables and the amount is increasing every year at a continual rate. The number of farms is steadily declining. The water rates on all the islands have gone up as much as 130 percent. The price of land has gone up to the point where people can't even afford to get land to farm. The water systems being developed here on Maui County right now are going to the resort areas. Nothing is being done in the agricultural areas of Maui.
>
> You talk about educating people as to the advantages of tourism, but there is no mention at all about educating people to the fact that tourism is a dead-end road and that's what you want us to pursue here on Maui.[10]

After studying the projected development of an enormous destination resort complex on the relatively (tourism) undeveloped island of Molokai, Life of the Land, a Honolulu environmental organization, warned of imminent disaster for the local residents. Their statement probably constitutes the most candid critique of the destination resort phenomenon ever made in Hawaii.

> Kaluakoi is a huge land speculation deal. Its purpose is to make millions of dollars from the sale of land. The name of the game is sale and resale. First Kaluakoi will build one hotel and one golf course. This will raise the value of the surrounding land. Then Kaluakoi will put up another hotel, another condominium and another. The profits will go to the Molokai Ranch and the Louisiana Land and Exploration Company.
>
> They are in Molokai just to make money by selling and developing the land. They don't know the people who live on Molokai and they don't care about them. They are only interested in making MONEY FROM SALE AND EXPLOITATION OF OUR LAND.
>
> Kaluakoi means airports, highways, gas stations, curio shops, neon lights, plastic leis, rising crime, broken homes. Kaluakoi means the end of Molokai's Hawaiian lifestyle. We have to begin to fight to protect this lifestyle.[11]

In a very real sense, it is the airlines that have created Hawaii as a tourism center. Without the powerful catalytic agents of aircraft technology, airline promotions, and special fare arrangements the expansion of the industry—from a clientele of 15,000 in 1946 to 4 million in 1979—would be inconceivable. In the late 1950s, when the airlines were desperately searching for destinations that would attract new passengers to fill their greatly expanded seating capacity, Hawaii loomed as one of the brightest potential stars. But airlines executives expressed displeasure at what they viewed as the lack of accommodation. As one Pan Am vice-president commented, "Our major problem is that we'll have seats available this summer and next that we can't sell because there aren't enough beds."[12] Another told Island business and political leaders, "You must have more facilities to accommodate tourists and you ought to get working on them now."[13]

When hotel construction escalated in the early 1960s, the airlines used a variety of strategems to induce travel to Hawaii. In 1960 Pan Am launched its "through plan" discounts to the "Neighbor Islands." Then came the "thrift flights," tremendously popular among West Coast residents, who could travel to Hawaii for only $100; United and Northwest also offered a series of group discounts.[14] As business boomed, the airlines expanded their operations, and by 1963 Pan Am alone was offering 10,000 seats a week to Hawaii.

Control over air routes to Hawaii became an intensely political issue. The Big Five had tried to monopolize the route in the 1930s, but lacked the necessary political muscle. Pan Am, however, succeeded in monopolizing air service from the late 1930s until shortly after World War II. An oligopoly of three companies then exercised dominion until the late 1960s, when a number of other airlines had sufficient political power at the highest levels of national decision making (Presidents Johnson and Nixon intervened personally) to grab a piece of the action. The intensity of the struggle tells us how lucrative the Hawaiian market was perceived to be—it has been referred to by one authority as "perhaps the most bitterly fought and protracted in the history of the Civil Aeronautics Board."[15]

The most powerful airline in Hawaii today is United Airlines, which owns some of the Islands' most luxurious hotels and delivers one out of every two passengers to what it refers to as "Our Little Corner of the World." Moreover, as the largest continental airline with a Hawaiian route, United operates a huge feeder system into Hawaii from 112 cities in 34 states.[17] In 1976, the Hawaii route furnished 10 percent of the airline's volume and 13 percent of its profits.[18] So crucial is the Hawaiian route for the biggest airline in the United States that when United lost money in 1972, the loss was attributed to "Hawaiian red ink." The impact of the spring 1979 machinists' strike, which grounded United in Hawaii (and elsewhere), provides some insight into the sort of power United wields. The strike had severe repercussions on the entire Island economy. As the *Honolulu Star-Bulletin* noted, "The current machinist's strike against United Airlines has by itself come close to causing a minor recession here."[19] Throughout the islands, hotel occupancies fell—the Kapalua Bay Hotel dived from 100% occupancy to 40%—while tour companies operated at a fraction of capacity and layoffs were common.

The intensified competition among airlines gave rise to a structural dilemma that faced all the airlines with Island routes. At a time when income per seat was falling (Continental was offering $85 flights between Hawaii and the West Coast), aircraft with huge capacities (over 350 seats in the 747s) were going on the market and the airlines were confronted with increasing overhead costs. Volume had never been more essential. Edward Barnett, former dean of the University of Hawaii Travel Industry Management School, explained the dilemma with sledgehammer logic:

> When Pan American Airways buys 747s at over $20 million apiece [$60 million by 1980], that is capital investment that requires that others or even their own Inter-Continental Hotels must build multi-million dollar hotels to have sufficient pukas [slots] into which they can place the delivered bodies. Multiply this by all the major airlines and we are talking about a lot of capital. . . . To make this pay off, to lower unit fixed costs of handling one individual on an individualistic basis, there must be VOLUME. We are leaving the CLASS MARKET for the CLASS MASS MARKET.[20]

The primary response on the airlines' part was vertical integration into Hawaiian tourism and intensification of promotionals. As the chairman of a United Airlines' subsidiary, Western International Hotels, explained in 1971, "For United Airlines, Hawaii is terribly important. So we are spending more money than ever to promote the Islands. The airlines are promoting the dickens out of your state."[21] And indeed, United spent $12 million in 1981 alone promoting Hawaii. By 1968 Pan Am was introducing a sophisticated electronics system connected to all the major hotels. With one phone call, the prospective traveler in Los Angeles or Sydney could obtain air reservations, ground transportation, sightseeing tours, and hotel accommodations.[22] Hotel integration followed close behind. Both Pan Am's Inter-Continental (sold in 1981) and United Airlines' Western International became heavyweights in the Hawaiian hotel industry. TWA bought the Kahala Hilton, Continental Air and Hyatt teamed up at the Waikiki Gateway, and American Airlines and Dillingham did the same for the Ala Moana. Regarding Hawaii as one of their largest potential markets, airline executives were determined to maintain and extend their operations there. An American Airlines vice-president commented, "We will move ahead energetically with a strong and continuing program to attract mainland tourists to Honolulu and San Francisco.

We will not be satisfied with simply competing for existing traffic."[23]

The airlines also launched furious multi-media campaigns to lure tourists to Hawaii, relying on their intimate associates, the travel agents and tour operators, to achieve adequate volume on their routes. Metropolitan-based travel agencies and tour organizations have thus become increasingly vital to the functioning of Island tourism. As early as 1957 the Governor's Advisory Committee on the Tourist Industry noted that "because of the increased volume of package tours to Hawaii, mainland tour agencies are achieving an increasing influence on the pattern of tourist travel and expenditure in Hawaii."[24] When the airlines adopted a policy of making commissions on package tours to Hawaii lucrative enough to provide travel agents with a real incentive to sell them, Island tourism boomed. By 1967, 27 percent of Hawaii's tourists were arriving on package tours, and by the mid-1970s many hotels were utterly dependent upon tour groups for financial solvency. Well over one-half of the clientele in many Waikiki hotels consists of the package tour crowd, especially during the summer. In addition, the airlines systematically import travel agents from the United States and Japan in an effort to encourage their selling of the Islands. As an example, in 1970 United and Quantas brought in two thousand U.S. travel agents to promote Hawaii as a gateway for package tours of the South Pacific; four years later nine hundred were taken to Maui for a "Maui Showcase" promotion.

The airlines are thus the most powerful single force in Hawaiian tourism today. They have the power to make or break the industry. They deliver over 99 percent of the tourists, they own or are linked with some of the largest and most profitable hotels and destination resort areas, and they dominate the promotional activities. United was instrumental in creating the Hawaii Island Visitors' Information Association (HIVIA), a publicly financed vehicle whose key positions were filled by United officials and whose funds are used to conduct joint promotions.[25] Fujio Matsuda, former director of the State Department of Transportation and the current president of the University of Hawaii, has been a director of United since 1975.

Above all else, the airlines are located in the metropole and subject to direction from their owners and directors. They regard Hawaii purely and simply as a profitable tourism destination, and they will be content if it remains a tourism society for the indefinite future. As a top company executive remarked in 1976, "Nobody cares whether Waikiki is a concrete jungle. They come here for the beaches, the scenery, the flowers, the great year-round weather, sightseeing, dining, and entertainment."[26]

Most tourism investment in Hawaii is from the United States, but there is also a considerable amount from non-U.S. sources, and its extent—as well as Hawaii's inability to control or stop it—is a powerful component of tourism dependency. The presence of over $3 billion in foreign capital, almost completely concentrated in the tourism–land development sector, is another way in which local participation in Hawaii's key economic sectors is denied and linkages between tourism and the rest of the Islands' economy limited.

Although there is substantial Hong Kong, Australian, and Canadian capital investment, it is the two hundred and fifty Japanese companies controlling two-thirds of all foreign assets that dominate. Japanese penetration of Hawaii has occurred within the framework of Japanese expansion throughout the Pacific Rim. In each area, it has been in those sectors of the economy deemed most profitable, and in Hawaii this has of course meant tourism–land development.

It was in the early 1970s that a number of factors coalesced to spur Japanese interest in the Hawaiian Islands, including a sharp increase in the disposable income of many Japanese and a taste for spending some of it on foreign travel. At the same time, liberalization of currency restrictions and the devaluation of the dollar vis-à-vis the yen made traveling abroad both easier and cheaper. By 1971 over 1.3 million Japanese were taking their vacations overseas,[27] and Hawaii quickly became one of their favorite destinations—120,000 arrived in 1970, 235,000 in 1972, and 455,000 in 1975.[28]

The Japanese tourism corporations were determined to monopolize this potentially lucrative trade. Since the tourism industry in Japan is controlled by a handful of powerful corporations closely tied to some of the largest Japanese industrial and banking firms, they simply transferred their vertically integrated system to Hawaii, starting in the early 1960s but increasing sharply in the early 1970s—to the point where by the 1980s they controlled a score of hotels and more than 15 percent of the industry's rooms.[29]

Kokusai Kogyo, the most prominent Japanese investor in the Islands, is a gigantic travel conglomerate, with 2,300 buses and 1,300 cabs under its control, in addition to hotels, golf courses, automobile interests, and airlines. Its dominant figure is Kenji Osano, known in Japan as the "King," a notorious power broker in Japanese ruling-class politics, patron of former Prime Minister Tanaka and the most prominent figure convicted in the Lockheed payoff scandals, largest civilian stockholder in Japan Airlines, and a major investor in Korea, the United States, and Southeast Asia.[30] Through Kokusai Kogyo, Osano has also become a major economic power in Hawaii (and was rather appropriately given the keys to the city by the mayor of Honolulu after his first large-scale investment). Osano purchased the Sheraton Hawaii chain of hotels in 1964 for $105 million and eventually came to control about one-fifth (or 4,900) of the total hotel rooms in Waikiki, including 75 percent of the choice beachfront hotel properties, running from Diamond Head to Kuhio Beach.[31] Other hotels were purchased or built by such Japanese giants as Tokyu, Seibu, and Japan Airlines.

Ultimately the Japanese tourism operation in Hawaii achieved a degree of vertical integration unrivalled even by U.S. capital. Indeed, it has become so well integrated that when one speaks of "leakages" it is in reference not to leakages from the host area, Hawaii, as is customary, but rather to leakages from the *Japanese* economy. The vast majority of Japanese tourists (81 percent in 1971) come to Hawaii on prepaid package tours of four-to-six or six-to-eight days, arrive and depart via Japan Airlines, stay in Japanese-owned hotels, and tour Hawaii with Kintetsu International, a Japanese tour operator. A fair proportion of retail trade is carried on in Japanese-owned department stores.[32] For the new monied class of Japanese corporate executives, there is a range of luxury amenities, including half-a-dozen Japanese-owned golf courses, the most luxurious of which is the Honolulu International Country Club, "an exclusive club with plush facilities and an immaculately manicured 18-hole golf course," complete with thick English carpets and Italian stained glass ceilings. Memberships sell for $12,000 each.[33] And for those affluent enough to afford a "piece of the rock," Asahi Development Corporation offers its Waikiki condominium units on the Tokyo market for upward of a quarter of a million dollars each. The system even extends to the construction of hotels. When Kenji Osana decided to expand two of his hotels, he brought in a close corporate ally, the Ohbayashi Construction Company. Seibu, another Japanese conglomerate, plans to use one of its subsidiaries, the largest landscaping firm in Japan, to landscape its huge residential-resort complex at Makena, Maui, and plans to use another to build the hotel.[34] And investments in tourism are only the most obvious of the Japanese holdings, which include local banks, automobiles, and camera dealerships, the market for polyester fibers, and large retail and shopping centers.

Although there are some local supporters of the Japanese—including John Bellinger, whose First Hawaiian Bank has played a strong role in attracting Japanese capital—this is by no means the popular sentiment, judging by a number of polls showing that a large majority of local residents are against further Japanese investment. Rather than simply indicating narrow-minded national chauvinism or racism, this strong feeling reflects an understanding that Japanese tourism operations contribute only to the development of the Japanese economy and to the profits of Japanese corporations, along with a few local allies.

The twin foundations upon which the profitability of Hawaiian tourism rests are massive government subsidies and a labor structure that generally gives workers low wages, uncertain employment, and poor working conditions. Government subsidies, discussed earlier, were of course one of the key aspects of the "New Hawaii" economic model. Given Hawaii's relatively small population and slender resources, the extent of that support has been truly staggering. A 1972 state report provides some insight on the figures:

> Expenditures for visitor-related capital improvement projects from Fiscal Year 1960 through Fiscal Year 1970 totaled $167.8 million or 27% of all capital expenditures for the decade. Actual and proposed expenditures reveal a total public commitment of $560.8 million in projects which were initiated to support the visitor industry.[35]

Funding has gone for a wide range of infrastructural and related costs, and tourism interests have been given virtual *carte blanche* to tap the public treasury. At a time when tourism sites are inter-changeable and tourism investment capital is difficult to find, the tourism developer–financier holds all the aces: Hawaii can be played off against Mexico, where four thousand new hotel rooms are being built each year, or against Fiji, Tahiti, or a dozen other places. The president of Unitours, for instance, warned the Hon-olulu Chamber of Commerce that Hawaii compared unfavorably with Mexico in certain key areas. "Tourism," he said, "is not some-thing handed to you on a silver platter. The tourism industry is here to stay and it should be cultivated, nurtured, and allowed to grow." Not only have the Hawaiian taxpayers financed airports, sewerage systems, roads, harbors, the bulk of the costs of the Hawaii Visitors' Bureau, and multimillion dollar Waikiki "facelift-ing" projects, but they have also footed the bill at the university and community colleges for training thousands of future tourism in-dustry workers in everything from cooking to management.

And even this is no longer enough. Destination resort tourism demands increased government subsidies: located far from existing facilities and built on a monumental scale, destination re-sorts need the kinds of public services that even the Waikiki hotels never needed. Says Honolulu County planner Wilfred Chow:

> Residents have absorbed the cost of providing more public services and facilities for the use of visitors. Infrastructural costs are particu-larly high on the Neighbor Islands and on rural Oahu, where resort developments have been allowed and even encouraged to scatter by water, sewage and highway inputs and zoning decisions. Resort de-velopment in outlying areas results in higher public costs, but permits developers to acquire less expensive land. State and local taxes in Hawaii are among the highest in the nation.[36]

Other public resources go to tourism as well. On Molokai the state's decision to funnel up to 2 million gallons of water daily to the golf courses, hotels, and restaurants at Kaluakoi has effectively dimin-ished the potential for a diversified agriculture and food self-sufficiency.

If Hawaiian tourism is among the world's most profitable, it is largely because of the sacrifices of those who labor for its expatriate owners. Even in a relatively low-wage state like Hawaii (average wages in 1979 were 8.4 percent below the national average), hotel workers have consistently been among the lowest paid: in 1967 they had average weekly earnings of $73.58, the second lowest wage of any industry in the state (only workers in laundries, also a tourism-related industry, were paid less). A decade later their weekly wage had risen to an average of $137.38 (still the second lowest), but the gap between hotel workers and those in better paid industries was widening. Workers in communications and utilities earned an average of $311.28 in 1977 and those in manufacturing earned $209.38. A major factor is the limited number of hours hotel employees are given work: an average of 33.6 a week in 1966, which had decreased to 31.8 in 1977.[37] One-quarter of all tourism workers are part-timers, few by choice. For the hotel, the ability to cut down on the workers' hours, lay them off when convenient, and force them on to split shifts represents a major source of flexibility; for the worker, it means frustration and hardship.

In late 1977, a time when the cost of living for an urban family of four in Honolulu was 27 percent higher than in the mainland United States, the Hawaiian family needed $13,280 for a "lower family budget" and $20,883 for an "intermediate" budget.[38] The great majority of hotel workers were earning (including tips) substantially less than the lower budgetary figure. Even the businessman's journal, *Pacific Business News,* expressed some misgivings at tourism wage levels: "Either there is considerable tipping to augment these wages, or a great many workers are now at the poverty level, which makes us wonder if greatly increasing employment in tourism is the answer to Hawaii's needs."[39] Of course, this neatly ignores the fact that the low wages in the tourism industry have been a prime incentive for the movement of investment from plantation agriculture to tourism. In 1982, to cite some recent ILWU figures, office janitors and field hands in the sugar industry received $6.39 per hour, while hotel maids and kitchen workers received $4.93 and pool attendants $4.87; warehouse workers in the sugar sector got $7.72, while hotel cashiers got $5.62; and so on down the line.[40]

There are few in Hawaii who work in tourism of their own volition. A 1972 State Department of Planning and Economic Development study said as much: "In view of the low wages offered by the industry, it is doubtful whether young people who have a choice will be willing to remain on their home islands to work in hotels."[41] But wages are only one cause of such deep alienation.

Another is that tourism jobs are basically dead-end, since virtually all top management—and sometimes even middle management, especially in the hotel chains and airlines—are imported from the metropole. As a waiter in a Waikiki hotel remarked, "The trouble is you have to remain a coolie here. You can stay here and work for twenty years and receive maybe a few slight raises. There are no promotions for the people at the bottom of the hotel and hotel retail industries. The industry has its problems and one of its worst is the hierarchy." A third reason for alienation is the job pace at which the work must be done. A room maid at the Princess Kaiulani said, "We do fifteen rooms in six hours. That is hard. Your pace is so fast that you can't do the rooms properly."[42] Moreover, there is the humiliation of catering to people with whom one's only tie is the cash nexus. In the tourism industry, the old adage that the "client is always right" has been raised to the level of gospel. Dave Thompson, ILWU education director and a long-time trade unionist, voiced the hidden anger felt by workers demeaned by the role of servant: "There is an important dimension of self-image. The tourists want the black face to play at being dumb. It is very damaging for a person to have to play that role. How do we convince the local people that they are more sophisticated and humane than these red-neck tourists?"[43]

There is a deep fear among many in Hawaii today, a fear born of terrible despair, that they must labor in the hotels if they want to stay in the Islands. They know that during the past two decades tens of thousands of young people have left rather than work on the "new plantations." Even propaganda by the Visitors' Industry Education Council (run by the hotel industry) to the effect that tourism is beneficial to Hawaii's people and that tourism work is rewarding cannot, in the words of a hotel owner, "erase the impression that tourism jobs are demeaning."[44] A Hawaiian construction worker voiced the fear so many feel: "Brothers and sisters, people of Hawaii, is it not time to admit that our islands, our homes, our lives are being directed by powers we cannot control. What will happen when there is no longer any land to build upon? We will have to take jobs catering to tourists. We will carry their bags, make their beds, cook for them. What a sorry existence for a once proud people."[45]

It is extremely revealing that even during times of severe unemployment, hotel jobs in Hawaii remain unfilled. A worried Amfac vice-president complained that "West Maui is labor short. There are 50 to 200 job openings a day on Kaanapali. We may have to subsidize to get labor."[46] And a high state official admits, "It may be that some of the local people simply don't want jobs in tourism."[47] As a result, tourism developers have been going to places where the people have no choice but to work in tourism (or leave). When Chinn Ho was examining the feasibility of locating a large resort complex at Makaha, a journalist reported that "Ho puts the availability of help up at the top of the list. He considers the fact that the Leeward Oahu area is one of the highest unemployment areas as a real asset."[48] Further, most of the jobs being created in tourism today—57 percent according to one report[49]—are being filled by female workers, particularly in the menial and low-paying (housekeeping, food preparation, etc.) areas, because women are perceived as being more easily exploitable than men and because their low wages can be rationalized on the basis of their being so-called secondary wage earners. The industry is also anxious to employ as many foreigners as possible—immigrant Filipinos constitute one-half of the Waikiki workforce—since they too can be readily controlled and intimidated. In 1968 *Beacon Magazine* found a number of Filipina maids in a Waikiki hotel so enraged at their conditions that they were talking of murdering a supervisor. One of the maids explained her despair: "We cannot do anything but work because we have nothing left back there and we have very little here. We are treated like animals sometimes. Rush, rush, all the time. No time to breathe in. I cry because if I do not cry, then maybe I get mad and maybe say something and they fire me."[50]

Use of the term "new plantation" to describe the hotel and resort areas is validated by the strong cultural division of labor reminiscent of the plantation days—only now it is imported Caucasian hotel managers, Hawaiian entertainers and tour bus drivers, and Filipina maids. This is only part of the powerful cultural division of labor among ethnic groups displayed by Hawaiian society *in toto,* where the bureaucratic-professional middle class is dominated by Asians and Caucasians and the blue-collar working class is largely Hawaiian, Filipino, Samoan, immigrant Asian, and Pacific Islander. The following table gives the breakdown for the major ethnic groups in 1977.[51]

Ethnic Stock	Percent of population	Percent of group in professional and technical occupations	Percent of group in service occupations
Caucasian	27.5	20.9	12.8
Japanese	25.8	17.5	9.5
Filipino	10.7	6.3	22.2
Chinese	4.8	20.1	14.0
Hawaiian and part-Hawaiian	17.0	15.6	39.9

The workers in Hawaii's tourism industry are not eager hosts delighted to welcome guests into their place, to share with them some of the joys and sorrows of being human. They are proletarians tied by the cash nexus to the clientele they serve and the overseas corporations they work for. And their alienation, poor living conditions, and daily drudgery are at the source of the industry's profits. In view of all this, it is remarkable how friendly and helpful they remain in their human relationships on the job.

The fact that the taxpayers and workers of Hawaii underwrite an industry that repatriates huge sums of capital back to the metropole is one part of the story; the other is that the substantial financial and other resources drained from the public coffers preclude the opportunity to establish economic foundations other than tourism. Thus with each passing year, the uneven development of the Hawaiian economy becomes more pronounced. The following state figures reveal dramatically the extent to which Hawaii has become dependent on tourism.

Within the space of a decade, tourism changed from an industry providing somewhat more income than agricultural commodities (and substantially less than defense) to an industry almost five times that of agriculture and almost twice that of defense. And this pat-

Hawaii's Direct Income from Major Exports[52]
(in millions of dollars)

	Total	Sugar and molasses	Pineapple	Defense	Tourism
1967	1,255.0	180.3	133.3	561.4	380.0
1977	3,320.0	226.8	161.6	1,086.6	1,845.0

tern is intensifying: a state study estimates that "by 1985, as much as 49 percent of overseas income might be derived from visitor expenditures."[53] Tourism, conceived of by those who had formulated the "New Hawaii" model in the 1950s as an industry that would balance the Territory's overreliance on sugar, pineapples, and the military, has, on the contrary, come to dwarf the rest of the economy. Even *Hawaii Business* expressed some dismay at this trend in a 1978 article: "For what has helped to make tourism's ascent so conspicuous in the last three years is the alarmingly poor showing of such runner-up industries as sugar and construction. . . . The industry's preeminence is causing some well-justified nervousness."[54]

Overdependence upon tourism, a notoriously fragile and tenuous industry, means extreme vulnerability to any of the interlocking crises—monetary, stagflationary, shortages, etc.—that are undermining global capitalism. As a City and County of Honolulu study noted, "There is no industry standing in the wings ready to come on stage should the economy's leading star, the visitor industry, falter."[55] Controlled by metropolitan agencies and highly sensitive to economic tremors, Hawaiian tourism has consistently demonstrated its fundamental instability. A 1977 state study found that, "Since 1955, the annual percentage growth rate in the number of visitors to Hawaii fluctuated by 10 percent or more, a total of nine times. This uneven growth contributes to the boom/bust growth in construction and related activities."[56] During the 1970-72 recession, when many resorts were losing money and large numbers of hotel workers were laid off, unemployment levels rose to over 6 percent. The 1975-76 economic crisis was considerably worse: in early 1976, as hotel occupancy rates declined to under 60 percent, the "official" Big Island unemployment rate soared to over 12 percent.[57] "The Big Island's visitor industry is still looking for enough warm bodies to fill its many rooms with two, three, and more big hotels looming ahead," was the gloomy comment of *Hawaii Business*. With a huge backlog of 10,000 unsold condominium units and hotel building at a standstill, unemployment in construction, Hawaii's third largest industry, rose to 40 percent. The 29,000 on-site construction workers of 1974 had been reduced to 18,000 by 1976. Many workers exhausted their unemployment insurance benefits and were forced to seek work on the mainland.

A devastating combination of sharply higher air fares and reduced real income in the metropole brought on still another tourism debacle in the early 1980s. In 1980, occupancy fell by 7.9
percent and the number of arriving tourists declined for the first
time since Pearl Harbor. The next year, 1981, witnessed a further
decline. Hotel lobbies and restaurants were nearly empty; hundreds of workers were laid off. "Right now the future is totally
blind," said a veteran Waikiki hotelier. "It's crazy, totally crazy. . . .
This is the worst recession we've ever had." Only the "under-
ground" economy of the Big Island—based on marijuana—kept
hundreds of families solvent. Hilo's Banyan Drive hotel strip was so
empty that hotel rooms were being converted into offices. A Hyatt
executive noted, "I don't know how to create a market when one
doesn't exist."[58] The response to this was "Hawaii 1982," a $4 mil-
lion media blitz financed by the tourism corporations and the state,
coordinated by Sheraton, United Airlines, and Bank of Hawaii
executives, and aimed at the huge U.S. market. Hawaiian tourism
may experience some bouyant periods in the coming years, but the
cycles of boom and bust will occur more frequently and the troughs
will be ever deeper. Tourism as an industry can only decline as the
general crisis of capitalism escalates.

Rage and frustration are also sources of vulnerability for the
industry, and these have been growing apace. Resentment is nurtured by the loss of access to land, by the debasement of Polynesian
culture—now we see the culture of the "plastic lei." No one has
expressed the metropolitan attitude toward Hawaiian culture better than Continental Airlines President Stanley Kennedy during a
speech to a group of Pacific Islanders. Explaining how his airline
was promoting Hawaiian tourism in the United States and exhorting his audience to follow the Hawaiian model, he made this statement:

> The arts and crafts, foods and so forth of Hawaii not only are used in
> those kinds of promotions, but in major state fairs across our country,
> large tents are being set up that feature Hawaii exclusively.
>   You must develop some kind of a symbol. We talk about the symbol
> of Diamond Head, the symbol of the lei. . . . You have to have some
> kind of a monocle to hang your advertising and your promotions
> on.[59]

The basic contempt for, and commoditization of, Hawaiian culture implicit in these words is the attitude of the tourism industry in general. Local people understand it only too well.

There are a host of other ways in which local residents feel abused and threatened by tourism, from the endless lines of tour buses emitting fumes along the major highways of every island, to the usurpation by tourists of some of the finest beaches. Not surprisingly, then, the well-financed efforts of the Visitors' Industry Education Council and other propaganda arms of the tourism industry to maintain a "good public attitude" toward tourism (the so-called aloha spirit) have not stopped the change in the attitude of Hawaii's people from one of benevolent neutrality to one of resentment and rage. Speaking of the "warmth and friendliness" of people in tourism societies during a 1975 conference on tourism in California, Peter Sanborn, former project manager of Amfac's Kaanapali Resort, admitted, "I have seen those qualities eroding rapidly in Hawaii. . . . The Hawaiian people, too, are some of the friendliest people I have encountered. But I have seen a great change occur since 1965."[60] Herbert Hiller, former president of the Caribbean Travel Association and now a tourism consultant, observed the same process in the Caribbean and drew a general conclusion from this phenomenon: "As soon as tourism is around long enough to reveal itself, people begin to assault it. Tourism begins to collapse when people express rage."[61]

These expressions of rage assume two forms, both dangerous to the viability of the industry. The first response involves spontaneous individual or small group actions against the industry, including destruction of hotel property and the construction equipment on hotel sites, the innumerable robberies and assaults against tourists, the rock-throwing by teenagers at the tour busses along the Kalanianaole Highway, and the increasing surliness of tourism workers toward the clientele. The second response, organized political struggle, could be far more important in the long run. The first sizeable struggle over eviction from the land in recent Hawaiian history occurred in Oahu's Kalama Valley in 1971 when local farmers' and workers' homes and land were cleared to make way for an extensive subdivision-hotel complex. Since then, fights over rezoning and eviction have taken place on almost every island. Most of these struggles have been unsuccessful—ethnic divisions and poor leadership have divided the resisters, while the corporations and local politicians have been able to mobilize huge resources to counter the demonstrations. Nevertheless, there have been a number of striking victories by cohesively organized groups. For instance, in 1981, when Standard Oil of California sought to build a luxury condominium in previously resort-free east Molokai, a local group organized island-wide to block it. After months of petitions, marches, and public hearings that mobilized large numbers of people, a notoriously pro-development Maui County Land Board was forced to turn the developer's application down.

The common thread here is the awakening of an anti-developer, anti-tourism consciousness, a desire to reassert local control and local integrity among large numbers of people. This was apparent during the demonstrations against the construction of the TH-3 highway in the early 1970s and from the wide support later evoked by the struggle of residents living in Windward Oahu's Waiahole-Waikane valleys to save their homes and farms from subdivision development. When the mayor of Kauai, in defiance of a November 1980 referendum (of more than 2:1) against allowing a huge Japanese developer, Hasegawa Komuten, to construct a luxury resort at Nukolii, agreed to let construction continue, there were large-scale protests, followed by arrests on the construction site. In what has become a typical scene at public hearings on land-use questions, a carpenter at a State Growth meeting on Maui told state officials pointblank, "I'd rather be unemployed than work on the jobs that are destroying Hawaii. The type of development that you plan is destroying it."[62] There is a basis being laid for a new politics that repudiates the "New Hawaii" developmental model and seeks to mobilize its victims (and non-victims) for economic, political, and social change that will benefit all the people. A new constituency is gradually emerging for a break with Hawaii's role as a dependent tourism society.

Conclusion: 1983

It is necessary to create sober, patient men and women who do not lose hope before the worst horrors and who are not excited by rubbish.

Antonio Gramsci, *Prison Notebooks*

We have seen throughout the history of Hawaii a pattern associated with each new stage of economic activity in the Islands. Decision-making has been progressively removed from the people and invested in the metropole. During the earlier plantation era, when international capitalism was much weaker and less expansionist, the local elite monopolized local industries and kept a large proportion of Hawaii's export revenues inside the Islands. Even the sugar planters, dependent as they were upon mainland sugar quotas and prices, still exercised strong local authority in many key areas. This is now gone. The Big Five complex are nearly all metropole-owned, while the state and county governments function increasingly as agents of international capital. Every major economic enterprise in Hawaii, from the department stores to the hotels to the paper company to the utilities to the bakeries, is controlled by overseas capital. And, in a related phenomenon, as Hawaii passed from one economic base to another, and increasingly as it moved from plantation agriculture to tourism, local culture and local nuances were swept away; Hawaiians became integrated, as workers and consumers, into the North American colossus.

This leads us to conclude that the contemporary period is the age of almost complete dependency in Hawaii, and that tourism more than any other factor is at the root of this dependency. Jafar Jafari, who has made an extensive study of the effects of tourism across the world, notes that the value of tourism in enhancing the economic development of an area depends upon whether it can be "tamed": "The question is whether it can be controlled with

186

sufficient intelligence that the damaging influences are contained and the positive effects enhanced."[1] This book has been an extended attempt to demonstrate that this has not been possible in Hawaii, and to show that the consequences of that failure are momentous. Virtually every manifestation of dependent tourism that can be found in Jamaica, Puerto Rico, Guam, or Fiji can also be found in Hawaii. This includes overseas control, direction, and ownership of the industry's major sectors; the dominant role played by the metropolitan agencies in establishing and defining the tourism destination and the form that tourism takes; the low wages that maintain the industry's high profits; and the overdependence upon tourism which makes for uneven development and extreme vulnerability to changes in the economic climate. It also includes the social crisis caused by tourism's ravishing of the local culture, environment, and lifestyle, and by its disastrous effect on the availability of housing and land to the local people. Finally, there are the negative costs of an industry that receives huge government subsidies, monopolizes public resources, and excludes other options.

Evidence of the failure of the "New Hawaii" model is abundant. We need only turn to the state's own reports for confirmation. *The Hawaii State Plan,* a multi-volume document dealing with a wide range of socioeconomic concerns, was issued in 1977. It reads like a counsel of despair. And it no longer even bothers to pretend that Hawaii is an independent economy: "A major proportion of Hawaii's income and employment, especially that related to Hawaii's current primary industry—tourism—is heavily dependent on outside forces, and the state's inelastic demand for commodity exports, mainly foodstuffs, is also largely dependent on economic and political forces outside the state."[2]

The dominant thrust of the study is that Hawaii is helpless on all fronts. On tourism, for instance, the report states that "little or nothing can be done in Hawaii to prevent potentially adverse overseas events that might cause a decline in Hawaii's tourism."[3] On food production, it reports that "it is clear that Hawaii's economic self-sufficiency is low and very probably declining. Local agriculture is clearly declining in self-sufficiency since the growth in production has not kept pace with the growth in consumption."[4] (In fact, by 1981, 60 percent of the vegetables, 76 percent of the fruits, and 72 percent of the meat and poultry consumed by Islanders were imported—and this is an agricultural area. The state's paper commitment to building a diversified agriculture has been undermined by its policy of promoting massive resort development in rural areas while keeping funding for agriculture low. The export of flowers and papayas, rather than the production of food crops, has been given priority.) And on employment, the report acknowledges that Hawaii's tourism-based society cannot create sufficient jobs to employ the state's youth, and makes a recommendation that is more suitable to a Third World nation than a state of the United States: The state should "strongly encourage outmigration now while Hawaii's population of young adults and recent arrivals is still relatively mobile."[3]

Seldom has there been such a stark admission of official failure; seldom has a government document shown so strikingly the bankruptcy of its own development model. Clearly, the Hawaiian Islands of Sheraton, Marriott, United Airlines, Kenji Osano, and Prudential cannot, and are not, the Hawaii of its own people. Yet ultimately it is only the people of Hawaii who can break the long chain of dependent development, who can build a society in which decisions are made by local people, based on their contribution to the well being and integrity of the majority of the citizens. But to do this they must formulate a comprehensive political program and economic strategy, with enough vision and good sense to attract the support of the growing number of disenfranchised. They will need to present an alternative based on public control of a humanized tourism industry; a diversified and self-sufficient agriculture; the elimination of the huge U.S. military presence and stockpile of nuclear weapons on Oahu, and the conversion of thousands of acres of military-owned and controlled land to productive agricultural and commercial use; and the creation of a government that will serve the community and be based on values quite different from those we see now. And, not the least, they will need to build an organization capable of implementing such a program.

Epilogue:
The Harsh Nineties

The economy now is self-serving and out of control.
—Hayden Burgess, native Hawaiian leader (1992)

Tourism is our number one industry today, and we have to do whatever we can to accomodate it.
—Senator Mamoru Yamasaki (1992)

Exactly one decade has passed since *Hawaii: Islands Under the Influence* first appeared. A more tumultuous set of years could scarcely be imagined: empires thought invincible have disintegrated, the Cold War ended, western Europe moved toward (partial) reunification, economic and technological revolutions occurred, AIDS achieved pandemic proportions, widespread outbreaks of ethnic warfare began, and so much else.

But the Islands remain under the influence. So much, in fact, that the (once scorned) dependency thesis is now treated seriously in the most curious of places. In 1992, Hawaii's lieutenant-governor, Benjamin Cayetano, was disturbed enough by the book's theme to distribute copies to the state legislature. Recently, the editor of *Hawaii Business* was bemoaning "the degree to which we have become observers of our own economic destiny."[1] Then, a University of Hawaii business school professor complained of Hawaii's "one-export-commodity developing country model."[2] To appreciate this sudden "illumination," we should briefly consider the Islands' recent relationship with its two dominant centers: the United States and Japan.

Ronald Reagan came to office in 1981 with a pledge to restore U.S. global primacy and high levels of economic growth. The economic upturn of 1984 appeared to vindicate his "morning in America" rhetoric, and Reagan was reelected by a landslide. Economic growth rolled on month after consistent month, and in 1988 George Bush was elected president on the strength of this performance.

189

The expansion, however, was deeply flawed. Economic growth rates were lower than during the Carter years. Reaganist tax, spending, and regulatory and trade policies helped intensify swelling market inequalities between the wealthiest Americans and everyone else. The living standards of the lower 60 percent either stagnated or declined. Americans found it increasingly difficult to retain middle-class status in a restructured labor market dominated by low-wage, part-time, temporary, and contract job categories. Millions of respectably paid blue- and white-collar jobs were automated, exported, or simply terminated. Home ownership, the badge of middle-class respectability, declined, especially among the young.[3]

The expansion was also flawed by the nature of its financing. Reagan policymakers reduced taxes and poured $1.5 trillion (1981–86) into military budgets; the national debt tripled. Corporations and individuals took on unprecedented amounts of debt. The nation borrowed 3 percent of its gross national product from abroad to meet its consumption needs, thus mortgaging the future to the present. By the 1990s, federal debt payments alone were over $300 billion annually. In a significant range of critical industries and technologies, U.S. companies became increasingly uncompetitive with foreign rivals. The Reagan-Bush period, in retrospect, amounted to a grand evasion of a desperately needed restructuring of the nation's class hierarchy and value structures.[4]

Meanwhile, an effortlessly dynamic Japan, Inc. sustained its postwar trajectory of high productivity, savings, and economic growth. Japanese manufacturers seized greater market shares in automobiles, electronics, and semiconductors from U.S. firms, and Japanese corporations and banks primarily financed the gaping deficits; inevitably, they wound up owning a multitude of lucrative properties and productive assets in the United States, including Columbia Pictures, Rockefeller Center, and a considerable stash of treasury bonds.[5]

Both the artificial Reaganist prosperity and the swiftly rising Japanese sun converged on Hawaii to make the late 1980s a period of dynamic but brief economic growth. The optimism and increased affluence of the rich and upper middle classes in North America and the unabashed hedonism spawned by Reaganism and the media spiraled Hawaiian tourism (particularly the luxury variety) upward.

Driven by favorable federal tax laws and heady prospects for profits in Hawaii's economy, construction of hotels and office buildings escalated rapidly. Westward-gazing California capitalists were deeply involved: a prime example was Los Angeles corporate raider David Murdock, who gained control over Castle and Cooke and proceeded to obsessively transform the pineapple island of Lanai into a luxury hotel/condominium complex.[6]

This coincided with a Japanese tourism explosion generated by prosperity and government encouragement to travel abroad. Tourists from Japan soon constituted one-quarter of all visitors arriving in Hawaii. Many Japanese companies, attracted by this ready-made clientele and the possibilities of phenomenal growth, began buying up prime resort properties and developing spanking new ones. Financing was a key incentive. The startling strength of the yen versus the dollar and the huge cash resources of Japanese banks and their low interest rates made investing in Hawaii real estate and tourism remarkably inviting. The $1.8 billion Japanese firms invested in 1988 jumped to some $4.4 billion the following year.[7]

Two landmark neighbor-island hotels, the Mauna Kea Beach and the Kaluakoi, were snapped up by Seibu. Companies new to Hawaii, such as Azabu (Hyatt Regency Waikiki, Maui Marriott) and Otaku (Holiday Inn Waikiki, Hawaiian Regent), suddenly emerged as major players. In late 1989, deep-pockets Nansay Hawaii bought $300 million worth of real estate in Hawaii Kai, downtown Honolulu, and Kauai.[8] Japanese firms now owned substantial amounts of prime downtown Honolulu commercial space, including the Amfac Center. Probably nothing symbolized the massive Japanese presence better than the Ko Olina mega-project on Oahu's Ewa coast, which will eventually resemble a mini-Waikiki conglomeration of 4,000 hotel rooms (seven luxury hotels) and 4,000 resort condominium units. In return for million-dollar fees, well-connected local lawyer-powerbrokers continued to play a critical role in negotiating the Japanese corporate entree. Back in the early 1980s, Japanese capital had already owned a fair slice of the Island economy. In addition to hotels and real estate, Daiei, for instance, purchased Honolulu's mammoth Ala Moana Shopping Center for $370 million. After 1986, although 95 percent of investment by Japanese companies remained in land and tourism, Japanese ownership diffused throughout the economy to control insurance companies, supermarkets, department stores, the Burger King fast food chain, Spencecliff restaurants, and even locally famous names such as the Columbia Inn Restaurant and Love's Bakery.[9]

As the 1990s began, Japanese investors owned over $8 billion in Hawaii's assets; this included one-third of the state's hotel units and one-half of downtown Honolulu office space. These investors were estimated to be responsible for nearly half the state's economic activity.[10]

This mighty infusion made the economy thrive. Areas like South Kohala and North Kona on the Big Island and Maui's Wailea-Kihei were the scene of burgeoning luxury hotels and phenomenal population growth. Between 1986 and 1989, the Hawaii state gross product rose 32 percent; state government revenue surpluses approached one-half billion dollars by 1989.[11] Construction doubled its dollar volume in these three years and moved past the military to become Hawaii's second-largest industry, employing a work force of well over 30,000.[12]

The economic boom of the late 1980s, however, did no more to solve Hawaii's basic problems than had earlier booms. Between 1987 and 1990, the median price of a single-family Oahu home appreciated 90 percent from $185,000 to $352,000.[13] A rapid rise in rents and the sheer absence of enough housing units literally pushed marginal working-class people out of the housing market; larger numbers of homeless became noticeable around beach areas and parks on Oahu. In a Maui designated by tourism developers for upscale, luxurious resorts, the housing crunch was so excruciating that hotels had to provide subsidized housing to attract employees. The frantic growth of tourism on Maui and West Hawaii's "Gold Coast" overwhelmed road and sewer infrastructure.[14]

Hence, the anti-Japanese backlash, when it came, was intense. Many genuinely feared that Hawaii was indeed becoming a de facto Japanese prefecture. In this environment, Japanese investors could be scapegoated for ills they had little responsibility for, such as the residential housing crisis. It didn't matter that only a tenuous relationship existed between skyrocketing residential prices and rents and some limited Japanese purchases of residential properties. The sinister figure of one Japanese billionaire pointing out properties to be snatched up as he cruised the streets of Honolulu's luxurious Kahala area became imprinted in the public mind. A host of stories, sometimes genuine, circulated about business-suited men arriving on doorsteps, suitcases bulging with money. Japanese firms were also more reasonably accused of discriminatory hiring against non-Japanese and mistreatment of female workers. Always sensitive to votes garnered by posturing on issues like these, Honolulu Mayor Frank Fasi loudly advocated restrictions on Japanese investments, then demanded a $100 million ransom from Japanese firms seeking to construct golf courses on prime Oahu lands.[15]

Beyond the political grandstanding and elements of anti-Japanese racism, however, lay the very real and historic conflicts between overseas forces and the majority of Hawaii's people over basic priorities. Japanese interests mainly wanted new resort playgrounds in Hawaii to accomodate the tourist rush, profitable investments, well-watered golf courses for Japanese executives to play on, condominiums to winter in, and so forth. Hawaii's people, however, were concerned with affordable new housing, decent jobs, and recreational opportunities. The two simply could not be reconciled. How telling that Governor John Waihee was politely listened to and ignored when he visited Japan to plead for more investment in research, development, and high-tech and less in tourism.

Meanwhile, the state government remained committed to the existing economic model. Waihee, who became governor in 1987, widely advertised himself as an energetic leader but proved to be unimaginative, a procrastinator, and deeply tied to the financial interests of the top echelons of the Democratic party. Buoyed by the huge state revenue surpluses and virtually full employment of the 1987–90 period, he chose to take few new initiatives. Reform of a hideously bureaucratic and inept public educational system floundered. The state's reliance on a policy of forcing developers to allocate a portion of new developments to "affordable homes" (price range $90,000–$140,000) did not not begin to stem the mushrooming housing crisis. Honolulu remained the least affordable metropolitan housing market in the United States.[16] In a situation where families in the $60,000 to $100,000 income range were classified "gap group," working-class, single-parent renters were at constant risk of homelessness.[17]

Rather than charting a new course, Waihee's major concern seemed to be awarding lucrative jobs throughout the state bureaucracy to his political cronies. The nonaccountability of the influential had never been more apparent. Among the most blatant cases was the failure to prosecute Judge Russell Nagata for altering a public document to protect a Bank of Hawaii lobbyist. The routine award of nonbid contracts to leading construction-industry donors to John Waihee's political chest was a scandal.[18] Perhaps the most revealing incident was the refusal of nine women who had accused powerful U.S. Senator Daniel Inouye of sexual harrassment to come forth publically. In a "one-party government," said Professor Neal Milner, in examining their reluctance, "everything depends upon behaving yourself."[19]

Despite the arrival in the 1980s of an excellent crop of principled, progressive new Democrats—JoAnn Yukimura, Gary Gill, Steve Holmes, Mazie Hirono, David Hagino, Roy Takumi, Jim Shon, and Mike McCartney, to name a few—the party remained the prisoner of large corporate interests and personal interlocks. The Bishop Estate, Bank of Hawaii, and First Hawaiian Bank retained immense clout among the leadership. After forty years in power, the Democratic establishment was patently bankrupt; it could offer no alternative vision of Hawaii's future.

The Hawaii as "high-tech center" fantasy continued to be nurtured by political insiders such as former State Department of Business, Economic Development and Tourism (DBEDT) head Kent Keith. Groping abroad for overseas capital, DBEDT announced it was "looking to direct it into certain areas where it is needed, like hi-tech or marine products."[20] Against the wishes of local residents, the Waihee administration promoted a Big Island space launch-site project. The state shelled out millions to build a Manoa Valley "Innovation Center" and to subsidize some companies of dubious worth. Meanwhile, 90 percent of the 256-acre high-tech park at Mililani, developed by Keith in his reincarnation as Castle and Cooke manager, lay unoccupied. Originally designed to accomodate 12,000 workers, it held 350.[21] Lacking low operating and living costs, sufficient venture capital, and nearness to major markets, Hawaii's latest thrust toward high-tech wizardry remained as doomed as earlier ones had been.

Sometime in 1989, the U.S. mainland went into recession, or, as some would have it, "contained depression." Japanese economic activity in Hawaii's $12 billion tourism and $3.7 billion construction industries initially provided a strong buffer. Unemployment rates remained a fraction of national figures. Japanese investment continued at high levels ($2.8 billion in 1990), and visitors from Japan reached almost one-third of the total tourist count.[22] This contributed to the popular illusion that the Japanese and California connections made Hawaii "recession proof." The Gulf War, however, revealed the fragility of this base. Tourism plunged a dramatic 13.5 percent during early 1991, and hotel occupancies fell below profitable minimums.[23] Following the war, the stubborn inability of a mainland economy, burdened by years of mismanagement and astronomical debt, to regain momentum sabotaged tourism's recovery. Crucial here was the unprecedented decline of the California economy. In a February 1993 speech in Santa Monica, Bill Clinton opined that "unless California is revived, the nation can't recover." This is doubly true for a Hawaii dependent upon the Golden State's money and tourists. California's problems—an unprecedented downturn in its real estate–finance–aerospace–defense–high-tech industries, race riots, natural disasters, huge deficits, and cutbacks in the state public sector—have simply become Hawaii's. The number of mainland tourists coming to Hawaii dropped alarmingly during the 1990s.

The second pillar had been Japan's seemingly inexhaustible prosperity and financial resources. Suddenly, the Tokyo stock market crash, accompanied by a stark fall in real estate values and a rash of bankruptcies, dissipated the euphoria. In Japan, official policy encouraged a general tightening of speculative activity and lending abroad. Meanwhile, the fall of the yen vis-à-vis the dollar discouraged overseas investment. Large investors in Hawaii, such as Azabu, Asahi Jyuken, and TSA International, found themselves overextended, their financial structures tottering. They proceeded to freeze or cut back on planned developments such as Ko Olina, Kawela Bay, and the Keeaumoku superblock in Honolulu. What new investment did emerge was directed toward Australia, Florida, and Hong Kong.[24] An apostate Frank Fasi journeyed to Tokyo to plead for renewed investment.

In a portent of the future, the higher end, luxury hotels bore the brunt of the downturn. Tourists became more price-conscious and more were repeat Hawaii visitors, and they stayed in cheaper accommodations. Functioning at half-occupancy, the "upscale" resorts desperately offered free nights and cars to attract clientele.[25] Nothing halted the malaise, and 1992 saw a 5 percent drop in tourist arrivals from the dismal 1991. The 7 million tourists of 1990 became the 6.4 million of 1992.[26] Hotel workers were laid off. The vacuum of Japanese money spelled *finis* for the building boom. As building tapered off, the swollen work force of architects, ironworkers, carpenters, and laborers was drastically reduced. A stagnant real estate market forced layoffs in that sector, too. Facing billion dollar losses internationally, United Airlines, the dominant Hawaii-bound carrier, was laying off local employees. Aloha Airlines, also in the red, announced a hiring freeze.[27]

Tourism was faltering even as sugar and pineapple production in Hawaii moved toward extinction; the first months of 1993 saw the closing of the Big Island's Hamakua sugar plantation, throwing over 600 people out of work, and the abrupt end of Dole's Lanai pineapple operations, affecting 160 more.[28]

The impacts of negative growth were felt along a broad spectrum. State and county revenues had large shortfalls; $115 million was cut from the $4 billion 1992 state budget. Essential social welfare programs lost funding; 2,100 individuals and families were being cut from the welfare rolls in 1993.[29] Mental health services were pared down. Ranking officials at the State Human Services Department (cut 15 percent) told me: "We don't have adequate funds to take care of our families now." The Department of Education, in need of new funds to implement an innovative decentralization program, was instead cut back. The University of Hawaii budget was declared frozen through the mid-nineties.

Meanwhile, a tourism-addicted government frantically scrambled to prop up the industry. The Hawaii Visitors Bureau received an emergency $6 million in 1991 to run a blitz of advertisements and a $22 million allocation for 1992–93.[30] Plans were made to build a mammoth convention center to capture that business. The state was pumping almost $3 billion into a multiyear airport enlargement program. Certainly, this might keep the construction interests, who were the major Democratic party campaign contributors, in work. But the projections the program was based

upon—a 33 percent rise in tourism by the year 2000 and a reinfla-
tion of sagging duty-free revenues—were wildly optimistic,[31] not
so much because (as some feared) the new, longer range jets would
overfly Hawaii, but because Hawaii's tourism constituency is
shrinking.

The 1990–92 recession savaged white collars, professionals, and
middle managers; many lost their jobs or became underemployed.
Because corporations in virtually every industry have adopted
strategies of globalism and minimalization, these positions will not
be recreated.[32] Recent college graduates and MBAs are entering a
hostile labor market overloaded with talent and experience. Thus,
the people who form the natural base of Island tourism are major
victims of the ongoing U.S. economic crisis. Visitors will come in
diminished numbers and spend more modestly when they do come.
The restructuring of the U.S. labor market and the forced retreat
from debt-laden, hedonistic consumption must have a telling long-
term impact on tourism; so will the difficult structural problems
faced by California's core industries. And will a Japanese economy
battered by bad loans, overcapacity, stagnant sales and profits,
and unprecedented layoffs continue to generate ever-increasing
planeloads of tourists? Recession or not, revival or not, a return to
the years of high annual tourism growth is unlikely.[33]

Economic distress is accelerating the remarkable number of local
people who leave Hawaii each year. Out-migration remains the
most acute indictment of the failure of the "New Hawaii" model.
Increasingly commented upon in the 1990s, out-migration is a
sign that many locals now find living in the Islands untenable. The
unstable, low-wage job structure and soaring cost of living
differential (38 percent higher than the mainland) is propelling all
sorts of people to become ex-residents.[34] Attractive because of its
relatively dirt-cheap land and homes, and as unlikely as it may
seem, Las Vegas has become a center of the Hawaii diaspora. Most
serious is the noticeable exodus, characterized by one observer as
"brain drain," of educated young people. Nowadays, ask a class
of high school or college students how many of them plan to leave
the Islands, and there is a flurry of hands.

These are conditions laden with danger. "We are the nation's
experiment in multiculturalism," remarks one of Hawaii's most
perceptive political analysts, Professor Dan Boylan.[35] Indeed,

at a time of worldwide ethnic/racial polarization and violence, Hawaii can legitimately claim to be one densely multiethnic society that works. But even relatively tolerant and civilized ethnic relations are prone to disintegrate under a political economy as harsh as Hawaii's. Ultimately, it is the desperate land/housing situation more than any other single factor that has the most potential to poison relations; witness the ugly confrontation of January 1993 between mostly non-Hawaiian condominium owners protesting prices charged by the Bishop Estate to buy their leaseholds and pro-estate Hawaiians determined to defend estate programs. Announcements of sign-ups for affordable Oahu housing sites draw hundreds of home-hungry families and occasional scenes of hysteria.

There also remain strong forces that fortify Hawaii's integrity of place and possibilities for movement away from the vise of complete dependency. "Localism" continues to thrive; it constitutes a genuine alternative to "the complete assimilation" of Hawaii's people by overseas capital and culture and for retention of integrity of place. Unified by Hawaiian Creole English, music, food, lifestyle, collective memory, the ocean, and (as Eric Yamamoto says) "the goodness of Hawaii," localism stands in opposition to the agendas and projects of overseas corporations and their collaborators in the Hawaii establishment.[36] If not reduced to anti-*haole* or anti-Japanese bigotry, it will certainly be a force to be reckoned with.

The hugely successful campaign to save Oahu's Sandy Beach from unsightly development was one straw in the wind. The intense debate over (and 1992 rejection of) a wasteful and unneeded fixed rail system in Honolulu marked the first massive setback for unlimited growth on Oahu. On Maui, Kauai, and the Big Island, proponents of limited growth and environmental concerns have challenged airport-road expansion, gained some popular support, and captured political offices. Lanaians for Sensible Growth have emerged to challenge David Murdock's enclave resort plans there. Running on an antidevelopment–grassroots democracy–community-based economics platform, Hawaii's fledgling Green Party did surprisingly well in the 1992 election.

The Hawaiian sovereignty movement is now clearly the most potent catalyst for change. During the late 1980s and early 1990s, sovereignty was transformed from an outlandish idea propagated by marginal groups into a legitimate political position supported by a majority of native Hawaiians. The vast outpouring around the events in January 1993 commemorating the centennial of the overthrow of the monarchy was a convincing demonstration of this rising consciousness. One sovereignty organization, Ka Lahui Hawaii, already views itself as a separate nation from that of the United States and demands that Hawaiian self-determination be patterned along the lines of the Native Americans' "nation within a nation." The land base would consist of one-half the 1.4 million acres of ceded lands, in addition to 200,000 acres of Hawaiian Homes lands.[37] Dr. Kekuni Blaisdell (Ka Pakaaka) of the pro-Hawaiian Sovereignty Group calls for nothing less than "control of our lands and natural resources."[38]

The way in which the sovereignty question is played out will have a profound impact on Hawaii's future. Despite the existence of the state-controlled Office of Hawaiian Affairs, it will be increasingly difficult for state authorities to coopt or discredit the movement. Restoration of lands will have a major impact upon land and housing policy and use in the Islands.

The consequences of failure will be harsh. If the sovereignty movement splinters badly, frustrates the high expectations of its members, or polarizes non-Hawaiians against it, there is a potential for the kind of internal feuding or interethnic violence that could balkanize the movement. (Certain anti-*haole*, anti-Asian sovereignty leaders may be unwittingly preparing an environment for this.)

Yet the potential ramifications of a "Kanaka Maoli" entity are stunning. Given the continuing thread of Polynesian communalism, it can fundamentally challenge long dominant values. There is Kekuni Blaisdell's insistence on a foundation of "spirituality, not materialism"; the advocacy by Hayden Burgess (Poka Laenu) of a "human, rather than a capital based economy."[39] Self-sufficiency and controls on tourism and multinationals take prominent places on the current agenda, and no wonder. Many native Hawaiians have strong reservations about an economic/cultural system that dispossessed their people and a hundred years after annexation locates them on the rock bottom of the Islands' multiethnic hierarchy.

Ultimately, to be effective, sovereignty calls for a coalition; it will have to be done as a joint project by native Hawaiians and non-Hawaiians and in the name of creating a different Hawaii nei. "We indigenous and non-indigenous peoples are in a constant search for spiritual development which has not ended," says Hayden Burgess. "We must all share in that continuing quest as partners. We look forward to that challenge."[40]

The ultimate challenge, of course, is to safeguard and enhance the goodness and specialness of the Islands. This means the people of Hawaii will need to draw upon their varied cultural traditions, communitarian spirit, good sense, and humor. In a world afflicted by myriad ethnic/racial hatreds, this feat will not go unnoticed.

Notes

Introduction

1. Lawrence Fuchs, *Hawaii Pono: A Social History*, p. 449.
2. Gavan Daws, *Shoal of Time: A History of the Hawaiian Islands*, p. 395. Daws later modified this view, advocating a new scholarship that "would put Hawaii in a national and world context to show the kinds of relationships and interdependencies that actually and increasingly determine how life is lived here." See *Hawaii Observer*, March 24, 1977, p. 32.

Chapter 1. To Kealekukua Bay and Beyond

1. *The Voyages of Captain Cook Around the World* (London: John Tallis and Co., *circa* 1800), p. 232.
2. Edwin G. Burrows, *Hawaiian-Americans*, p. 15.
3. James Cook and James King, *A Voyage to the Pacific Ocean*, p. 244.
4. Kathleen Dickenson Mellen, *The Gods Depart*, p. 49.
5. Quoted in Theodore Morgan, *A Century of Economic Change*, p. 48.
6. Ibid., p. 62.
7. Cited in Ralph S. Kuykendall, *The Hawaiian Kingdom, 1778–1854*, p. 27.
8. Ibid., p. 42.
9. Cited in ibid., pp. 65, 47.
10. Elizabeth Withington, *The Golden Cloak*, p. 31.

Chapter 2. A Tale of Sandalwood and Whaling

1. Dorothy Shineberg, *They Came for Sandalwood*, p. 12.
2. Theodore Morgan, *Century of Economic Change*, p. 72.
3. Samir Amin, *Accumulation on a World Scale*, vol. 2, p. 379.

4. Richard O'Connor, *Pacific Destiny*, p. 43.
5. Quoted in Kuykendall, *Hawaiian Kingdom, 1778–1854*, p. 88.
6. James Jackson Jarves, *History of the Hawaiian Islands*, p. 109.
7. Quoted in Kuykendall, *Hawaiian Kingdom, 1778–1854*, p. 145.
8. Morgan, *Century of Economic Change*, p. 277.
9. Quoted in Kuykendall, *Hawaiian Kingdom, 1778–1854*, p. 90.
10. Ibid.
11. Quoted in ibid.
12. Ibid.
13. Morgan, *Century of Economic Change*, p. 75.
14. Ibid., p. 114.
15. Ibid., p. 78.
16. Louis Crampon, *Hawaii's Visitor Industry: Its Growth and Development*, p. 62.
17. Morgan, *Century of Economic Change*, p. 51.
18. *The Friend*, July 1, 1844.
19. Edward P. Scott, *The Saga of the Sandwich Isles*, p. 37.
20. *The Polynesian*, June 6, 1840.
21. Morgan, *Century of Economic Change*, p. 142.

Chapter 3. Dispossession of a People

1. Kuykendall, *Hawaiian Kingdom, 1854–1874*, p. 101.
2. Morgan, *Century of Economic Change*, p. 87.
3. Harold W. Bradley, *The American Frontier in Hawaii*, p. 415.
4. Quoted in Theon Wright, *The Disenchanted Isles*, p. xiii.
5. Kuykendall, *Hawaiian Kingdom, 1854–1874*, p. 121.
6. Quoted in Morgan, *Century of Economic Change*, p. 92.
7. William Rice Castle, *The Life of Samuel Northrop Castle*, p. 29.
8. Scott, *Saga of the Sandwich Isles*, p. 38.
9. Quoted in Jarves, *History of the Hawaiian Islands*, p. 204.
10. Jean Hobbs, *A Pageant of the Soil*, p. 31.
11. Kuykendall, *Hawaiian Kingdom, 1854–1874*, p. 145.
12. Ibid.
13. Morgan, *Century of Economic Change*, p. 227.
14. Quoted in Sylvester Stevens, *American Expansion in Hawaii, 1842–1898*, p. 32.
15. Quoted in ibid., p. 33.
16. Quoted in Morgan, *Century of Economic Change*, p. 187.
17. Neil M. Levy, "Native Hawaiian Land Rights," *California Law Review* 63 (July 1975): 853.

18. Laura Fish Judd, *Honolulu Sketches of Life in the Hawaiian Islands,* p. 167.
19. Mellen, *Gods Depart,* p. 36.
20. Levy, "Native Hawaiian Land Rights," p. 856.
21. Morgan, *Century of Economic Change,* p. 137.
22. Ibid., p. 178.
23. Quoted in John H. Bodley, "Alternatives to Ethnocide: Human Zoos, Living Museums, and Real People," in Elias Sevilla-Casas, ed., *Western Exploitation and Indian Peoples,* p. 37.
24. Karl Marx, *Capital,* p. 834.
25. Cited in Paul Jacobs and Saul Landau, *To Serve the Devil,* p. 25.
26. Quoted in Kuykendall, *Hawaiian Kingdom, 1854–1874,* p. 258.
27. Burrows, *Hawaiian-Americans,* pp. 149–152.
28. *The American Way* (May-October 1971), p. 13.

Chapter 4. The Rise of King Sugar

1. Morgan, *Century of Economic Change,* p. 139.
2. Quoted in Cecil Tilton, *The History of Banking in Hawaii,* p. 26.
3. Ralph Davis, *The Rise of the Atlantic Economies,* p. 257.
4. Quoted in Stevens, *American Expansion in Hawaii,* p. 34.
5. Morgan, *Century of Economic Change,* p. 179.
6. Ibid., p. 145.
7. Quoted in Kuykendall, *Hawaiian Kingdom, 1854–1874,* p. 142.
8. Manley Hopkins, *Hawaii,* p. 43.
9. Quoted in A. G. Alexander, *Koloa Plantation and Hawaii,* pp. 4–5.
10. Quoted in *Honolulu Record* (1952).
11. Quoted in Kuykendall, *Hawaiian Kingdom, 1874–1893,* p. 376.
12. Quoted in Merze Tate, *Hawaii: Reciprocity or Annexation,* p. 4.
13. Quoted in Kuykendall, *Hawaiian Kingdom, 1874–1893,* p. 387.
14. O'Connor, *Pacific Destiny,* pp. 81, 104.
15. Kuykendall, *Hawaiian Kingdom, 1778–1854,* p. 386.
16. Quoted in O'Connor, *Pacific Destiny,* p. 104.
17. Ibid.
18. Quoted in Kuykendall, *Hawaiian Kingdom, 1854–1874,* p. 208.
19. Ibid., p. 194.
20. O'Connor, *Pacific Destiny,* p. 105.
21. Quoted in Castle, *Life of Samuel Northrop Castle,* p. 173.
22. Jarves, *History of the Hawaiian Islands,* p. 204.
23. Kuykendall, *Hawaiian Kingdom, 1854–1874,* p. 30.

24. From a speech made during the campaign of 1873.
25. Ibid., p. 226.
26. Thomas Black Clark, *Hawaii: The 49th State*, p. 80.
27. Judd, *Honolulu Sketches*, p. 202.
28. Harold Kent, *Charles Reed Bishop: Man of Hawaii*, p. xii.
29. Quoted in Kuykendall, *Hawaiian Kingdom, 1854–1874*, p. 27.
30. Ibid., p. 35.
31. Quoted in Tate, *Hawaii: Reciprocity or Annexation*, p. 118; italics added.
32. Ibid., front jacket.
33. Morgan, *Century of Economic Change*, p. 206.
34. John Anthony Mollett, *Capital in Hawaiian Sugar: Its Formation and Relation to Labor and Output*, p. 28.
35. Jacob Adler, *Claus Spreckels, The Sugar King of Hawaii*, p. 97.
36. Kent, *Charles Reed Bishop*, p. 83.
37. William Taylor, "The Hawaiian Sugar Industry," p. 16.
38. Quoted in Adler, *Claus Spreckels*, p. 169.
39. Ibid., p. 81.
40. Jacob Adler and Gwynn Barrett, eds., *The Diaries of Walter Murray Gibson*, vol. 1, p. xii.
41. Quoted in Kuykendall, *Hawaiian Kingdom, 1854–1874*, p. 225.
42. Ibid., p. 256.
43. Adler, *Claus Spreckels*, p. 248.
44. Ibid., pp. 169–70.
45. Kuykendall, *Hawaiian Kingdom, 1874–1893*, pp. 282–87.
46. Merze Tate, *The United States and the Hawaiian Kingdom*, p. 70.
47. Kent, *Charles Reed Bishop*, p. 63.
48. Quoted in Harold Kent, *Dr. Hyde and Mr. Stevenson*, p. 213.
49. Adler and Barrett, eds., *Diaries of Walter Murray Gibson*, p. 159.
50. Ethel M. Damon, *Sanford Ballard Dole and His Hawaii*, p. 201.
51. Quoted in Kent, *Dr. Hyde and Mr. Stevenson*, p. 220.
52. Kuykendall, *Hawaiian Kingdom, 1874–1893*, p. 423.

Chapter 5. The Pear Is Ripe

1. Quoted in William Appleman Williams, *The Contours of American History*, p. 346.
2. William Appleman Williams, *The Roots of the Modern American Empire*, p. 41.
3. Williams, *Contours of American History*, p. 338.
4. Bureau of the Americas, *Hawaii*, pp. 88–89.

5. Ibid., p. 68.
6. Quoted in Kuykendall, *Hawaiian Kingdom, 1874–1893*, p. 508.
7. Quoted in Williams, *Roots of the Modern American Empire*, p. 248.
8. Quoted in Kuykendall, *Hawaiian Kingdom, 1874–1893*, p. 245.
9. Ibid., p. 487.
10. U.S. Congress, *Papers and Documents Relating to the Hawaiian Islands*, p. 191.
11. Quoted in William Adam Russ, Jr., *The Hawaiian Revolution, 1893–94* p. 125.
12. Ibid., p. 55.
13. The Alexander quote is from Russ, *Hawaiian Republic*, p. 129; the Thurston quote is from *A Handbook*, pp. 1–2; and the Cruzan quote is from Kuykendall, *Hawaiian Kingdom, 1874–1893*, p. 177.
14. Quoted in Adler, *Claus Spreckels*, p. 221.
15. Quoted in Damon, *Sanford Ballard Dole*, p. 322.
16. Quoted in Kuykendall, *Hawaiian Kingdom, 1874–1893*, p. 569.
17. Ibid., p. 588.
18. U.S. Congress, *Papers and Documents Relating to the Hawaiian Islands*, p. 48.
19. Lucien Young, *The Boston at Hawaii*, p. 182.
20. Quoted in Julius W. Pratt, *Expansionists of 1898*, p. 134.
21. Quoted in Samuel Weaver, *Hawaii U.S.A.*, p. 103.
22. Wright, *Disenchanted Isles*, p. 13.
23. Russ, *Hawaiian Revolution*, p. 2.
24. Wright, *Disenchanted Isles*, pp. 17–19.
25. Quoted in Russ, *Hawaiian Republic*, p. 62.
26. Lorrin Thurston, *Annexation to the United States*, p. 31.
27. Quoted in Wright, *Disenchanted Isles*, pp. 17–19.
28. Russ, *Hawaiian Republic*, p. 209.
29. Quoted in O'Connor, *Pacific Destiny*, p. 202.
30. *San Francisco Evening Bulletin*, January 30, 1893.
31. Quoted in Williams, *Roots of the Modern American Empire*, p. 432.
32. Quoted in Russ, *Hawaiian Republic*, p. 186.
33. Quoted in ibid., p. 237.
34. Quoted in *Expansionists of 1898*, p. 274.
35. Quoted in Russ, *Hawaiian Republic*, p. 368.

Chapter 6. Big Five Territory

1. University of Hawaii, Legislative Reference Bureau, *Public Land Policy in Hawaii: A Historical Analysis*, p. 32.

2. Ronald Chilcote and Joel Edelstein, *Latin America: The Struggle with Dependency and Beyond*, p. 594.
3. *Honolulu Star-Bulletin Centenary Issue*, April 14, 1920.
4. *Honolulu Record* (1950).
5. "Men and Women of Hawaii 1935," *Honolulu Star-Bulletin* (1936). Also corporate reports.
6. Frank J. Taylor et al., *From Land and Sea*, p. 137.
7. Fuchs, *Hawaii Pono*, p. 202.
8. Ibid., p. 230.
9. Ibid., pp. 230–35.
10. Ibid., p. 232.
11. *Honolulu Record* (1950).
12. Lawrence M. Judd, *Lawrence M. Judd and Hawaii*, p. 192.
13. *The Navy and the Massie-Kahahawai Case* (Honolulu: Honolulu Public Record Office, 1951), p. 17.
14. U.S. Congress, *Hearings on Statehood for Hawaii*, pp. 289–93, 401–10.
15. *Honolulu Record* (1953).
16. Quoted in Thomas B. Healey, *The Republican Party in Hawaii*, p. 31.
17. Quoted in Kuykendall, *Hawaiian Kingdom, 1874–1893*, p. 635.
18. Judd, *Lawrence M. Judd and Hawaii*, p. 59.
19. *Public Land Policy in Hawaii*, p. 32.
20. W. A. Kinney, *Hawaii's Capacity for Self-Government All but Destroyed*, p. 3.
21. Ray Stannard Baker, "Wonderful Hawaii: A World Experimental Station," *The American* (November 1911), p. 28.
22. Quoted in Richard Alan Liebes, "Labor Organization in Hawaii," p. 32.
23. Samuel Weinman, *Hawaii: A Case of Imperialist Plunder*, p. 33.
24. Taylor et al., *From Land and Sea*, p. 143.
25. Quoted in Wright, *Disenchanted Isles*, p. 34.
26. "Public Land Policy in Hawaii," *Honolulu Advertiser*, February 25, 1945.
27. Wright, *Disenchanted Isles*, p. 31.
28. Fuchs, *Hawaii Pono*, p. 174.
29. Joseph Barber, Jr., *Hawaii: Restless Rampart*, p. 38.
30. Marilyn Vause, "The Hawaiian Home Commission Act, 1920," p. 106.
31. *Crossroads of the Pacific*, April 19, 1912, p. 4.
32. *Honolulu Record* (1954).
33. Baker, "Wonderful Hawaii," p. 32.
34. Quoted in Henry Franck, *Roaming in Hawaii*, p. 232.
35. Barber, *Hawaii: Restless Rampart*, pp. 56–57.
36. Ibid, p. 42.
37. Quoted in T. B. Hardy, *Wallace Rider Farrington*, p. 57.

38. Baker, "Wonderful Hawaii," *The American* (December 1911), p. 207.
39. *Honolulu Record* (February 1951).
40. Quoted in William L. Abbott, *The American Labor Heritage*, p. 89.
41. Alexander MacDonald, *Revolt in Paradise*, pp. 40–41.
42. *Crossroads of the Pacific*, May 17, 1912.
43. Barber, *Hawaii: Restless Rampart*, p. 46.
44. Ibid.
45. Weinman, *Hawaii: A Case of Imperialist Plunder*, pp. 1–3.
46. *Honolulu Record* (1952).
47. Quoted in MacDonald, *Revolt in Paradise*, p. 133.
48. Sophie Judd Cooke, *Sincerely Sophie*, p. 68.
49. Baker, "Wonderful Hawaii," p. 207.
50. *Ibid.*, p. 30.
51. Fuchs, *Hawaii Pono*, p. 55.
52. *Honolulu Record* (1951).
53. Judd, *Lawrence M. Judd*, p. 59.
54. S. D. Porteus and Marjorie Babcock, *Temperament and Race*, p. 52.
55. Ibid., p. 336.
56. Ibid., p. 66.
57. Ibid., p. 70.
58. Ibid.
59. Quoted in MacDonald, *Revolt in Paradise*, p. 126.
60. Quoted in ibid., p. 128.
61. Quoted in Liebes, "Labor Organization in Hawaii," p. 32.
62. Hardy, *Wallace Rider Farrington*, p. 67.
63. Fuchs, *Hawaii Pono*, p. 213.
64. William Rice Castle, *Hawaii Past and Present*, p. 248.
65. MacDonald, *Revolt in Paradise*, p. 130.
66. Lillian Symes, "The Other Side of Paradise," *Harpers Monthly* (1930), p. 44.
67. MacDonald, *Revolt in Paradise*, p. 138.
68. Liebes, "Labor Organization in Hawaii," p. 81.
69. Barber, *Hawaii: Restless Rampart*, pp. 81–95.
70. Quoted in ibid., p. 87.
71. Quoted in MacDonald, *Revolt in Paradise*, p. 259.
72. Chilcote and Edelstein, *Latin America*, p. 601.
73. Eric Hanley, "Rice, Politics and Development in Guyana," in Ivar Oxaal et al., eds., *Beyond the Sociology of Development*, p. 131.
74. *Thrumm's Hawaiian Almanac and Annual 1916* (Honolulu: Thomas G. Thrumm), p. 27.
75. Ibid., 1936, p. 26.
76. Ibid.

77. Ibid., 1916, p. 26; 1936, pp. 25–26.
78. Ibid., 1936, p. 23.
79. Ibid.
80. Edward Joesting, *An Uncommon History of Hawaii*, p. 291.
81. Robert Schmidt, "Unemployment Rates in Hawaii During the 1930s," *Hawaiian Journal of History* 10 (1976): 92.
82. Mollett, *Capital in Hawaiian Sugar*, p. 12.

Chapter 7. The Pacific Rim Strategy

1. *Northwest Passage* 18 (July 1978): 3.
2. Richard Barnet and Ronald Muller, *Global Reach*, p. 16.
3. Quoted in O'Connor, *Pacific Destiny*, p. 464.
4. Ibid., p. 457.
5. Quoted in Noam Chomsky, *At War with Asia*, p. 8.
6. Gabriel Kolko, *Main Currents in Modern American History*, p. 159.

Chapter 8. The Great Corporate Transformation

1. *Honolulu Advertiser*, May 13, 1959.
2. Ibid.
3. John W. Vandercook, *King Cane*, p. 185.
4. *Honolulu Advertiser*, August 21, 1953.
5. Ibid., March 30, 1954.
6. Ibid., March 26, 1958.
7. Ibid., October 4, 1962.
8. *Hawaii Business and Industry* (July 1968), p. 17.
9. *Honolulu Star-Bulletin*, February 9, 1962.
10. *Honolulu Record* (1957).
11. *Beacon* (1962).
12. *Honolulu Advertiser*, January 15, 1964.
13. *Honolulu Star-Bulletin and Advertiser*, April 17, 1966.
14. *Hawaii Business* (April 1973).
15. *Economic Salon* (March 1972), p. 34.
16. Simpich, *Dynasty in the Pacific*, p. 155.

17. *ILWU Dispatcher* (1973).
18. *Dillingham Corporation Special Report,* February 1, 1977.
19. *Dillingham Quarterly* 1 (March-May 1976): 5.
20. *Dillingham Quarterly* (Winter 1971), p. 5.
21. Ibid., p. 15.
22. *Honolulu Star-Bulletin,* October 29, 1968.
23. *Pacific Business News,* June 17, 1963.
24. *Honolulu Star-Bulletin and Advertiser* (1973).
25. *Hawaii Business* (January 1978).
26. *Hawaii Business* (February 1976).
27. Simpich, *Dynasty in the Pacific,* p. 158.
28. Taylor et al., *From Land and Sea,* p. 206.
29. *Forbes,* June 1, 1971.
30. Simpich, *Anatomy of Hawaii,* p. 162.
31. *ILWU Dispatcher* (September 1973).
32. North American Committee on Latin America (NACLA), *Latin America and Empire Report* (September 1974).
33. Ibid.
34. *San Jose Maverick* (March 1970).
35. Paul Rupert, "Corporate Feast in the Pacific," *Pacific Report and World Empire Telegram* (March 1970), p. 2.
36. *Honolulu Star-Bulletin and Advertiser,* April 21, 1974.
37. Simpich, *Anatomy of Hawaii,* p. 110.
38. Ruth Tabrah, "The Day the District Died," *Gathering Place* (May 1971).
39. *Modern Times* (March 1978), p. 6.
40. State of Hawaii, Department of Taxation, *Hawaii Income Patterns 1973.*
41. *Fortune* (June 1960).
42. *Honolulu Magazine* (October 1967), p. 26.
43. *Hawaii Business* (July 1971), p. 32.
44. Ibid. (November 1977), p. 47.
45. Ibid. (October 1977), p. 66.
46. Laura Brown and Walter Cohen, "Hawaii Faces the Pacific," *Pacific Studies Center Bulletin* (January–February 1975), p. 6.

Chapter 9. The Era of Consensus

1. *Special Message on Policies for Capital Improvements for the State of Hawaii,* Governor William Quinn to the legislature, May 1961, p. 2.
2. *Honolulu Advertiser,* February 17, 1960.
3. Joyce Kolko, *America and the Crisis of World Capitalism,* p. 120.

4. *Honolulu Advertiser* (1961).
5. *Honolulu Star-Bulletin,* January 27, 1961.
6. *Honolulu Star-Bulletin,* April 10,1960, January 3, 1964; *Honolulu Advertiser,* February 12, 1961.
7. State of Hawaii, Department of Taxation, *Hawaii Income Patterns 1973,* p. 52.
8. Ibid., p. 55; Thomas Creighton, *The Lands of Hawaii: Their Use and Misuse,* p. 66.
9. *Honolulu Star-Bulletin,* September 25, 1961.
10. *Honolulu Advertiser,* August 8, 1960, July 6, 1962.
11. Ibid., September 3, 1957.
12. Club 15, *East Meets West in Hawaii* (Honolulu: 1965), pp. 1–3.
13. *Honolulu Advertiser,* September 20, 1957.
14. *Honolulu Advertiser,* April 30, 1950; *Honolulu Star-Bulletin,* May 1, 1950.
15. Wright, *Disenchanted Isles,* pp. 114–15.
16. Speech to the 442nd Regiment meeting, October 1974.
17. Wright, *Disenchanted Isles,* p. 96.
18. *Honolulu Advertiser,* November 4, 1954.
19. *Honolulu Star-Bulletin,* November 4, 1954.
20. Wright, *Disenchanted Isles,* p. 287.
21. *Honolulu Star-Bulletin,* November 5, 1954.
22. *Honolulu Advertiser,* November 12, 1954
23. George Cooper, untitled manuscript, 1982.
24. *Honolulu Record* (1955).
25. *Honolulu Advertiser,* September 16, 1957.
26. *Honolulu Star-Bulletin,* March 14, 1967
27. *Honolulu Record* (1951).
28. Joyce Walker, *A Rhetorical Analysis of the Epidetic Speeches of Jack Hall,* p. 103.
29. Edward L. H. Johannessen, *The Hawaiian Labor Movement: A Brief History,* p. 150.

Chapter 10. If the Price Is Right . . .

1. *Honolulu Star-Bulletin,* December 4, 1962.
2. Ibid.
3. Ibid., February 19, 1964.
4. Ibid., December 19, 1964.
5. *Honolulu Advertiser,* October 31, 1963; *Honolulu Star-Bulletin,* May 15, 1964.

6. *Pacific Business News*, October 20, 1969, p. 1.
7. *Honolulu Advertiser* (1969).
8. *Pacific Business News*, October 15, 1965.
9. *Honolulu Advertiser*, June 7, 1963.
10. *Honolulu Star-Bulletin*, October 11, 1963.
11. Ibid., October 30, 1970.
12. *Honolulu Advertiser*, January 19, 1964.
13. *Time*, February 26, 1965, p. 66
14. Wright, *Disenchanted Isles*, p. 239.
15. *Honolulu Advertiser*, August 4, 1970.
16. *Honolulu Star-Bulletin*, February 26, 1976.
17. State of Hawaii, Department of Planning and Economic Development, *Hawaii Economic Review*, p. 7.
18. *Honolulu Star-Bulletin*, December 14, 1960, and October 1, 1961,
19. Ibid., February 4, 1961.
20. Ibid., December 22, 1960.
21. Ibid.
22. John Witeck, "The East-West Center: An Intercult of Colonialism," *Hawaii Pono Journal* (May 1971), p. 3.
23. *Honolulu Advertiser*, November 27, 1970.
24. *Pacific Business News*, September 8, 1969.
25. State of Hawaii, Department of Planning and Economic Development, *State of Hawaii Data Book, 1977*.
26. Ibid.
27. *Pacific Business News*, September 25, 1967.
28. *Hawaiian Ethos* (Berkeley, CA.) (1971), p. 7.
29. Speech to the 1974 East-West Center Conference on the Impact of Tourism in the Pacific.
30. Creighton, *Lands of Hawaii*, p. 187.
31. Republican Party Central Committee, *Annual Almanac and Government Guide of Hawaii*. This is the source for all occupational materials on the 1969 legislature.
32. *Honolulu Advertiser*, June 18, 1961.
33. The Ho quote is from Honolulu Star-Bulletin, *Men and Women of Hawaii*, p. v; the Horita quote is from *Economic Salon* (September 1972), p. 12.
34. Honolulu Star-Bulletin, *Men and Women of Hawaii*.
35. *Hawaii Business* (August and September 1970).
36. Tom Coffman, "Hawaii's High Priced Politics," *Honolulu Advertiser*, February 13, 1973.
37. Ibid.
38. *Modern Times* (October 1977).
39. Interview with Dr. Willis Butler, 1972.

40. State of Hawaii, Commission on Manpower and Unemployment, *Unemployment and Welfare in Hawaii*, pp. 1–3.
41. Ibid., p. 1.
42. *Hawaii Observer*, February 3, 1976, p. 1, and January 20, 1976, p. 6.
43. *Honolulu Star-Bulletin*, February 10, 1977.
44. Ibid.
45. *Hawaii Business* (April 1977).
46. *Honolulu Star-Bulletin*, February 10, 1977.
47. *Pacific Business News*, March 14, 1977; *Honolulu Star-Bulletin*, August 28, 1977.
48. *Honolulu Star-Bulletin*, February 5, 1979.
49. Ibid., January 26, 1977.
50. State of Hawaii, Commission on Manpower and Employment, *Unemployment and Welfare*, p. 31.
51. *Hawaii Herald*, April 13, 1973.
52. *Modern Times* (October 1977).
53. *Honolulu Observer*, February 18, 1975.
54. Gov. George Ariyoshi, *State of the State Address, 1977*.
55. Ibid.
56. *Honolulu Star-Bulletin*, January 27, 1979.
57. *Pacific Business News*, March 14, 1977.
58. *Honolulu Star-Bulletin*, May 5, 1952.
59. State of Hawaii, Department of Planning and Economic Development, *The Hawaii State Plan 1977*, p. 2.
60. *Hawaii Observer*, October 13, 1976, pp. 12, 13.
61. *Pacific Business News*, January 22, 1976.
62. 1954 Democratic Party Platform, *Honolulu Star-Bulletin*, May 3, 1954.
63. *Hawaii Observer*, March 20, 1976, pp. 10–12.
64. *Honolulu Star-Bulletin*, May 5, 1952.
65. *Honolulu Advertiser*, July 15, 1959.
66. *Hawaii Business* (September 1978), p. 16.
67. *Pacific Business News*, May 1, 1972, p. 4.
68. John Kelly, *Hawaii: Showcase of Imperialism, Land Alienation, and Foreign Control*, p. 24.
69. *Hawaii Observer* (1976)

Chapter 11. A Tourism Society

1. Crampon, *Hawaii's Visitor Industry*, p. 131.
2. *Honolulu Star-Bulletin*, January 5, 1959.

3. *Hawaii Business* (April 1978).
4. *Hawaiian Ethos* (May 1971), pp. 5–6.
5. *Hawaii Business* (April 1978).
6. *Honolulu Star-Bulletin*, August 30, 1976.
7. City and County of Honolulu, Department of General Planning, *The Interim Report on the Future of Oahu's Economy*, p. 62.
8. *Pacific Business News*, December 23, 1976; *Economic World* (May 1976), p. 36.
9. *Hawaii Business* (May 1979), p. 21.
10. *The Valley Isle*, August 10–23, 1977,
11. Quoted in *Another Voice* (Honolulu), June 20, 1974.
12. *Honolulu Advertiser*, March 31, 1960.
13. Ibid., April 19, 1959.
14. *Honolulu Star-Bulletin*, September 19, 1962.
15. Simpich, *Anatomy of Hawaii*, p. 99.
16. *Hawaii Business* (April 1978), p. 14.
17. Ibid. (February 1979), p. 17.
18. Ibid. (December 1976), p. 40.
19. *Honolulu Star-Bulletin*, May 10, 1979.
20. University of Hawaii, School of Travel Industry Management, *Reader*.
21. *Pacific Business News*, March 1, 1971, p. 2
22. Ibid., June 17, 1968.
23. Ibid., June 8, 1970.
24. State of Hawaii, Governor's Advisory Committee on the Tourism Industry, *The Role of Government in the Development of Hawaii's Visitor Industry*, p. 6.
25. *Hawaii Observer*, June 10, 1975, p. 1.
26. *Honolulu Star-Bulletin*, July 28, 1976.
27. Francisco Quesada, *The Mechanism and Economics of Tourism*, p. 4.
28. Robert Heller, *The Economic and Social Impact of Foreign Investment in Hawaii*, p. 50.
29. Ibid., pp. 56–62; *Economic World* (January 1978); *Hawaii Observer* (June 1974).
30. *Honolulu Star-Bulletin*, August 5, 1976.
31. Ibid.
32. *Hawaii Observer*, March 24, 1977.
33. *Economic World* (June 1977), p. 22.
34. Ibid. (November 1977), p. 13.
35. State of Hawaii, Department of Planning and Economic Development, *Tourism in Hawaii*, p. 64.
36. Willard Chow, "Tourism and Regional Planning: The Legend of

Hawaii," paper given at the Fifth Annual Pacific Regional Science Conference, Vancouver, August 1977, p. 2.

37. State of Hawaii, Department of Planning and Economic Development, *State of Hawaii Data Book, 1978*, p. 183.
38. Ibid.
39. *Pacific Business News*, December 25, 1967, p. 4.
40. Hawaii Employers Council, cited in *Hawaii Business* (July 1982).
41. State of Hawaii, Department of Planning and Economic Development, *Tourism in Hawaii*, p. 51.
42. Personal interviews.
43. Hawaii Committee for the Humanities, *Discusssion on Tourism*, Waikiki, April 1977.
44. *Honolulu Star-Bulletin*, September 23, 1976.
45. *Hawaii Free Peoples' Press*, April 30, 1969.
46. *Honolulu Advertiser*, October 25, 1977.
47. Ibid.
48. *Hawaii Business and Industry* (January 1968), p. 18.
49. R. Merrill, *Hotel Employment and the Community in Hawaii*, p. 51.
50. *Beacon* (October 1968), p. 23.
51. The source for these figures is Operation Manorg, College of Education, University of Hawaii, *Hawaii Ethnic Information*. Like all censuses that give ethnic breakdown, these should be viewed with caution.
52. State of Hawaii, Department of Planning and Economic Development, *Hawaii State Data Book, 1978*, p. 190.
53. State of Hawaii, Department of Planning and Economic Development, *Growth Policies Plan 1974–84*, p. 14.
54. *Hawaii Business* (January 1978), p. 15.
55. City and County of Honolulu, Department of General Planning, *Interim Report*, p. 21.
56. *Hawaii Business*, November 1976.
57. State of Hawaii, Department of Planning and Economic Development, *The Hawaii State Plan 1977*, pp. 15–21.
58. Quoted in *Hawaii Business*, various issues in 1981.
59. In the proceedings of the Pacific Islands Tourism Conference, 1974.
60. Bryan Farrell, ed., *The Social and Economic Impact of Tourism on Pacific Communities*, pp. 17–28.
61. Personal interview.
62. *The Valley Isle*, August 10–23, 1977, p. 4.

Conclusion: 1983

1. Jafar Jafari, *The Role of Tourism in the Socioeconomic Transformation of Developing Countries*, p. 161
2. State of Hawaii, Department of Planning and Economic Development, *The Hawaii State Plan 1977, Sociocultural Advancement*, p. 85.
3. Ibid., *The Economy*, pp.15–22.
4. Ibid.
5. Ibid., p.5.

Epilogue: The Harsh Nineties

1. Diane Chang, *Hawaii Business* (June 1991).
2. David McClain, "Hawaii's Competitiveness," in Randall W. Roth, ed., *The Price of Paradise: Lucky We Live Hawaii* (Honolulu: Mutual Publishing, 1992), p.10.
3. See Katherine Newman, *Falling From Grace: The Experience of Downward Mobility in the American Middle Class* (New York: The Free Press, 1988); Thomas Justen, "The Distribution of Wealth in the U.S. Economy," pt. 2, *Economic Outlook* (Spring 1988); Bureau of Labor Statistics, *BLS Reports on Worker Displacement* (December 1988) Washington, D.C.; Gary Wills, *Reagan's America;* Chris Tilly, *Short Hours Short Shrift: Causes and Consequences of Part-Time Work* (Washington, D.C.: Economic Policy Institute, 1990); Paul Krugman, *The Age of Diminished Expectations: U.S. Economic Policy in the 1990s* (Cambridge: Massachussets Institute of Technology Press, 1990).
4. See Robert Pollin, *Deeper in Debt: The Changing Condition of U.S. Households* (Washington, D.C.: Economic Policy Institute, 1990); Philip Mattera, *Prosperity Lost* (Reading, Mass.: Addison Wesley, 1987).
5. Joyce Kolko, *Restructuring the World* (New York: Pantheon, 1988), pp.84–87; Krugman, *The Age of Diminished Expectations*, pp. 115–131.
6. Bill Wood, "Pied Piper in Pin Stripes," *Hawaii Investor* (March 1988), p.17.
7. Tom Yoneyama and Susan Hooper, "The Japaning of Hawaii," *Hawaii Business* (January 1990), pp. 14–16
8. Mari Taketa, "Sitting Tight," *Hawaii Business* (June 1992), pp. 50–53.
9. James Maki and Marcia Y. Sakai, "Foreign Investment," in Randall Roth, ed., *The Price of Paradise*, pp. 33–37; Bill Wood, "We Will Now Do a Slowdown," *Hawaii Investor* (November 1990), pp. 29–32; see also Yoneyama and Hooper, "The Japaning of Hawaii."

10. Bill Wood, "The Over Achievers," *Hawaii Investor* (July 1990), p. 6; see also Yoneyama and Hooper, "The Japaning of Hawaii."
11. Ibid.
12. Mari Taketa, "Sweating Out the Slump," *Hawaii Business* (March 1992), pp. 26–27.
13. Lou Rose, "Speculators," in Roth, ed., *The Price of Paradise*, pp. 18–21.
14. Donne Dawson, "A Roof Over Maui's Head," *Hawaii Investor* (November 1990), pp. 14–21.
15. David Callies, "Development Fees," in Roth, ed., *The Price of Paradise*, p. 169.
16. David McClain, "Hawaii's Competitiveness," in Roth, ed., *The Price of Paradise*, pp. 23–25; "Housing Takes its Biggest Pay Bite Here in Honolulu," *Honolulu Star-Bulletin and Advertiser*, February 2, 1992.
17. "Single Parent Renters Struggle to Find Housing," *Honolulu Star-Bulletin and Advertiser*, September 6, 1992.
18. Ian Lind, "Architects and Engineers Provide Bulk of Democratic Funds," *Monitor* 3 (1) (December 1992), p. 1.
19. Richard Borrecca, "Rock the Boat and Surfer," *Honolulu Star-Bulletin*, December 18, 1992.
20. Ellen Paris, "Hawaii Calls," *Hawaii Investor* (October 1992), pp. 24–26.
21. Lisa Ishikawa, "High Tech Wanna Be," *Hawaii Business* (February 1992), pp. 48–51.
22. See Maki and Sakai, "Foreign Investment," Wood, "The Over Achievers," and Yoneyama and Hooper, "The Japaning of Hawaii"; Daniel Martin, "Construction's New Frontier," *Hawaii Business* (March 1991), pp. 42–45.
23. Susan Hooper, "Waiting Out the Slump," *Hawaii Business* (June 1991), p. 18.
24. Mari Taketa, "Taming of the Yen," *Hawaii Business* (June 1992), p. 39; see also Taketa, "Sweating Out the Slump."
25. Mari Taketa, "New Moves for Tourism," *Hawaii Business* (May 1992), pp. 26–28.
26. "Hawaii Tourism No Rebound Yet," *Honolulu Star-Bulletin*, January 22, 1993; "Whither the Mighty Yen," *Hawaii Business* (March 1991), p. 71.
27. "UAL Stock Soars on Plans to Reduce Costs," *Honolulu Star-Bulletin*, January 7, 1993.
28. *Hawaii Investor* (January 1993), pp. 46–52; Kelly Arbor, "Paty Marks End of Pineapple Era," *Honolulu Star-Bulletin*, November 14, 1992.
29. *Hawaii Advertiser*, February 25, 1993.

30. Ellen Paris, "Hawaii Calls," *Hawaii Investor* (October 1992), pp. 24–26.
31. Bill Wood, "Airport Expansion," in Roth, ed., *The Price of Paradise,* p. 229.
32. See Robert Reich, *The Work of Nations: Preparing Ourselves for 21st Century Capitalism* (New York: Knopf, 1991); see Peter F. Drucker, *Managing for the Future: The 1990s and Beyond* (New York: Dutton, 1992).
33. *Hawaii Investor* (January 1993), pp. 46–52; "Japanese Recession Prompts Corporations to Take Radical Steps," *Wall Street Journal,* February 24, 1993.
34. Walter Miklius, "Outmigration," and "Too Many Moving Away," *Honolulu Star-Bulletin and Advertiser,* October 11, 1992.
35. Susan Yim, "Hawaii's Ethnic Rainbow: Shining Colors Side By Side," *Honolulu Advertiser,* 1992.
36. Eric Yamamoto, "The Significance of Local," *Social Process in Hawaii* 27 (1979), pp. 102–114.
37. Haunani Kay-Trask, "Money Cannot Substitute for Hawaiian Land Base," *Honolulu Star-Bulletin and Advertiser,* January 17, 1993. In a poll conducted by the *Honolulu Star-Bulletin* (January 6, 1993) one-half of the native Hawaiians polled favored sovereignty; 26 percent were opposed.
38. *Hawaii Business* (January 1992), p. 71.
39. Ibid., p. 72
40. Hayden Burgess, in statement before Pacific Asian Council For Indigenous Affairs, December 10, 1992.

Bibliography

1. Public Documents

City and County of Honolulu, Department of General Planning, *The Interim Report on the Future of Oahu's Economy*. Honolulu, 1976.

State of Hawaii, Commission on Manpower and Unemployment, *Unemployment and Welfare in Hawaii*. Honolulu, 1977.

State of Hawaii, Department of Planning and Economic Development, *Hawaii Economic Review*. Honolulu, September–October 1968.

State of Hawaii, Department of Planning and Economic Development, *Hawaiian International Services Agency Annual Report*. Honolulu, 1969.

State of Hawaii, Department of Planning and Economic Development, *Growth Policies Plan 1974–84*. Honolulu, 1978.

State of Hawaii, Department of Planning and Economic Development, *State of Hawaii Data Books, various years*.

State of Hawaii, Department of Planning and Economic Development, *The Hawaii State Plan 1977*. Honolulu, 1978.

State of Hawaii, Department of Planning and Economic Development, *Tourism in Hawaii*. Honolulu, 1972.

State of Hawaii, Department of Taxation, *Hawaii Income Patterns 1973*. Honolulu, 1974.

State of Hawaii, Governor's Advisory Committee on the Tourism Industry, *The Role of Government in the Development of Hawaii's Visitor Industry*. Honolulu, 1957.

University of Hawaii, Legislative Reference Bureau, *Public Land Policy in Hawaii: A Historical Analysis*. Honolulu, 1969.

University of Hawaii, School of Travel Industry Management. *Reader*. Honolulu, 1973.

U.S. Congress, Senate, *Papers and Documents Relating to the Hawaiian Islands*. Senate Executive Document No. 76, 52nd Congress, 1893.

U.S. Congress, *Report of the Hawaiian Commission 1898*. Washington, D.C., 1898.

U.S. Congress, *Hearings on Statehood for Hawaii*. Washington, D.C., 1948.

219

2. Books and Theses

Abbott, William L. *The American Labor Heritage.* Honolulu: University of Hawaii Industrial Relations Center, 1967.

Adler, Jacob. *Claus Spreckels, The Sugar King in Hawaii.* Honolulu: University of Hawaii Press, 1966.

Adler, Jacob and Gwynn Barrett, eds., *The Diaries of Walter Murray Gibson.* Vol. 1, 1886, Vol. 2, 1887. Honolulu: University of Hawaii Press, 1966.

Alexander, A. G. *Koloa Plantation and Hawaii.* Honolulu, 1937.

Amin, Samir. *Accumulation on a World Scale,* 2 vols. New York: Monthly Review Press, 1974.

Barber, Joseph, Jr. *Hawaii: Restless Rampart.* Indianapolis: Bobbs-Merrill Company, 1940.

Barnet, Richard and Ronald Muller. *Global Reach.* New York: Simon and Schuster, 1974.

Bradley, Harold W. *The American Frontier in Hawaii.* Gloucester, Mass.: Peter Smith, 1968.

Bureau of the Americas, *Pan American Handbook No. 85: Hawaii.* Washington, D.C., 1897.

Burrows, Edwin G. *Hawaiian-Americans.* New Haven: Yale University Press, 1947.

Castle, William Rice. *Hawaii Past and Present.* New York: Dodd, Mead and Co., 1917.

———*The Life of Samuel Northrop Castle.* Honolulu: Hawaiian Historical Society, 1960.

Chilcote, Ronald and Joel Edelstein. *Latin America: The Struggle with Dependency and Beyond.* Cambridge: Schenkman Publishing Company, 1974.

Clark, Thomas Black. *Hawaii: The 49th State.* Garden City, N.Y.: Doubleday, 1947.

Cook, James and James King. *A Voyage to the Pacific Ocean.* London: W. A. Strahan, 1784.

Cooke, Sophie Judd. *Sincerely Sophie.* Honolulu: Tongg Publishing Company, 1964.

Crampon, Louis. *Hawaii's Visitor Industry: Its Growth and Development.* Honolulu: University of Hawaii School of Tourism Industry Management, 1976.

Creighton, Thomas. *The Lands of Hawaii: Their Use and Misuse.* Honolulu, University of Hawaii, 1978.

Damon, Ethel M. *Sanford Ballard Dole and His Hawaii.* Honolulu: Hawaiian Historical Society, 1957.

Davis, Ralph. *The Rise of the Atlantic Economies.* Ithaca, N.Y.: Cornell University Press, 1974.

Daws, Gavan. *Shoal of Time: A History of the Hawaiian Islands.* New York: Macmillan, 1969.

Franck, Henry. *Roaming in Hawaii.* New York: Frederick A. Stokes and Company, 1937.

Fuchs, Lawrence. *Hawaii Pono: A Social History.* New York: Harcourt, Brace, and World, 1968.

Hardy, T. B. *Wallace Rider Farrington.* Honolulu: Honolulu Star-Bulletin, 1935.

Healey, Thomas B. "The Republican Party in Hawaii." Master's Thesis, University of Hawaii, 1965.

Heller, Robert. *The Economic and Social Impact of Foreign Investment in Hawaii.* Honolulu: University of Hawaii Economic Research Center, 1973.

Hobbs, Jean. *A Pageant of the Soil.* London: Stanford University Press, 1953.

Honolulu Star-Bulletin. *The Men and Women of Hawaii.* 1972

Hopkins, Manley. *Hawaii.* London: Green, Longman, and Roberts, 1862.

Jacobs, Paul and Saul Landau. *To Serve the Devil.* New York: Vintage, 1971.

Jafari, Jafar. *Role of Tourism in the Socioeconomic Transformation of Developing Countries.* Master's Thesis, Cornell University, 1974: published by the author.

Jarves, James Jackson. *History of the Hawaiian Islands.* Honolulu: Henry M. Whitney, 1872.

Joesting, Edward. *An Uncommon History of Hawaii.* New York: W. W. Norton, 1972.

Johannessen, Edward L. H. *The Hawaiian Labor Movement: A Brief History.* Boston: Bryce Humphries, 1956.

Judd, Laura Fish. *Honolulu Sketches of Life in the Hawaiian Islands.* Honolulu: Honolulu Star-Bulletin, 1928.

Judd, Lawrence M. *Lawrence M. Judd and Hawaii.* Rutland, Vt.: C. E. Tuttle, 1957.

Kelly, John. *Hawaii: Showcase of Imperialism, Land Alienation, and Foreign Control.* Honolulu: private printing, 1974.

Kent, Harold. *Charles Reed Bishop, Man of Hawaii.* Honolulu: Kamehameha Schools Press, 1966.

Kent, Harold. *Dr. Hyde and Mr. Stevenson.* Rutland, Vt.: C. E. Tuttle, 1973.

Kinney, W. A. *Hawaii's Capacity for Self-Government All but Destroyed.* Salt Lake City: Frank L. Jensen, 1927.

Kolko, Gabriel. *Main Currents in Modern American History.* New York: Harper and Row, 1976.

Kolko, Joyce. *America and the Crisis of World Capitalism.* Boston: Beacon Press, 1974.

222 / Noel J. Kent

Kuykendall, Ralph S. *The Hawaiian Kingdom, 1778–1854.* Honolulu: University of Hawaii Press, 1938.

—————. *The Hawaiian Kingdom, 1854–1874.* Honolulu: University of Hawaii Press, 1966.

—————. *The Hawaiian Kingdom, 1874–1893.* Honolulu: University of Hawaii Press, 1967.

Liebes, Richard Alan. "Labor Organization in Hawaii." Master's Thesis, University of Hawaii, 1938.

MacDonald, Alexander. *Revolt in Paradise.* New York: S. Daye & Co., 1944.

Mellen, Kathleen Dickenson. *The Gods Depart.* New York: Hastings House, 1956.

Merrill, R. *Hotel Employment and the Community in Hawaii.* Honolulu, n.d.

Mollett, John Anthony. *Capital in Hawaiian Sugar. Its Formation and Relation to Labor and Output.* Honolulu, 1961.

Morgan, Theodore, *A Century of Economic Change.* Cambridge: Harvard University Press, 1948.

O'Connor, Richard. *Pacific Destiny.* Boston: Little, Brown and Co., 1969.

Oxaal, Ivar et al., eds. *Beyond the Sociology of Development.* Boston: Routledge and Kegan Paul, 1975.

Porteus, S. D. and Marjorie Babcock. *Temperament and Race.* Boston: Richard Badger, 1926.

Pratt, Julius W. *Expansionists of 1898,* Baltimore: Johns Hopkins University Press, 1936.

Quesada, Francisco. *The Mechanisms and Economics of Tourism.* Manila: Manila Book Store, 1976.

Republican Party Central Committee. *Annual Almanac and Government Guide of Hawaii.* Honolulu, 1969.

Russ, William Adam. *The Hawaiian Republic, 1894–98.* Selingsgrove, PA.: Susquehanna University Press, 1956.

—————. *The Hawaiian Revolution, 1893–94.* Selingsgrove, PA: Susquehanna University Press, 1956.

Scott, Edward P. *The Saga of the Sandwich Islands.* Lake Tahoe, Nevada: Sierra Tahoe Publishing Company, 1968

Sevillas-Casas, Elias, ed. *Western Exploitation and Indian Peoples.* The Hague: Mouton, 1977.

Shineberg, Dorothy. *They Came for Sandalwood.* London: Melbourne University Press, 1967.

Simpich, Frederick. *Anatomy of Hawaii.* New York: Avon Books, 1973.

—————. *Dynasty in the Pacific.* New York: McGraw-Hill, 1974.

Stevens, Sylvester. *American Expansion in Hawaii, 1842–1898.* New York: Russell and Russell, 1945.

Tate, Merze. *Hawaii: Reciprocity or Annexation.* East Lansing: Michigan State University Press, 1968.

―――. *The United States and the Hawaiian Kingdom.* New Haven: Yale University Press, 1965.

Taylor, Frank J. et al. *From Land and Sea.* San Francisco: Chronicle Books, 1976.

Taylor, William. "The Hawaiian Sugar Industry." Ph.D. diss., University of California, 1935.

Thurston, Lorrin. *Annexation to the United States.* Washington, D.C., 1898.

Tilton, Cecil. *The History of Banking in Hawaii.* Honolulu: University of Hawaii Press, 1927.

Vandercook, John W. *King Cane.* New York: Harper and Bros., 1939.

Vause, Marilyn. "The Hawaiian Homes Commission Act, 1920." Master's Thesis, University of Hawaii, 1962.

Walker, Joyce. *A Rhetorical Analysis of the Epidetic Speeches of Jack Hall.* Honolulu: University of Hawaii Press, 1961.

Weaver, Samuel. *Hawaii U.S.A.* New York: Pageant Press, 1959.

Weinman, Samuel. *Hawaii: A Case of Imperialist Plunder.* Honolulu, 1934.

Williams, William Appleman. *The Contours of American History.* Cleveland: World Publishing Co., 1961.

―――. *The Roots of the Modern American Empire.* New York: Vintage Books, 1969.

Withington, Elizabeth. *The Golden Cloak.* Honolulu: Honolulu Star-Bulletin, 1953.

Wright, Theon. *The Disenchanted Isles.* New York: Dial Press, 1972.

Young, Lucien. *The Boston of Hawaii.* Washington: Gibson Bros. 1898.

Index

Adams, Brooks, 98
Adams, John Quincy, 19
Agriculture: dispossession and capitalist export, 32; 1890s, 58; 18th-century, 13–15; expressly for sale (mid-19th century), 22; liquidation of commercial, 110; for U.S. Pacific coast, 30–31; *see also* Plantation industry; Subsistence economy; Sugar industry
Airlines: in tourist trade, 170–74
Alaska (purchase), 42
Alexander, B. S., 53–54
Alexander, Samuel, 37
Alexander, William, 61
Allen, Elisha, 27
Amin, Samir, 4, 18
Anarchism, 57
Anderson, D. G., 160
Anderson, Eileen, 156
Annexation, 40–43, 55–68; Blaine on, 59; and the British, 15–16; ceremony of, 67–68; community for, 60–62; economic expansion following, 69; Hawaiians opposed to, 44, 64–68; lobbying for, and debate over, 65–67; and military bases, 54; paving way to, 54–55; reciprocity and, 46; Spreckels on, 52; and "yellow wave," 60–61
Annexationist League, 61–62
Ansai, Toshio, 148, 149
Aoki, Dan, 130, 163
Ariyoshi, George, 126, 155, 158–60, 163
Arkwright, Richard, 12
Armstrong, Richard, 27, 30–31
Ashford, C. W., 55
Asians, 39, 60–61, 82–86, 127–32, 180
Atherton, Frank Cooke, 71, 85
Atherton, J. B., 63
Australia, 111, 118, 165, 174

Bahamas, 111, 117
Baker, Ray Stannard, 74, 77, 83
Baldwin, Henry P., 33, 37, 49, 71
Balknap, George, 66
Baran, Paul, 4
Barnett, Edward, 172
Bayonet Constitution, 54, 55, 62
Beardslee, L. A., 68
Belcher, J. Henshaw, 29
Bellinger, John, 157–58, 176
Big Five: and air routes, 171; control maintained by, 69–91; government financing and, 142; International Longshoremen's and Warehousemen's Union and, 134–38; and land development, 148, 149 (*see also* Land development); monopoly control by, 74–75, 80, 81 (*see also* Pineapple industry; Sugar industry); and tourism, 166 (*see also* Tourism); transformation of, into multinationals, 103–21 (*see also* Multinational corporations); *see also* Plantation system
Bingham, Hiram, 29
Bishop, Charles, 37, 45, 48, 49, 54
Blaine, James, 59, 62
Blaisdell, Neil, 151
Blanding, Donald, 82
Blount, James, 63–64
Bodenheimer, Suzanne, 4
Bodley, John, 32
Bourgeoisie: Asian, 130; Big Five as part of, *see* Big Five; in conflict with monarchy, 43–44; control maintained by, 69–91; coup led by, 53–54; economy in hands of (by 1876), 47; financial apparatus of, 47–49 (*see also* Financial apparatus); government controlled by, 72–74, 149–53, 161–63; and International Longshoremen's and Warehousemen's

225

CPSIA information can be obtained
at www.ICGtesting.com
Printed in the USA
FSOW01n0321030116
15271FS